PYTHON PROJECT FOUNDATIONS- BUILDING AND EVOLVING RESEARCH MANAGEMENT APPLICATIONS - A SERIES OPENER

First edition. April 2, 2024.

Copyright © 2024 ATHEER Mahir.

ISBN: 979-8224320202

Written by ATHEER Mahir.

Also by ATHEER Mahir

Python Project Foundations
Python Project Foundations- Building and Evolving Research Management Applications - A Series Opener

Tech trends
Chat GPT Prompt Engineering With Tech Trends

Watch for more at https://www.linkedin.com/in/atheermahir/.

Table of Contents

To my father Prof. Dr Dawood Mahir

To everyone I have learned from, from my teachers, students, and colleagues in the academic and industrial fields in different countries.

Python Project Foundations- Building and Evolving Research Management Applications - A Series Opener

Volume 1

Atheer Mahir

Introduction

Embracing the Journey of Python Project Development

Welcome to "Python Project Foundations: Building and Evolving Research Management Applications - A Series Opener," a comprehensive guide designed for mid-level Python programmers who aspire to develop a complete and functional research project management application. This book serves as your starting point, a launchpad into the intricate world of Python programming, where concepts are not just explained but also woven into a real-world application. Here, you embark on a journey that transcends basic coding to embrace project planning, implementation, review, and future-proofing.

The Genesis of an Idea: Conceiving a Python Project

Every great application begins with an idea, a spark that ignites the process of creation. In this book, we start by diving into the genesis of our project - a research project management application. This idea isn't just a fleeting thought; it's a response to a real need in the academic and research community for efficient project management tools. We explore how this idea takes shape, morphing from abstract concepts into concrete plans, user stories, and architectural designs.

The journey through the initial chapters immerses you in the planning phase, where we dissect the project's requirements, including user stories and use cases. You'll witness the evolution of an idea as it gets translated into a working model, complete with stub code and initial implementations.

Navigating Through Implementation: The Heart of Development

As the narrative unfolds, you'll delve into the heart of Python programming. The implementation chapters are not just about writing code; they're about understanding the logic, structure, and nuances that make a Python project robust and scalable. Through various versions of implementation, you'll experience the trials and triumphs of coding. Each version brings new challenges and learning opportunities, highlighting the iterative nature of software development.

These chapters are more than just instructional; they're experiential. You'll encounter common issues and learn how to tackle them, gaining insights that only come from hands-on practice. The book guides you through refining and enhancing your code, offering practical tips and advanced techniques to elevate your programming skills.

First Big Review: A Critical Evaluation

In the realm of software development, reviewing and evaluating your work is as important as writing the code itself. The chapters dedicated to review and evaluation serve as critical checkpoints. Here, you assess the progress, identify gaps, and realign strategies. This process is not just about critiquing but also about learning and adapting.

The reviews are thorough, examining the project from various angles - functionality, scalability, user experience, and more. This comprehensive evaluation ensures that the application you build is not just functional but also efficient, user-friendly, and secure.

Charting the Path: Structuring a Python Project

Embarking on the development of a Python project is akin to setting off on an expedition. It requires not only a keen understanding of the programming language but also a strategic approach to project management. This book offers you a map and compass for this journey. We delve into the structuring of a Python project, breaking down complex requirements into manageable tasks and modules.

You'll learn about organising your codebase, creating a coherent and maintainable structure, and the significance of version control in tracking changes and collaborating effectively. The book guides you through setting up a development environment that mirrors real-world software development scenarios, preparing you for professional coding practices.

From Theory to Practice: Implementing and Refining the Application

As we progress, the book transitions from theoretical planning to practical implementation. You'll witness the transformation of abstract plans and requirements into tangible code. These chapters are not just about coding but about understanding the rationale behind each decision and its impact on the overall project.

Each implementation phase is accompanied by challenges and learning curves. You'll encounter common programming hurdles and learn how to overcome them with creativity and efficiency. The book emphasises the importance of refining and optimising your code, ensuring it not only works but excels in performance and reliability.

Embracing the Iterative Process: Reviews and Evolution

In the world of software development, the first draft is never the final product. The book embraces this iterative process, guiding you through successive reviews and revisions. Each review is an opportunity for growth, a chance to enhance and evolve your project. We examine various aspects of the application, from functionality and user experience to security and performance, ensuring a well-rounded and robust final product.

These iterative cycles are reflective of real-world software development, where applications are continuously improved based on user feedback, technological advancements, and changing requirements. You'll learn to adapt and evolve your project, keeping it relevant and effective.

Laying the Groundwork for Future Development

The final chapters of the book are not just a conclusion but a launchpad for future development. They open a gateway to advanced concepts and technologies that can elevate your project to the next level. You'll be introduced to forward-thinking ideas and emerging trends in Python programming, preparing you for the next steps in your development journey.

The book concludes with an emphasis on the continuous nature of learning in software development. The skills, insights, and experiences you gain from this project are stepping stones to more complex and challenging programming ventures.

Cultivating a Developer's Mindset: Learning Beyond the Code

In the odyssey of building a Python project, technical skills are just one part of the equation. This book emphasises cultivating a developer's mindset, an approach that goes beyond writing code to understanding the broader context of software development. You'll learn the importance of problem-solving, critical thinking, and creativity in programming. Each challenge encountered and solved not only improves the project but also hones your skills as a developer.

Navigating Through Challenges and Setbacks

The journey of developing the Python Research Manager is replete with challenges and setbacks, mirroring the real-world scenarios faced by developers daily. This book doesn't shy away from these difficulties; instead, it embraces them as integral to the learning process. You'll encounter issues ranging from simple bugs to complex architectural decisions, each providing a valuable learning opportunity. The process of troubleshooting and resolving these issues is detailed, offering insights into effective problem-solving strategies in software development.

Embracing Collaboration and Community

Software development is often a collaborative effort. This book highlights the significance of community involvement and teamwork in developing a successful project. You'll learn about the dynamics of working in a team, leveraging version control systems like Git for collaborative coding, and engaging with the programming community for feedback and support. The book underscores the value of collective wisdom and diverse perspectives in creating robust software solutions.

Preparing for the Future: A Stepping Stone to Advanced Development

As you reach the end of this book, the journey doesn't conclude; it merely transitions to the next phase. The final chapters set the stage for advancing your skills further. You'll be introduced to concepts and practices for professional-level development, preparing you for more complex projects and challenges ahead. The book serves as a stepping stone, providing the foundation upon which you can build a deeper and more nuanced understanding of Python programming and software development.

Conclusion: The Beginning of a Lifelong Journey

"Python Project Foundations: Building and Evolving Research Management Applications - A Series Opener" is more than just a guide to Python programming; it's an invitation to a lifelong journey of learning and growth in the field of software development. The project you've embarked upon in these pages is just the beginning. As you close this book, you'll be equipped not only with a functional Python application but also with a mindset geared towards continuous learning, innovation, and exploration in the vast and ever-evolving world of software development.

Most used glossary

Agile Methodology: A project management approach that involves breaking the project into small, iterative cycles or 'sprints,' promoting adaptive planning, evolutionary development, and continuous improvement.

API (Application Programming Interface): A set of protocols and tools for building software applications, allowing different software programs to communicate with each other.

Authentication: The process of verifying the identity of a user or process.

Automated Testing: The use of software tools to run tests on a software application automatically, checking for bugs or other issues.

Bcrypt: A password hashing function designed to build a cryptographic hash of a password.

CI/CD (Continuous Integration/Continuous Deployment): A method in software development where code changes are automatically tested and deployed to production.

Containerization: A lightweight alternative to full machine virtualization that involves encapsulating an application in a container with its own operating environment.

Docker: A tool designed to simplify the process of creating, deploying, and running applications by using containers.

Gantt Chart: A type of bar chart that illustrates a project schedule and shows the dependency relationships between activities and current schedule status.

GUI (Graphical User Interface): A user interface that includes graphical elements, such as windows, icons, and buttons.

Integration Testing: Testing in which individual software modules are combined and tested as a group.

Kubernetes: An open-source system for automating deployment, scaling, and management of containerized applications.

Load Testing: Testing an application's ability to perform under anticipated user loads.

Microservices Architecture: An architectural style that structures an application as a collection of loosely coupled services.

MS Teams: A communication platform in the Microsoft 365 family of products, offering chat, videoconferencing, file storage, and application integration.

OneDrive: A file hosting service and synchronisation service operated by Microsoft as part of its suite of Office Online services.

PyQt5: A set of Python bindings for The Qt Company's Qt application framework, used for developing graphical user interfaces (GUIs).

RBAC (Role-Based Access Control): A policy-neutral access control mechanism defined around roles and privileges.

Responsive Design: A design approach that ensures web applications render well on a variety of devices and window or screen sizes.

Scalability: The capability of a system, network, or process to handle a growing amount of work, or its potential to be enlarged to accommodate that growth.

SQL (Structured Query Language): A standard programming language for managing and manipulating databases.

SQLite: A C-language library that implements a small, fast, self-contained, high-reliability, full-featured, SQL database engine.

Unit Testing: Testing of individual software components or modules.

Usability Testing: Testing a product by observing users as they attempt to complete tasks with it.

User Acceptance Testing (UAT): The last phase of the software testing process where actual software users test the software to ensure it can handle required tasks in real-world scenarios.

Version Control: A system that records changes to a file or set of files over time so that specific versions can be recalled later.

Chapter 1 : Idea , Plan and basic implementation

Planning the Project

Introduction to Planning

Embarking on the development of the Research Project Management Application, our journey begins with meticulous planning. This phase lays the groundwork for the application, defining its purpose, scope, and the specific functionalities it aims to provide. Through careful planning, we ensure that the application not only meets the needs of its users but also adheres to technical feasibility and scalability.

User Stories

- Admin User:

- *"As an admin, I want to manage all user accounts to maintain system integrity."* Admins play a crucial role in overseeing the application's operations, ensuring user accounts are managed effectively and securely.

- Supervisor User:

- *"As a supervisor, I want to approve student registrations to control access."* Supervisors act as gatekeepers, ensuring only authorised students gain access to the system.

- *"As a supervisor, I want to assign and track student projects to monitor progress."* This story highlights the need for supervisors to manage and oversee student projects efficiently.

- Student User:

- *"As a student, I want to register and get my account approved to start using the app."* This story reflects the students' need for a straightforward and secure registration process.

- *"As a student, I want to view and update my project tasks to manage my research effectively."* It emphasises the application's role in aiding students in their research management.

- Mind Map Visualization: Imagine these stories branching off from their respective user roles, each branch then diverging further into detailed needs and functionalities.

Use Cases

Use cases provide a structural view of the application's functionalities, demonstrating how different user roles interact with the system.

- Account Management: Encompasses essential features like registration, login, and account approval processes.

- Project Management: Focuses on creating, assigning, tracking, and updating projects, a core component for both supervisors and students.

- File Management: Integration with OneDrive facilitates efficient handling of project files.

- Communication: Incorporates MS Teams for streamlined communication within the app.

- Reporting: Features for generating and viewing reports on progress and activities.

- Mind Map Visualization: Each use case unfolds into a series of actions that users can perform, further branching into specifics for different user roles.

Requirements

Functional Requirements:

- User Authentication: Central to the application, encompassing login, registration, and password management.

- User Management: Includes the creation, modification, and deletion of user accounts.

- Project Management: Tools for assigning, tracking, and updating projects.

- File Management: Seamlessly integrates with OneDrive for file handling.

- Communication: Embedded MS Teams functionality enhances in-app communication.

- Notifications: Alerts and notifications keep users informed of deadlines and updates.

Non-Functional Requirements:

- Usability: A focus on intuitive UI/UX design for ease of use.

- Performance: Ensuring the application's responsiveness and efficiency.

- Security: Robust measures for data protection and secure access.

- Scalability: Capable of accommodating an increasing load of data and users.

- Maintainability: Designed for easy updates and maintenance.

Program Architecture (with Conceptual Diagram)

Introduction to Layered Architecture

In the realm of software development, particularly for complex applications like the Research Project Management Application, adopting a layered architectural approach is pivotal. This architecture segregates the application into distinct, interconnected layers, each dedicated to a specific aspect of the application's functionality. This segregation not only streamlines development and maintenance but also enhances scalability and modularity. Let's delve into the layers that constitute the architecture of our application:

Front-End Layer

- Built using PyQt: The front-end, or the presentation layer of our application, is developed using PyQt. This choice provides a rich set of tools to create a user interface that is both aesthetically pleasing and user-friendly.

- Functional Modules: This layer comprises various modules catering to different aspects of user interaction, such as user authentication (login), user registration, and managing various aspects of project tracking and management. Each module is designed to provide an intuitive and seamless user experience.

Back-End Layer

- SQLite Database for Data Storage: The backbone of our application's data management, the SQLite database, resides in this layer. It serves as the central repository for all data, including user information, project details, and other relevant data.

- Python Modules for Core Functionalities: The back-end layer is powered by Python. It encompasses various modules that implement the application's business logic, such as authentication processes, project management operations, and user management. These modules interact with the database to retrieve, update, and manage data as per the application's requirements.

External Integrations Layer

- Integration with OneDrive and MS Teams APIs: To enhance the application's functionality and to provide additional services, it integrates with external APIs. This includes cloud storage services like OneDrive for file management and Microsoft Teams for communication and collaboration features. These integrations extend the capabilities of the application, providing a more robust and feature-rich user experience.

Architecture Diagram

- A Layered Visual Representation: To encapsulate the architecture succinctly, a conceptual diagram is presented. This diagram visually represents the layered structure, illustrating how the front-end interface, back-end logic, database, and external integrations interact. It provides a clear and concise overview of the application's architecture, demonstrating the separation of concerns and the flow of data and control across the application.

Requirements:

To build a comprehensive research project management application, especially for managing and tracking student research projects, we need to define detailed requirements. These requirements will encompass various aspects of the application, including functional and non-functional requirements.

Functional Requirements

1. User Roles and Authentication

- Different user roles: Admin, Supervisor, Student.

- Secure login and authentication system.

- Ability for students to register using their email address.

- Supervisor's approval required for activating student accounts.

- Supervisor's can track all students' work as a table with links to each student.

- Supervisor or admin can produce a One-time password generation for initial login, with an option to change it later by user.

2. User Management (Admin Specific)

- Ability for admin to add, edit, or remove user accounts.

- Admin oversight of all user registrations and approvals.

3. Project Management

- Functionality for supervisors and students to create, view, and manage research projects.

- Ability for supervisors to assign projects to students.

- Tracking project progress and deadlines.

4. Gantt Chart Integration

- Integration of Gantt charts for project timeline visualisation.

- Options to import and export Gantt charts, preferably from/to Excel.

5. File Management with OneDrive Integration

- Ability for users to link, upload, and access project files from OneDrive.

6. Communication via MS Teams

- Integration with MS Teams for direct communication within the app.

- Features like sending messages and scheduling meetings.

7. Notifications and Alerts

- Automated alerts for upcoming deadlines, new messages, or project updates.

8. Reporting

- Generation of progress reports and activity logs for both supervisors and students.

Non-Functional Requirements

1. Usability
- User-friendly interface with intuitive navigation.
- Clear and consistent design across the application.
2. Performance
- Fast response times for user interactions.
- Efficient handling of database queries and external API calls.
3. Security
- Secure handling of user data and authentication information.
- Compliance with data protection regulations.
4. Scalability
- Ability to handle an increasing number of users and data volume.
- Flexible design to add new features or modify existing ones.
5. Maintainability
- Well-structured and documented code for easy maintenance.
- Modular design to facilitate updates and bug fixes.
6. Compatibility
- (Optional) Cross-platform compatibility for different operating systems.
7. Backup and Recovery
- Regular backups of the database.
- Mechanisms for data recovery in case of system failure.

Additional Considerations

- Testing and Validation: Rigorous testing, including unit tests, integration tests, and user acceptance tests, to ensure reliability and correctness.

- User Training and Documentation: Comprehensive user manuals and documentation for both end-users and system administrators.

These detailed requirements will guide the development of the research project management application, ensuring that it meets the needs of its users effectively and provides a robust, secure, and user-friendly platform for managing student research projects.

Planning the Project (updated)

User Stories

- Admin User:

- "As an admin, I want to manage all user accounts to maintain system integrity."

- Supervisor User:

- "As a supervisor, I want to approve student registrations to control access."

- "As a supervisor, I want to assign and track student projects to monitor progress."

- Student User:

- "As a student, I want to register and get my account approved to start using the app."

- "As a student, I want to view and update my project tasks to manage my research effectively."

- Mind Map: Visualise these stories branching off from each role (Admin, Supervisor, Student), with each branch detailing specific needs and functionalities.

Use Cases

- Account Management: Registration, login, password change, account approval.

- Project Management: Creating, assigning, tracking, and updating projects.

- File Management: Uploading, downloading, and linking files with OneDrive.

- Communication: Messaging and meeting scheduling via MS Teams.

- Reporting: Generating and viewing progress and activity reports.

- Mind Map: Each use case branches out to show specific actions users can perform, with sub-branches for different user roles.

Requirements

- Functional Requirements:
- User Authentication: Login, registration, password management.
- User Management: Account creation, modification, deletion.
- Project Management: Project assignment, tracking, updates.
- File Management: OneDrive integration for file handling.
- Communication: MS Teams integration.
- Notifications: Alerts for deadlines and updates.
- Non-Functional Requirements:
- Usability: Intuitive UI/UX.
- Performance: Quick response and efficient operations.
- Security: Data protection and secure access.
- Scalability: Handling increasing data and user load.
- Maintainability: Easy to update and maintain.

Program Architecture

- Front-End:

- Built using PyQt.

- Modules for login, registration, project management, etc.

- Back-End:

- SQLite database for data storage.

- Python modules for different functionalities (auth, project management).

- External Integrations:

- APIs for OneDrive and MS Teams.

- Architecture Diagram: A layered diagram showing the front-end interface, back-end logic, database, and external integrations.

Stub Code (version 1)

Sample Structure

database.py
Database setup and schema definition

auth.py
Authentication and user management logic

project_management.py
Project management functions

communication.py
MS Teams integration functions

file_management.py
OneDrive file handling functions

main.py (PyQt Application)
Main application window and event handling

Example of main.py:

```python
import sys
from PyQt5.QtWidgets import QApplication, QMainWindow
class MainWindow(QMainWindow):
def __init__(self):
super().__init__()
self.initUI()
def initUI(self):
self.setWindowTitle('Research Project Management App')
# ... UI setup ...
if __name__ == '__main__':
app = QApplication(sys.argv)
mainWin = MainWindow()
mainWin.show()
sys.exit(app.exec_())
```

This planning phase sets a strong foundation for your application development. For visual diagrams like mind maps and architectural overviews, tools like Lucidchart, Draw.io, or even hand-drawn sketches can be used to visualise the concepts effectively.

Implementation:

Creating a complete front-end and back-end for a research project management application is quite extensive, and providing the full code here would be impractical. However, I can guide you through structuring the project and key components that should be included in your files. You can then expand on these foundations based on your specific requirements.

Project Structure:

Front-End (PyQt) Files
- main.py: Main application window and user interface.
- login_window.py: Interface for user login.
- registration_window.py: Interface for student registration.
- supervisor_window.py: Interface for supervisor approvals.
- student_window.py: Interface for student project management.
- admin_window.py: Interface for admin account management.

Back-End Files
- database.py: Handling database connections and schema.
- auth.py: Authentication, registration, and user management logic.
- project_management.py: Logic for managing projects and tasks.
- communication.py: Handling MS Teams integration.
- file_management.py: Managing OneDrive file interactions.

24

Key Components:

1. Front-End (PyQt) Sample Structure (main.py)

```python
import sys
from PyQt5.QtWidgets import QApplication, QMainWindow
# Import other custom window classes
from login_window import LoginWindow
from registration_window import RegistrationWindow
# ... other imports ...
class MainWindow(QMainWindow):
def __init__(self):
super().__init__()
# Initialise the main window
self.initUI()
def initUI(self):
self.setWindowTitle('Research Project Management App')
self.setGeometry(100, 100, 800, 600)
# ... setup other UI components ...
# ... other methods ...
# Application Initialization
def main():
app = QApplication(sys.argv)
main_window = MainWindow()
main_window.show()
sys.exit(app.exec_())
if __name__ == '__main__':
main()
```

2. Back-End Sample Structure (auth.py)

```python
import sqlite3
from werkzeug.security import generate_password_hash, check_password_hash
# Initialize database connection
conn = sqlite3.connect('app.db')
c = conn.cursor()
def register_user(email, role):
# ... user registration logic ...
pass
def verify_user(email, password):
# ... user verification logic ...
pass
def approve_user(email):
# ... supervisor approval logic ...
pass
# ... other authentication-related functions ...
```

Implementing the Full Application:

Implementing the complete application involves the following steps:

1. Designing the UI:

- Use PyQt to design each window and interface (login, registration, project management, etc.).

2. Building the Backend Logic:

- Implement the necessary functions in each backend file (auth.py, database.py, etc.).

3. Connecting Front-End and Back-End:

- Ensure the frontend interfaces interact correctly with the backend logic.

4. Testing:

- Test each part of the application thoroughly, both individually and as a whole.

5. Iterative Development:

- Develop and test iteratively, adding features and refining the application.

6. Documentation and Final Touches:

- Document the code and application usage.

- Add final touches to improve usability and aesthetics.

Final Notes:

- The sample code provided above is foundational. You will need to expand upon it based on your specific requirements.

- Focus on one component at a time to ensure each part is fully functional before moving on to the next.

- Regular testing and user feedback can greatly assist in refining the application.

Stub Code (version 2)

Creating stub code for each file in a comprehensive application like the research project management app involves laying out the basic structure and some placeholder functions. Here's a foundational setup for each of the main files in your project:

1. Front-End (PyQt) Files

main.py:

```python
import sys
from PyQt5.QtWidgets import QApplication, QMainWindow
# Import other custom window classes (to be created)
# from login_window import LoginWindow
# from registration_window import RegistrationWindow
# ... other imports ...
class MainWindow(QMainWindow):
    def __init__(self):
        super().__init__()
        self.initUI()
    def initUI(self):
        self.setWindowTitle('Research Project Management App')
        self.setGeometry(100, 100, 800, 600)
        # ... setup other UI components ...
    # ... other methods ...
# Application Initialization
def main():
    app = QApplication(sys.argv)
    main_window = MainWindow()
    main_window.show()
    sys.exit(app.exec_())
if __name__ == '__main__':
    main()
```

login_window.py:

```python
from PyQt5.QtWidgets import QWidget
# ... other PyQt imports ...
class LoginWindow(QWidget):
def __init__(self):
super().__init__()
self.initUI()
def initUI(self):
# Setup the layout and widgets for login
pass
```

registration_window.py:

```python
from PyQt5.QtWidgets import QWidget
# ... other PyQt imports ...
class RegistrationWindow(QWidget):
def __init__(self):
super().__init__()
self.initUI()
def initUI(self):
# Setup the layout and widgets for registration
pass
```

2. Back-End Files

database.py:

```python
import sqlite3
# Database setup and connection
conn = sqlite3.connect('app.db')
def setup_database():
# Create tables and initialise the database
pass
if __name__ == '__main__':
main()
```

auth.py:

```python
import sqlite3
from werkzeug.security import generate_password_hash, check_password_hash
# Database connection
conn = sqlite3.connect('app.db')
def register_user(email, password):
# Logic for registering a user
pass
def verify_user(email, password):
# Logic for verifying a user's login
pass
def change_password(email, new_password):
# Logic for changing a user's password
pass
```

project_management.py:

```python
import sqlite3
# Database connection
conn = sqlite3.connect('app.db')
def create_project(title, description, supervisor_id):
# Function to create a new project
pass
def get_project(project_id):
# Function to get details of a specific project
pass
```

communication.py:

```python
# Functions related to MS Teams integration
def send_message(team_id, message):
# Send a message to a MS Teams channel
pass
def schedule_meeting(team_id, meeting_details):
# Schedule a meeting in MS Teams
pass
```

file_management.py:

```python
# Functions related to OneDrive file handling
def upload_file(file_path, onedrive_path):
# Upload a file to OneDrive
pass
def download_file(onedrive_path, local_path):
# Download a file from OneDrive
pass
```

Notes for Development:

- Each of these files contains only basic structure and placeholder functions. You'll need to implement the actual logic for each part.

- The front-end files (main.py, login_window.py, etc.) will handle user interaction and should be designed to be user-friendly and intuitive.

- The back-end files (database.py, auth.py, etc.) will contain the core functionality of your application, interacting with the database and external services.

- Ensure that you test each component thoroughly as you develop it, and integrate them step by step.

- Remember to handle exceptions and edge cases, especially in database operations and external API interactions.

This foundational code sets the stage for the development of the research project management application. You can build upon this stub code to create the full functionalities as per the project requirements.

Version 1 of implementation:

```python
main.py
# Import required libraries
import sqlite3
import sys
from PyQt5.QtWidgets import QApplication, QMainWindow, QPushButton, QLabel, QLineEdit

# Importing backend functions
from backend import verify_login, register_user
# Import backend modules
from project_management import create_project, get_projects_by_supervisor
# Main Window Class
class MainWindow(QMainWindow):
    def __init__(self):
        super().__init__()
        # Initialise the main window
        self.initUI()
    def initUI(self):
        # Initialize window, buttons, fields
        self.setWindowTitle('Research Project Management App')
        self.setGeometry(100, 100, 800, 600)
        self.addLoginWidgets()
    def addLoginWidgets(self):
        # Add login widgets (labels, text fields, buttons)
        self.username_label = QLabel('Username', self)
        self.username_field = QLineEdit(self)
        self.password_label = QLabel('Password', self)
        self.password_field = QLineEdit(self)
        self.login_button = QPushButton('Login', self)
        self.login_button.clicked.connect(self.login)
    def login(self):
        # Get user input from login fields
        username = self.username_field.text()
        password = self.password_field.text()
        # Verify login
        if verify_login(username, password):
            print("Login successful!")
            # Proceed to the next part of the application
        else:
            print("Login failed. Try again.")
    def some_function_to_handle_projects(self):
        # Example usage of project management functions
        create_project("AI Research", "Research on AI algorithms", 1)
        projects = get_projects_by_supervisor(1)
```

```python
print(projects)
# Application Initialization
def main():
app = QApplication([])
main_window = MainWindow()
main_window.show()
app.exec_()
if __name__ == '__main__':
main()

auth.py
'''User Authentication and Management (auth.py):
Manages user authentication and user-related operations.
Functions for user login, registration, password encryption, and role management.'''
import sqlite3
from werkzeug.security import generate_password_hash, check_password_hash
# Database connection
conn = sqlite3.connect('app.db')
def register_user(email, password):
# Logic for registering a user
pass
def verify_user(email, password):
# Logic for verifying a user's login
pass
def change_password(email, new_password):
# Logic for changing a user's password
pass

backend.py
# This is the backend.py file
# ... (include the user authentication code here) ...
import sqlite3
from werkzeug.security import generate_password_hash, check_password_hash
# Database setup for users
conn = sqlite3.connect('app.db')
c = conn.cursor()
c.execute('''CREATE TABLE IF NOT EXISTS users
(id INTEGER PRIMARY KEY, username TEXT, password TEXT, role TEXT)''')
conn.commit()
# Function to register a new user
def register_user(username, password, role):
hashed_password = generate_password_hash(password)
c.execute("INSERT INTO users (username, password, role) VALUES (?, ?, ?)",
(username, hashed_password, role))
conn.commit()
```

```python
# Function to verify user login
def verify_login(username, password):
c.execute("SELECT password FROM users WHERE username=?", (username,))
user = c.fetchone()
if user and check_password_hash(user[0], password):
return True
return False
# Example usage
register_user("testuser", "securepassword", "student")
is_authenticated = verify_login("testuser", "securepassword")
print("User authenticated:", is_authenticated)

communication.py
'''Communication (communication.py):
Handles MS Teams integration.
Functions for sending messages, scheduling meetings, and maintaining communication logs.'''
# Functions related to MS Teams integration
def send_message(team_id, message):
# Send a message to a MS Teams channel
pass
def schedule_meeting(team_id, meeting_details):
# Schedule a meeting in MS Teams
pass

database.py
'''Database Management (database.py):
Handles all database-related operations.
Includes functions to create tables, insert data, query data, etc.
Example tables: Users, Projects, Tasks, Gantt Chart Entries.'''
import sqlite3
# Database setup and connection
conn = sqlite3.connect('app.db')
def setup_database():
# Create tables and initialise the database
pass

file_management.py
'''File Management (file_management.py):
Manages interactions with OneDrive for file storage.
Includes functions for uploading, downloading, and retrieving file links.'''
# Functions related to OneDrive file handling
def upload_file(file_path, onedrive_path):
# Upload a file to OneDrive
pass
def download_file(onedrive_path, local_path):
# Download a file from OneDrive
```

```
pass
gantt_chart.py
'''Gantt Chart Operations (gantt_chart.py):
Dedicated to handling Gantt chart data.
Functions for importing, exporting, and manipulating Gantt chart information.'''
login_window.py
from PyQt5.QtWidgets import QWidget
# ... other PyQt imports ...
class LoginWindow(QWidget):
def __init__(self):
super().__init__()
self.initUI()
def initUI(self):
# Setup the layout and widgets for login
pass
project_management.py
'''Project Management (project_management.py):
Contains logic for managing projects and tasks.
Functions for creating, updating, and deleting project details and tasks.'''
import sqlite3
# Initialise connection to the database
conn = sqlite3.connect('app.db')
def create_project(title, description, supervisor_id):
"""

Create a new project.
"""

c = conn.cursor()
c.execute("INSERT INTO projects (title, description, supervisor_id) VALUES (?, ?, ?)",
(title, description, supervisor_id))
conn.commit()
def get_projects_by_supervisor(supervisor_id):
"""

Retrieve all projects under a specific supervisor.
"""

c = conn.cursor()
c.execute("SELECT * FROM projects WHERE supervisor_id=?", (supervisor_id,))
return c.fetchall()
# Add more functions as needed for updating and deleting projects, managing tasks, etc.
registration_window.py
from PyQt5.QtWidgets import QWidget
# ... other PyQt imports ...
class RegistrationWindow(QWidget):
```

```python
def __init__(self):
    super().__init__()
    self.initUI()
def initUI(self):
    # Setup the layout and widgets for registration
    pass
```

When I ran this code, I got this error:

Angry message

```
Traceback (most recent call last):
File "——/main.py", line 24, in <module>
from project_management import create_project, get_projects_by_supervisor
File "——t/project_management.py", line 41, in <module>
register_user("testuser", "securepassword", "student")
File "——/project_management.py", line 30, in register_user
conn.commit()
sqlite3.OperationalError: database is locked
```

Version 1 of issues:

The error sqlite3.OperationalError: database is locked typically occurs when an SQLite database is accessed simultaneously by multiple processes or threads, or when a single process tries to make conflicting accesses. In your application, it seems like this might be happening due to multiple connections being opened to the same SQLite database across different files. Let's address this and other potential improvements:

Solutions and Suggestions:

Centralised Database Connection:

● Instead of opening a new database connection in each file (backend.py, project_management.py, etc.), consider centralising the database connection in database.py and importing it into other modules.

● This will ensure that all database interactions go through a single connection, reducing the likelihood of the 'database is locked' error.

Use Context Managers for Database Operations:

● Modify the database operations to use context managers (with statement). This ensures that connections are properly closed after operations, which can help prevent locking issues.

Review and Refactor backend.py and auth.py:

● It seems like backend.py and auth.py might have overlapping functionalities (both handle user authentication). Consider merging these files or clearly separating their responsibilities to avoid redundancy.

Handle Exceptions:

● Implement exception handling in your database operations to catch and manage errors like the one you're encountering.

```python
main.py
# Import required libraries
import sqlite3
import sys
from PyQt5.QtWidgets import QApplication, QMainWindow, QPushButton, QLabel, QLineEdit

# Importing backend functions
from backend import verify_login, register_user
# Import backend modules
from project_management import create_project, get_projects_by_supervisor
# Main Window Class
class MainWindow(QMainWindow):
    def __init__(self):
        super().__init__()
        # Initialise the main window
        self.initUI()
    def initUI(self):
        # Initialize window, buttons, fields
        self.setWindowTitle('Research Project Management App')
        self.setGeometry(100, 100, 800, 600)
        self.addLoginWidgets()
    def addLoginWidgets(self):
        # Add login widgets (labels, text fields, buttons)
        self.username_label = QLabel('Username', self)
        self.username_field = QLineEdit(self)
        self.password_label = QLabel('Password', self)
        self.password_field = QLineEdit(self)
        self.login_button = QPushButton('Login', self)
        self.login_button.clicked.connect(self.login)
    def login(self):
        # Get user input from login fields
        username = self.username_field.text()
        password = self.password_field.text()
        # Verify login
        if verify_login(username, password):
            print("Login successful!")
            # Proceed to the next part of the application
        else:
            print("Login failed. Try again.")
    def some_function_to_handle_projects(self):
        # Example usage of project management functions
        create_project("AI Research", "Research on AI algorithms", 1)
        projects = get_projects_by_supervisor(1)
```

```python
print(projects)
# Application Initialization
def main():
app = QApplication([])
main_window = MainWindow()
main_window.show()
app.exec_()
if __name__ == '__main__':
main()

auth.py
'''User Authentication and Management (auth.py):
Manages user authentication and user-related operations.
Functions for user login, registration, password encryption, and role management.'''
import sqlite3
from werkzeug.security import generate_password_hash, check_password_hash
# Database connection
conn = sqlite3.connect('app.db')
def register_user(email, password):
# Logic for registering a user
pass
def verify_user(email, password):
# Logic for verifying a user's login
pass
def change_password(email, new_password):
# Logic for changing a user's password
pass
```

Updated backend.py (Using Centralised Connection)

```python
backend.py
# This is the backend.py file
# ... (include the user authentication code here) ...
# Updated backend.py (Using Centralised Connection)
from database import get_db_connection
from werkzeug.security import generate_password_hash, check_password_hash
def register_user(username, password, role):
conn = get_db_connection()
hashed_password = generate_password_hash(password)
with conn:
conn.execute("INSERT INTO users (username, password, role) VALUES (?, ?, ?)",
(username, hashed_password, role))
communication.py
'''Communication (communication.py):
```

Handles MS Teams integration.

Functions for sending messages, scheduling meetings, and maintaining communication logs.'''

```python
# Functions related to MS Teams integration
def send_message(team_id, message):
# Send a message to a MS Teams channel
pass
def schedule_meeting(team_id, meeting_details):
# Schedule a meeting in MS Teams
pass
```

Modified database.py (Centralised Database Connection)

```python
database.py
'''Database Management (database.py):
Handles all database-related operations.
Includes functions to create tables, insert data, query data, etc.
Example tables: Users, Projects, Tasks, Gantt Chart Entries.'''
import sqlite3
def get_db_connection():
conn = sqlite3.connect('app.db')
return conn

file_management.py
'''File Management (file_management.py):
Manages interactions with OneDrive for file storage.
Includes functions for uploading, downloading, and retrieving file links.'''
# Functions related to OneDrive file handling
def upload_file(file_path, onedrive_path):
# Upload a file to OneDrive
pass
def download_file(onedrive_path, local_path):
# Download a file from OneDrive
pass

gantt_chart.py
'''Gantt Chart Operations (gantt_chart.py):
Dedicated to handling Gantt chart data.
Functions for importing, exporting, and manipulating Gantt chart information.'''

login_window.py
from PyQt5.QtWidgets import QWidget
# ... other PyQt imports ...
class LoginWindow(QWidget):
def __init__(self):
super().__init__()
```

```python
self.initUI()
def initUI(self):
# Setup the layout and widgets for login
pass
```

Updated project_management.py (Using Context Managers)

```python
project_management.py
'''Project Management (project_management.py):
Contains logic for managing projects and tasks.
Functions for creating, updating, and deleting project details and tasks.'''
from database import get_db_connection
def create_project(title, description, supervisor_id):
conn = get_db_connection()
with conn:
conn.execute("INSERT INTO projects (title, description, supervisor_id) VALUES (?, ?, ?)",
(title, description, supervisor_id))
def get_projects_by_supervisor(supervisor_id):
conn = get_db_connection()
with conn:
projects = conn.execute("SELECT * FROM projects WHERE supervisor_id=?",
(supervisor_id,)).fetchall()
return projects

registration_window.py
from PyQt5.QtWidgets import QWidget
# ... other PyQt imports ...
class RegistrationWindow(QWidget):
def __init__(self):
super().__init__()
self.initUI()
def initUI(self):
# Setup the layout and widgets for registration
pass
```

Additional Suggestions:

- Database Transactions: Be mindful of transactions in SQLite. Use conn.commit() where necessary to ensure changes are saved.

- Code Organization: Keep your code organised and modular. Each file should have a clear purpose and responsibility.

- Asynchronous Operations: If your application scales and requires handling multiple requests simultaneously (like in a web application), consider moving to a more robust database solution like PostgreSQL or MySQL, or implement an asynchronous SQLite access pattern.

- Testing: After making these changes, thoroughly test your application to ensure all parts are working harmoniously and the database lock issue is resolved.

By implementing these changes, you should be able to resolve the database lock issue and improve the overall structure and robustness of your application.

When i ran the code I got this window

Version 2 of implementation:

The number and structure of front-end and back-end files in your project should be guided by the principles of modularity, clarity, and maintainability. Here are some suggestions on how you might want to structure your files and whether to increase or decrease the number of files:

Front-End Files (PyQt)

1. Main Application Window (main.py):

- Should be your entry point. It can instantiate and manage the primary window and navigation.

2. Separate Windows/Dialogs for Each Major Function:

- Login Window: For user authentication.

- Registration Window: For new user registrations.

- Project Dashboard: For managing and viewing projects and tasks.

- Gantt Chart Viewer/Editor: If the Gantt Chart is a central feature.

- User Management (Admin): Specifically for admin to manage users.

- File Management Interface: For handling file uploads/downloads.

- Communication Interface: For messages and meeting scheduling.

3. UI Components:

- Consider separating complex UI components into their own files if they are large or reused.

4. Resource Files:

- If your UI uses images, custom styles, or other resources, organise these in separate resource files or directories.

Back-End Files

1. Database Connection (database.py):

- Centralise the database connection and configurations here.

2. Authentication Module (auth.py):

- For handling user authentication, registration, and password management.

3. User Management Module:

- Separate file if there are complex operations related to user management, especially for the admin role.

4. Project Management Module (project_management.py):

- Focuses on project and task-related functionalities.

5. Gantt Chart Module (gantt_chart.py):

- If Gantt charts have complex logic or operations, a dedicated file is justified.

6. File Management Module (file_management.py):

- For OneDrive integration and file handling logic.

7. Communication Module (communication.py):

- For handling MS Teams or other communication integrations.

General Suggestions

- Modularity: Each file should represent a distinct aspect of your application. Avoid having overly large files that handle multiple functionalities.

- Cohesion: Functions and classes in each file should be closely related to each other.

- Single Responsibility Principle: Each module or class should have responsibility over a single part of the functionality provided by the software.

- Avoid Redundancy: Ensure that there is no overlapping functionality across different files.

- Scalability and Maintenance: The structure should support easy addition of new features and maintenance.

Given these guidelines, assess whether your current file structure adheres to these principles. If a file is becoming too large or handling too many responsibilities, consider breaking it down. If several small files are tightly coupled and always change together, they might be combined.

In summary, the decision to increase or decrease the number of files should be based on achieving a balance between modularity and simplicity, ensuring each part of your application is manageable, understandable, and maintains a clear purpose.

Version 3 of implementation:

Based on the suggestions for modularity, clarity, and maintainability, the files you would need for your research project management application can be structured as follows:

Front-End Files (PyQt)

1. main.py
- Main application window and the primary navigation logic.
2. login_window.py
- UI and logic for the user login process.
3. registration_window.py
- UI and logic for new user registrations.
4. project_dashboard.py
- UI for managing and viewing projects and tasks.
5. gantt_chart_window.py (if applicable)
- UI for viewing and editing Gantt charts.
6. admin_panel.py
- UI for admin to manage users and application settings.
7. file_management_window.py
- UI for handling file uploads and downloads.
8. communication_window.py
- UI for messaging and meeting scheduling (MS Teams integration).

Back-End Files

1. database.py
- Handles database connection and configuration.
2. auth.py
- Manages user authentication, registration, and password operations.
3. user_management.py
- (Optional) If additional complex user management features are needed.
4. project_management.py
- Logic for managing projects and tasks.
5. gantt_chart.py
- (Optional) Handles operations related to Gantt chart data.
6. file_management.py
- Logic for OneDrive integration and file handling.
7. communication.py
- Manages communication functionalities (e.g., MS Teams integration).

Additional Considerations

- Utility Files: If there are common functionalities or helpers used across different modules (like date handling, text processing), you can create a utils.py file.

- Resource Files: For storing and managing resources like images, icons, and stylesheets.

- Testing Files: Depending on your testing strategy, you might have separate files or directories for tests, e.g., test_auth.py, test_project_management.py, etc.

This structure ensures that each aspect of your application is organised into a specific area, making it easier to develop, test, and maintain. Each front-end file corresponds to a distinct part of the UI, and each back-end file encapsulates a specific set of functionalities related to the application's logic and data handling.

Version 4 of implementation:

Based on the previous discussion and including utility, resource, and testing files, the structure of your research project management application can be expanded as follows:

Front-End PyQt Files

1. main.py
- Main application window and navigation control.
2. login_window.py
- Interface and logic for user login.
3. registration_window.py
- Interface and logic for new user registration.
4. project_dashboard.py
- Interface for managing and viewing projects and tasks.
5. gantt_chart_window.py
- Interface for Gantt chart viewing and editing (if applicable).
6. admin_panel.py
- Interface for admin user management and application settings.
7. file_management_window.py
- Interface for file upload/download operations.
8. communication_window.py
- Interface for messaging and meeting scheduling.

Back-End Python Files

1. database.py
- Database connections and schema management.
2. auth.py
- User authentication and registration logic.
3. user_management.py
- Additional complex user management features (optional).
4. project_management.py
- Project and task management logic.
5. gantt_chart.py
- Gantt chart-related operations (optional).
6. file_management.py
- OneDrive integration and file handling.
7. communication.py
- MS Teams or other communication platform integration.

Utility Files

1. utils.py (or similar)

- Common helper functions and utilities used across the application.

Resource Files

1. resources/

- Directory containing resource files like images, icons, stylesheets, etc.

- You might have separate files for different types of resources, e.g., icons.py, styles.py.

Testing Files

1. tests/

- Directory for all your test files.

- Separate test files for each module, e.g., test_auth.py, test_project_management.py.

- You can use Python's built-in unittest framework or third-party libraries like pytest for writing tests.

Additional Considerations

- Documentation: Consider adding a docs/ directory for project documentation, user manuals, and developer guides.

- Configuration: For larger projects, a configuration file or directory (config.py or configs/) can be useful to manage settings.

This structure provides a comprehensive layout for your application, covering the primary functionalities, utility operations, and necessary resources. Testing files ensure that each component can be independently verified, which is crucial for maintaining software quality.

Version 5 of implementation:

Including documentation and configuration files, here's an expanded structure for your research project management application:

Front-End PyQt Files

1. main.py
- Main application window and navigation control.
2. login_window.py
- Interface and logic for user login.
3. registration_window.py
- Interface and logic for new user registration.
4. project_dashboard.py
- Interface for managing and viewing projects and tasks.
5. gantt_chart_window.py
- Interface for Gantt chart viewing and editing.
6. admin_panel.py
- Interface for admin user management and application settings.
7. file_management_window.py
- Interface for file upload/download operations.
8. communication_window.py
- Interface for messaging and meeting scheduling.

Back-End Python Files

1. database.py
- Database connections and schema management.
2. auth.py
- User authentication and registration logic.
3. user_management.py
- User management features.
4. project_management.py
- Project and task management logic.
5. gantt_chart.py
- Gantt chart-related operations.
6. file_management.py
- File handling and OneDrive integration.
7. communication.py
- Communication platform integration.

Utility Files

1. utils.py

- Common utilities and helper functions.

Resource Files

1. resources/
- Directory containing resource files (images, icons, stylesheets).

Testing Files

1. tests/

- Directory for test files (test_auth.py, test_project_management.py, etc.).

Documentation

1. docs/
- Directory for project documentation.
- Includes user manuals, developer guides, and API documentation.
- Consider using tools like Sphinx for Python documentation.

Configuration Files

1. config.py or configs/

- File or directory for managing application configurations.

- Includes settings like database connection info, API keys, and application parameters.

Additional Files

1. requirements.txt

- Lists all Python dependencies. Helpful for setting up the development environment.

2. README.md

- Overview of the project, setup instructions, and general information.

3. .gitignore

- Specifies files and directories to be ignored in version control (like *.pyc files, environment folders).

4. setup.py (optional)

- If you plan to distribute your application as a package, this file can be used to define package metadata and dependencies.

This comprehensive structure ensures that every aspect of your application is neatly organised, from core functionalities to configuration and documentation. This setup aids in maintainability, scalability, and clarity, both for development purposes and for potential contributors or future users of the application.

Version 6 of implementation:

including the additional files, here's a complete structure for your research project management application:

Front-End PyQt Files

1. main.py
- Main application window and navigation.
2. login_window.py
- User login interface and logic.
3. registration_window.py
- New user registration interface and logic.
4. project_dashboard.py
- Project and task management interface.
5. gantt_chart_window.py
- Gantt chart viewing and editing interface.
6. admin_panel.py
- Admin panel for user and application settings.
7. file_management_window.py
- Interface for file operations.
8. communication_window.py
- Interface for messaging and meetings.

Back-End Python Files

1. database.py
- Database connection and schema management.
2. auth.py
- Authentication and user management.
3. user_management.py
- Additional user management functionalities.
4. project_management.py
- Project and task management logic.
5. gantt_chart.py
- Gantt chart operations.
6. file_management.py
- File handling and OneDrive integration.
7. communication.py
- Communication functionalities.

Utility Files

1. utils.py
- Common utilities and helper functions.

Resource Files

1. resources/
- Resources like images, icons, stylesheets.

Testing Files

1. tests/
- Test cases for various modules.

Documentation

1. docs/
- User manuals, developer guides, API documentation.

Configuration Files

1. config.py or configs/
- Application configuration settings.

Additional Files

1. requirements.txt
- List of Python package dependencies.
2. README.md
- Project overview, setup instructions, and general info.
3. .gitignore
- Files and directories excluded from version control.
4. setup.py
- Package setup for distribution.
5. LICENSE
- Licence details for the project (e.g., MIT, GPL).
6. CHANGELOG.md
- Log of changes, updates, and bug fixes.
7. CONTRIBUTING.md
- Guidelines for contributing to the project.
8. .env or env.py
- Environment variables for sensitive or dynamic settings.

This structure provides a comprehensive and organised framework for your research project management application. It ensures that you have everything you need for effective development, deployment, and maintenance, as well as clear guidelines and documentation for any collaborators or users of the application.

Version 7 of implementation (with code):

Achieving a balance between modularity and simplicity for your application, here's a refined and final suggestion for the structure of your research project management application. This structure ensures that each component of the application is manageable, has a clear purpose, and maintains simplicity in design:

Front-End PyQt Files

1. main.py

- Main application window and primary navigation logic.

2. login_window.py

- User login interface and functionality.

3. registration_window.py

- New user registration interface and functionality.

4. dashboard_window.py

- Central dashboard for accessing different functionalities (projects, Gantt chart, file management, etc.).

5. admin_panel.py

- Interface for admin-specific functionalities like user management.

Back-End Python Files

1. database.py
- Centralised database connection and schema setup.
2. auth.py
- User authentication, registration, and password management.
3. project_management.py
- Handling project and task-related functionalities.
4. user_management.py
- Admin functionalities for managing user accounts.
5. communication.py
- Handling communication features (e.g., MS Teams integration).
6. file_management.py
- OneDrive integration and file handling operations.

Utility Files

1. utils.py

● Common helper functions and utilities used across the application.

Resource Files

1. resources/
● Directory for storing resources like images, icons, stylesheets.

Testing Files

1. tests/
● Test cases for various components of the application.

Documentation and Configuration

1. docs/
● User manuals, developer guides, and API documentation.
2. config.py
● Configuration settings for the application.

Additional Files

1. requirements.txt
● Python package dependencies.
2. README.md
● Overview of the project, setup instructions, and usage.
3. .gitignore
● Files and directories to be excluded from version control.
4. LICENSE
● Project licensing information.

Final Notes

● This structure is designed to be clear and logical, with each file and directory serving a distinct purpose.

● The front-end files are separated based on the major functionalities and interfaces of the application.

● The back-end files are modular, each handling a specific aspect of the application logic.

● Utility, resource, and testing files support the main application by providing common functions, assets, and tests.

● Documentation, configuration, and additional files ensure the application is easy to understand, configure, and use.

This final structure should provide a solid foundation for developing a robust and maintainable research project management application.

Implementing

Let's start by implementing the backend code for each file in your application. I'll provide basic implementations for each of these backend files. Remember, these are foundational structures, and you'll need to expand them based on your application's specific requirements.

1. Database Connection (database.py)

This file will handle the database connection and initial setup.

Front-End PyQt Files

main.py

```python
import sys
from PyQt5.QtWidgets import QApplication, QMainWindow
from login_window import LoginWindow
# Import other windows as needed
class MainWindow(QMainWindow):
    def __init__(self):
        super().__init__()
        self.initUI()
    def initUI(self):
        self.setWindowTitle('Research Project Management App')
        self.setGeometry(100, 100, 800, 600)
        self.login_window = LoginWindow(self)
        self.setCentralWidget(self.login_window)
def main():
    app = QApplication(sys.argv)
    main_window = MainWindow()
    main_window.show()
    sys.exit(app.exec_())
if __name__ == '__main__':
    main()
```

login_window.py

```python
from PyQt5.QtWidgets import QWidget, QLabel, QLineEdit, QPushButton, QVBoxLayout
from auth import verify_user
class LoginWindow(QWidget):
    def __init__(self, parent=None):
        super().__init__(parent)
        self.initUI()
    def initUI(self):
        layout = QVBoxLayout()
        self.email_label = QLabel('Email', self)
        self.email_input = QLineEdit(self)
        self.password_label = QLabel('Password', self)
        self.password_input = QLineEdit(self)
        self.password_input.setEchoMode(QLineEdit.Password)
        self.login_button = QPushButton('Login', self)
        self.login_button.clicked.connect(self.check_login)
        layout.addWidget(self.email_label)
        layout.addWidget(self.email_input)
        layout.addWidget(self.password_label)
```

```python
layout.addWidget(self.password_input)
layout.addWidget(self.login_button)
self.setLayout(layout)
def check_login(self):
email = self.email_input.text()
password = self.password_input.text()
if verify_user(email, password):
print("Login Successful!")
# Here you should switch to another window or dashboard
else:
print("Login Failed!")

registration_window.py
from PyQt5.QtWidgets import QWidget, QLabel, QLineEdit, QPushButton, QVBoxLayout
from auth import register_user
class RegistrationWindow(QWidget):
def __init__(self, parent=None):
super().__init__(parent)
self.initUI()
def initUI(self):
layout = QVBoxLayout()
self.email_label = QLabel('Email', self)
self.email_input = QLineEdit(self)
self.password_label = QLabel('Password', self)
self.password_input = QLineEdit(self)
self.password_input.setEchoMode(QLineEdit.Password)
self.register_button = QPushButton('Register', self)
self.register_button.clicked.connect(self.register)
layout.addWidget(self.email_label)
layout.addWidget(self.email_input)
layout.addWidget(self.password_label)
layout.addWidget(self.password_input)
layout.addWidget(self.register_button)
self.setLayout(layout)
def register(self):
email = self.email_input.text()
password = self.password_input.text()
# Assuming default role as 'student' and status as 'pending'
register_user(email, password, 'student', 'pending')
print("Registration Request Sent")

project_dashboard.py
from PyQt5.QtWidgets import QWidget, QLabel, QVBoxLayout
class ProjectDashboard(QWidget):
def __init__(self, parent=None):
```

```python
super().__init__(parent)
self.initUI()
def initUI(self):
layout = QVBoxLayout()
self.title = QLabel('Project Dashboard', self)
# Additional UI elements for project management here
# ...
layout.addWidget(self.title)
# Add other widgets to layout
# ...
self.setLayout(layout)
# Add methods to handle project management tasks
# ...
```

```python
admin_panel.py
from PyQt5.QtWidgets import QWidget, QLabel, QVBoxLayout, QPushButton
from user_management import get_all_users, activate_user
class AdminPanel(QWidget):
def __init__(self, parent=None):
super().__init__(parent)
self.initUI()
def initUI(self):
layout = QVBoxLayout()
self.title = QLabel('Admin Panel', self)
self.refresh_button = QPushButton('Refresh User List', self)
self.refresh_button.clicked.connect(self.refresh_user_list)
layout.addWidget(self.title)
layout.addWidget(self.refresh_button)
self.setLayout(layout)
def refresh_user_list(self):
users = get_all_users()
# Display the user list and add buttons or actions for user management
# You might want to use a QTableWidget or QListWidget to display users
print("Users:", users)
# Add more methods for admin functionalities
# ...
```

Back-End Python Files

```python
database.py
import sqlite3
def get_db_connection():
conn = sqlite3.connect('app.db')
return conn
```

```python
def setup_database():
    conn = get_db_connection()
    with conn:
        conn.execute('''
        CREATE TABLE IF NOT EXISTS users (
        id INTEGER PRIMARY KEY,
        email TEXT UNIQUE NOT NULL,
        password TEXT NOT NULL,
        role TEXT NOT NULL,
        status TEXT NOT NULL
        )
        ''')
    # Add other table creation statements as needed
    conn.close()
if __name__ == "__main__":
    setup_database()
```

auth.py

```python
import sqlite3
from werkzeug.security import generate_password_hash, check_password_hash
from database import get_db_connection
def register_user(email, password, role, status='pending'):
    conn = get_db_connection()
    hashed_password = generate_password_hash(password)
    with conn:
        conn.execute("INSERT INTO users (email, password, role, status) VALUES (?, ?, ?, ?)",
        (email, hashed_password, role, status))
def verify_user(email, password):
    conn = get_db_connection()
    with conn:
        user = conn.execute("SELECT password FROM users WHERE email=?", (email,)).fetchone()
        return user and check_password_hash(user[0], password)
def change_password(email, new_password):
    conn = get_db_connection()
    hashed_password = generate_password_hash(new_password)
    with conn:
        conn.execute("UPDATE users SET password=? WHERE email=?", (hashed_password, email))
```

project_management.py

```python
import sqlite3
from database import get_db_connection
def create_project(title, description, supervisor_id):
    conn = get_db_connection()
    with conn:
```

```python
conn.execute("INSERT INTO projects (title, description, supervisor_id) VALUES (?, ?, ?)",
(title, description, supervisor_id))
def get_project(project_id):
conn = get_db_connection()
with conn:
return conn.execute("SELECT * FROM projects WHERE id=?", (project_id,)).fetchone()
```

user_management.py

```python
import sqlite3
from database import get_db_connection
def get_all_users():
conn = get_db_connection()
with conn:
return conn.execute("SELECT * FROM users").fetchall()
def activate_user(user_id):
conn = get_db_connection()
with conn:
conn.execute("UPDATE users SET status='active' WHERE id=?", (user_id,))
```

communication.py

```python
def send_message(team_id, message):
# Integration with MS Teams API to send a message
# This is a placeholder for actual API integration
pass
def schedule_meeting(team_id, meeting_details):
# Integration with MS Teams API to schedule a meeting
# This is a placeholder for actual API integration
pass
```

file_management.py

```python
def upload_file(file_path, onedrive_path):
# Placeholder for method to upload a file to OneDrive
# Actual implementation would use OneDrive API
pass
def download_file(onedrive_path, local_path):
# Placeholder for method to download a file from OneDrive
# Actual implementation would use OneDrive API
pass
```

Utility Files

utils.py
Not yet

Configuration

config.py
Not yet
So far we got this GUI:

Version 8 of implementation (with code):

here are some suggestions for improving the GUI:

1. Layout and Spacing: The elements seem to be quite spaced out. Consider reducing the spacing between the form fields and the button to create a more cohesive look.
2. Font and Size: It might be helpful to use a slightly larger font size for better readability. Also, you might want to choose a font that's more modern if the default doesn't fit the aesthetic you're aiming for.
3. Color and Themes: The current colour scheme is very minimal. While that's not inherently bad, adding a bit of colour could help differentiate sections and make the interface more engaging. You can use colour to highlight important actions like the login button.
4. Icons and Imagery: Adding icons to the input fields can make it visually clearer what each field represents. For instance, an envelope icon next to the email input and a lock next to the password field.
5. Input Field Design: The input fields could use a design touch-up. Consider slightly rounded corners or a subtle shadow to give a sense of depth.
6. Button Design: The login button could be more prominent. You could use a colour that stands out from the rest of the layout to draw attention to the primary action.
7. Feedback on Action: Upon a login attempt, consider having a loading indicator or animation to inform the user that their request is being processed.
8. Consistent Design Language: Ensure that the look and feel are consistent throughout the application, including any messages or other windows that might pop up.
9. Responsive Design: If your application will be used on different screen sizes, make sure the layout is responsive and elements adjust appropriately.
10. Accessibility: Ensure that your application is accessible, with proper contrast ratios and support for keyboard navigation.

Implementing these suggestions would likely enhance the user experience and make the application more visually appealing.

Improving the code for a PyQt5 application involves enhancing the structure, maintainability, and functionality of the codebase. Below are specific suggestions for each file:

main.py

- Implement a more robust mechanism for window management to handle the transition between different windows seamlessly.

- Use a stack of widgets or a QStackedWidget to manage the different pages of your application.

login_window.py

- Utilise form validation to ensure data integrity before submission.

- Add feedback mechanisms like status messages or dialog boxes to communicate success or error states to the user.

- Separate business logic from UI code by implementing a controller or signals and slots.

registration_window.py

- Similar to login_window.py, include form validation and feedback mechanisms.

- Consider adding more fields to handle full registration details (e.g., name, confirmation of password, etc.).

- Use a signal to notify the main window to switch views upon successful registration.

project_dashboard.py

- Introduce a model-view-controller (MVC) pattern to separate the UI from the business logic.

- Use a QTableView or QListWidget to display projects dynamically.

admin_panel.py

- Use QTableView with a custom model to manage and display user data.

- Implement functionalities such as user activation and deletion within the UI.

database.py

- Use context managers (with statement) to handle database connections to ensure they are closed properly.

- Consider using an ORM (Object-Relational Mapper) like SQLAlchemy for more complex database operations.

auth.py

- Implement more robust error handling and logging for each operation.
- Separate database logic from authentication logic.

project_management.py and user_management.py

- Encapsulate database access within classes to avoid repetitive code.
- Implement error handling for database operations.

communication.py and file_management.py

- Prepare for actual API integration by implementing mock functions that simulate the behaviour of the API.

General Code Improvements:

● Error Handling: Add try-except blocks where appropriate to catch and handle exceptions, preventing the application from crashing unexpectedly.

● Logging: Incorporate logging throughout the application to aid in debugging and track user activities or errors.

● Input Validation: Strengthen input validation on both the front-end and back-end to prevent SQL injection and ensure data integrity.

● Modularization: Break down larger functions into smaller, more manageable functions to follow the Single Responsibility Principle.

● Comments and Documentation: Add comments and docstrings to functions and classes to explain their purpose, parameters, and return values.

● Constants and Configuration: Use a separate configuration file or constants module to manage application-wide settings.

● Password Security: Ensure that you are using a strong hashing algorithm for passwords and consider adding a salt to improve security.

Implementing these improvements will enhance the overall quality of your application code and make it easier to maintain and extend in the future.

Front-End PyQt Files

No significant changes needed here, but ensure that you handle transitions and window management properly.

main.py

```python
import sys
from PyQt5.QtWidgets import QApplication, QMainWindow
from login_window import LoginWindow
# Import other windows as needed
class MainWindow(QMainWindow):
def __init__(self):
super().__init__()
self.initUI()
def initUI(self):
self.setWindowTitle('Research Project Management App')
self.setGeometry(100, 100, 800, 600)
self.login_window = LoginWindow(self)
self.setCentralWidget(self.login_window)
def main():
app = QApplication(sys.argv)
main_window = MainWindow()
main_window.show()
sys.exit(app.exec_())
if __name__ == '__main__':
main()
```

login_window.py

```python
from PyQt5.QtWidgets import QWidget, QLabel, QLineEdit, QPushButton, QVBoxLayout
from PyQt5.QtWidgets import QMessageBox #update ver 8
from auth import verify_user
class LoginWindow(QWidget):
def __init__(self, parent=None):
# super().__init__(parent) # not working
# update to correct the error
super(LoginWindow, self).__init__(parent)
# Rest of your code...
self.initUI()
def initUI(self):
layout = QVBoxLayout()
self.email_label = QLabel('Email', self)
self.email_input = QLineEdit(self)
self.password_label = QLabel('Password', self)
self.password_input = QLineEdit(self)
self.password_input.setEchoMode(QLineEdit.Password)
```

```python
self.login_button = QPushButton('Login', self)
self.login_button.clicked.connect(self.check_login)
layout.addWidget(self.email_label)
layout.addWidget(self.email_input)
layout.addWidget(self.password_label)
layout.addWidget(self.password_input)
layout.addWidget(self.login_button)
self.setLayout(layout)
def check_login(self):
email = self.email_input.text()
password = self.password_input.text()
if verify_user(email, password):
print("Login Successful!")
# Here you should switch to another window or dashboard
else:
print("Login Failed!")
# update ver 8
def check_login(self):
email = self.email_input.text()
password = self.password_input.text()
if verify_user(email, password):
QMessageBox.information(self, 'Login Success', 'You have successfully logged in.')
# Transition to the next window
else:
QMessageBox.warning(self, 'Login Failed', 'The email or password is incorrect.')

registration_window.py
from PyQt5.QtWidgets import QWidget, QLabel, QLineEdit, QPushButton, QVBoxLayout
from auth import register_user
class RegistrationWindow(QWidget):
def __init__(self, parent=None):
super().__init__(parent)
self.initUI()
def initUI(self):
layout = QVBoxLayout()
self.email_label = QLabel('Email', self)
self.email_input = QLineEdit(self)
self.password_label = QLabel('Password', self)
self.password_input = QLineEdit(self)
self.password_input.setEchoMode(QLineEdit.Password)
self.register_button = QPushButton('Register', self)
self.register_button.clicked.connect(self.register)
layout.addWidget(self.email_label)
layout.addWidget(self.email_input)
```

```python
layout.addWidget(self.password_label)
layout.addWidget(self.password_input)
layout.addWidget(self.register_button)
self.setLayout(layout)
def register(self):
email = self.email_input.text()
password = self.password_input.text()
# Assuming default role as 'student' and status as 'pending'
register_user(email, password, 'student', 'pending')
print("Registration Request Sent")
# update ver 8
def register(self):
email = self.email_input.text()
password = self.password_input.text()
# Input validation would go here
if not email or not password:
QMessageBox.warning(self, 'Error', 'Email and password are required.')
return
# Assuming default role as 'student' and status as 'pending'
register_user(email, password, 'student', 'pending')
QMessageBox.information(self, 'Registration', 'Registration request sent.')
project_dashboard.py
from PyQt5.QtWidgets import QWidget, QLabel, QVBoxLayout
class ProjectDashboard(QWidget):
def __init__(self, parent=None):
super().__init__(parent)
self.initUI()
def initUI(self):
layout = QVBoxLayout()
self.title = QLabel('Project Dashboard', self)
# Additional UI elements for project management here
# ...
layout.addWidget(self.title)
# Add other widgets to layout
# ...
self.setLayout(layout)
# Add methods to handle project management tasks
# ...
admin_panel.py
from PyQt5.QtWidgets import QWidget, QLabel, QVBoxLayout, QPushButton
from user_management import get_all_users, activate_user
class AdminPanel(QWidget):
def __init__(self, parent=None):
```

```python
        super().__init__(parent)
        self.initUI()
    def initUI(self):
        layout = QVBoxLayout()
        self.title = QLabel('Admin Panel', self)
        self.refresh_button = QPushButton('Refresh User List', self)
        self.refresh_button.clicked.connect(self.refresh_user_list)
        layout.addWidget(self.title)
        layout.addWidget(self.refresh_button)
        self.setLayout(layout)
    def refresh_user_list(self):
        users = get_all_users()
        # Display the user list and add buttons or actions for user management
        # You might want to use a QTableWidget or QListWidget to display users
        print("Users:", users)
    # Add more methods for admin functionalities
    # ...
```

Back-End Python Files

No significant changes needed here, but ensure that you use context managers when interacting with the database to handle resources properly.

database.py

```python
import sqlite3
def get_db_connection():
    conn = sqlite3.connect('app.db')
    return conn
def setup_database():
    conn = get_db_connection()
    with conn:
        conn.execute('''
        CREATE TABLE IF NOT EXISTS users (
        id INTEGER PRIMARY KEY,
        email TEXT UNIQUE NOT NULL,
        password TEXT NOT NULL,
        role TEXT NOT NULL,
        status TEXT NOT NULL
        )
        ''')
        # Add other table creation statements as needed
    conn.close()
if __name__ == "__main__":
    setup_database()
```

```python
auth.py
import sqlite3
from werkzeug.security import generate_password_hash, check_password_hash
from database import get_db_connection
def register_user(email, password, role, status='pending'):
conn = get_db_connection()
hashed_password = generate_password_hash(password)
with conn:
conn.execute("INSERT INTO users (email, password, role, status) VALUES (?, ?, ?, ?)",
(email, hashed_password, role, status))
def verify_user(email, password):
conn = get_db_connection()
with conn:
user = conn.execute("SELECT password FROM users WHERE email=?", (email,)).fetchone()
return user and check_password_hash(user[0], password)
def change_password(email, new_password):
conn = get_db_connection()
hashed_password = generate_password_hash(new_password)
with conn:
conn.execute("UPDATE users SET password=? WHERE email=?", (hashed_password, email))
# update ver 8
def verify_user(email, password):
conn = get_db_connection()
try:
user = conn.execute("SELECT password FROM users WHERE email=?", (email,)).fetchone()
if user and check_password_hash(user['password'], password):
return True
else:
return False
except sqlite3.Error as e:
print(f"An error occurred: {e.args[0]}")
return False
```

Consider implementing classes that handle the logic here.

```python
project_management.py
import sqlite3
from database import get_db_connection
def create_project(title, description, supervisor_id):
conn = get_db_connection()
with conn:
conn.execute("INSERT INTO projects (title, description, supervisor_id) VALUES (?, ?, ?)",
(title, description, supervisor_id))
def get_project(project_id):
conn = get_db_connection()
```

```python
with conn:
    return conn.execute("SELECT * FROM projects WHERE id=?", (project_id,)).fetchone()
```

Consider implementing classes that handle the logic here.

user_management.py

```python
import sqlite3
from database import get_db_connection
def get_all_users():
    conn = get_db_connection()
    with conn:
        return conn.execute("SELECT * FROM users").fetchall()
def activate_user(user_id):
    conn = get_db_connection()
    with conn:
        conn.execute("UPDATE users SET status='active' WHERE id=?", (user_id,))
```

Ensure you follow best practices for interacting with external APIs, such as handling API exceptions and using secure methods to store API credentials.

communication.py

```python
def send_message(team_id, message):
    # Integration with MS Teams API to send a message
    # This is a placeholder for actual API integration
    pass
def schedule_meeting(team_id, meeting_details):
    # Integration with MS Teams API to schedule a meeting
    # This is a placeholder for actual API integration
    pass
```

Ensure you follow best practices for interacting with external APIs, such as handling API exceptions and using secure methods to store API credentials.

file_management.py

```python
def upload_file(file_path, onedrive_path):
    # Placeholder for method to upload a file to OneDrive
    # Actual implementation would use OneDrive API
    pass
def download_file(onedrive_path, local_path):
    # Placeholder for method to download a file from OneDrive
    # Actual implementation would use OneDrive API
    pass
```

Utility Files

utils.py

```python
'''Not yet'''
pass
```

Resource Files

resources/

- Directory for storing resources like images, icons, stylesheets.

Not yet

Testing Files

tests/
- Test cases for various components of the application.

Not yet

Documentation and Configuration

docs/

- User manuals, developer guides, and API documentation.

Not yet
config.py
'"Not yet"'
pass

Additional Files

requirements.txt

- Python package dependencies.

Not yet
README.md

- Overview of the project, setup instructions, and usage.

Not yet
.gitignore

- Files and directories to be excluded from version control.

Not yet

Not yet
LICENSE

- Project licensing information.

Final Notes

- This structure is designed to be clear and logical, with each file and directory serving a distinct purpose.

- The front-end files are separated based on the major functionalities and interfaces of the application.

- The back-end files are modular, each handling a specific aspect of the application logic.

- Utility, resource, and testing files support the main application by providing common functions, assets, and tests.

- Documentation, configuration, and additional files ensure the application is easy to understand, configure, and use.

This final structure should provide a solid foundation for developing a robust and maintainable research project management application.

Version 9 of implementation (with code):

Let's design the database.py module for your research project management application. This module will establish a database schema with tables for users, projects, tasks, and other related entities. I'll ensure to include constraints for data integrity, indexing for performance optimization, and secure storage for sensitive information.

Database Schema

Users Table: Store user information.

Projects Table: Details about each project.

Tasks Table: Individual tasks within each project.

UserProject Table: To associate users with projects (many-to-many relationship).

Other Entities: Depending on future requirements, you can add more tables.

Sample database.py Implementation

```python
database.py
import sqlite3
from werkzeug.security import generate_password_hash
def get_db_connection():
conn = sqlite3.connect('app.db')
conn.row_factory = sqlite3.Row # Access columns by name
return conn
def setup_database():
conn = get_db_connection()
with conn:
# Users Table
conn.execute('''
CREATE TABLE IF NOT EXISTS users (
id INTEGER PRIMARY KEY,
email TEXT UNIQUE NOT NULL,
password TEXT NOT NULL,
role TEXT NOT NULL,
status TEXT NOT NULL,
supervisor_id INTEGER,
FOREIGN KEY(supervisor_id) REFERENCES users(id)
)
''')
# Add indexing on frequently queried columns
conn.execute('CREATE INDEX IF NOT EXISTS idx_users_email ON users (email)')
# Projects Table
conn.execute('''
CREATE TABLE IF NOT EXISTS projects (
id INTEGER PRIMARY KEY,
title TEXT NOT NULL,
description TEXT,
start_date DATE,
end_date DATE
)
''')
# Tasks Table
conn.execute('''
CREATE TABLE IF NOT EXISTS tasks (
id INTEGER PRIMARY KEY,
project_id INTEGER,
title TEXT NOT NULL,
description TEXT,
status TEXT NOT NULL,
due_date DATE,
```

```
FOREIGN KEY(project_id) REFERENCES projects(id)
)
''')
# UserProject Table (Many-to-Many Relationship between Users and Projects)
conn.execute('''
CREATE TABLE IF NOT EXISTS user_project (
user_id INTEGER,
project_id INTEGER,
role TEXT,
FOREIGN KEY(user_id) REFERENCES users(id),
FOREIGN KEY(project_id) REFERENCES projects(id),
PRIMARY KEY (user_id, project_id)
)
''')
conn.close()
if __name__ == "__main__":
setup_database()
```

Explanation

- Data Integrity: The schema includes primary keys, foreign keys, and unique constraints to maintain data integrity.

- Indexing: An index is created on the email column of the users table for faster query performance, as this is likely to be a frequently queried column.

- Normalisation: The schema is normalised to reduce data redundancy. For example, user-project relationships are managed in a separate user_project table, facilitating a many-to-many relationship.

- Secure Storage: While this script sets up the database, password hashing is handled in the user registration logic, as shown in your auth.py.

This database.py file sets up a well-structured and scalable database for your application, considering key database design principles. You can run this script once to initialise your database, and then it will be ready for use by other parts of your application.

```python
login_window.py
from PyQt5.QtWidgets import QWidget, QLabel, QLineEdit, QPushButton, QVBoxLayout
from PyQt5.QtWidgets import QMessageBox #update ver 9 - 25 Dec 2023 20:44
from auth import verify_user
class LoginWindow(QWidget):
def __init__(self, parent=None):
# super().__init__(parent) # not working
# update to correct the error
super(LoginWindow, self).__init__(parent)
# Rest of your code...
self.initUI()
def initUI(self):
layout = QVBoxLayout()
self.email_label = QLabel('Email', self)
self.email_input = QLineEdit(self)
self.password_label = QLabel('Password', self)
self.password_input = QLineEdit(self)
self.password_input.setEchoMode(QLineEdit.Password)
self.login_button = QPushButton('Login', self)
self.login_button.clicked.connect(self.check_login)
layout.addWidget(self.email_label)
layout.addWidget(self.email_input)
layout.addWidget(self.password_label)
layout.addWidget(self.password_input)
layout.addWidget(self.login_button)
self.setLayout(layout)
def check_login(self):
email = self.email_input.text()
password = self.password_input.text()
if verify_user(email, password):
''' old
print("Login Successful!")
# Here you should switch to another window or dashboard
'''
# update ver 9 - 25 Dec 2023 20:48
QMessageBox.information(self, 'Login Success', 'You have successfully logged in.')
# Transition to the next window
# end ver 9 - update 25 Dec 2023 20:48
else:
''' old
print("Login Failed!")
'''
# update ver 9 - 25 Dec 2023 20:48
```

QMessageBox.warning(self, 'Login Failed', 'The email or password is incorrect.')
# end ver 9 - update 25 Dec 2023 20:48
# update ver 8
def check_login(self):
email = self.email_input.text()
password = self.password_input.text()
if verify_user(email, password):
QMessageBox.information(self, 'Login Success', 'You have successfully logged in.')
# Transition to the next window
else:
QMessageBox.warning(self, 'Login Failed', 'The email or password is incorrect.')

Now let's implement the GUI for your application with PyQt, we'll outline the structure for each of the requirements. I'll provide a general guide on how to create each GUI component and the transitions between them.

1. Login GUI with Help and Registration Options

- Components:

- Input fields for email and password.

- 'Login' button to submit credentials.

- 'Register' button to open the registration form.

- 'Help' button to show help messages or instructions.

- Implementation:

- Use QLineEdit for input fields, QPushButton for buttons.

- Connect the 'Register' button to a function that opens the registration window.

- Implement a QMessageBox or a separate QDialog for the 'Help' functionality.

2. Admin Login

- Backend Logic:

- In your verify_user function, check if the user's role is 'admin' and the password matches 'asd/123ASD'.

- Implement a method to change the admin's password.

3. Admin Dashboard GUI

- Components:

- Options to view and manage user accounts.

- Functionality to approve or modify user roles (student, moderator, administrator).

- Interface to add users to the system.

- Implementation:

- Use QTableWidget or QListWidget to display user accounts.

- Implement forms or dialogs for user role management and account creation.

4. Supervisor GUI

- Components:

- Overview of all students.

- Option to select a specific student for detailed view and management.

- Controls to modify student accounts or roles.

- Implementation:

- A list or table view (QListWidget or QTableWidget) to display students.

- Detailed view can be a new window or a detailed section in the same window.

5. Student Dashboard GUI

- Components:

- Display of student information, achievements, research sources, etc.

- Possibly sections or tabs for different categories of information.

- Implementation:

- Use QLabel for displaying static information.

- Implement tabs using QTabWidget for organising different categories of information.

- Integrate with the backend to fetch and display student-specific data.

Additional Notes

- Window Transitions: Handle transitions between different windows carefully. You might use a stacked layout (QStackedWidget) or open new windows/dialogs for different roles.

- Dynamic Content Loading: Fetch data dynamically based on the user's role and display it in the respective UI components.

- User Experience: Ensure a consistent look and feel across different windows for a seamless user experience.

Sample Code for Login Window

Here's a basic structure for your login window with registration and help options:

```
login_window.py
''' old
from PyQt5.QtWidgets import QWidget, QLabel, QLineEdit, QPushButton, QVBoxLayout
from PyQt5.QtWidgets import QMessageBox #update ver 9 - 25 Dec 2023 20:44
'''
# update ver 9 - 25 Dec 2026 23:55
from PyQt5.QtWidgets import QApplication, QMainWindow, QWidget, QLabel, QLineEdit, QPushButton,
QVBoxLayout, QMessageBox
from auth import verify_user
class LoginWindow(QWidget):
def __init__(self, parent=None):
# super().__init__(parent) # not working
# update to correct the error
super(LoginWindow, self).__init__(parent)
# Rest of your code...
self.initUI()
def initUI(self):
layout = QVBoxLayout()
self.email_label = QLabel('Email', self)
self.email_input = QLineEdit(self)
self.password_label = QLabel('Password', self)
self.password_input = QLineEdit(self)
self.password_input.setEchoMode(QLineEdit.Password)
self.login_button = QPushButton('Login', self)
self.login_button.clicked.connect(self.check_login)
layout.addWidget(self.email_label)
layout.addWidget(self.email_input)
layout.addWidget(self.password_label)
layout.addWidget(self.password_input)
layout.addWidget(self.login_button)
self.setLayout(layout)
def check_login(self):
email = self.email_input.text()
password = self.password_input.text()
if verify_user(email, password):
''' old
print("Login Successful!")
# Here you should switch to another window or dashboard
'''
# update ver 9 - 25 Dec 2023 20:48
QMessageBox.information(self, 'Login Success', 'You have successfully logged in.')
# Transition to the next window
# end ver 9 - update 25 Dec 2023 20:48
```

```python
else:
''' old
print("Login Failed!")
'''

# update ver 9 - 25 Dec 2023 20:48
QMessageBox.warning(self, 'Login Failed', 'The email or password is incorrect.')
# end ver 9 - update 25 Dec 2023 20:48
# update ver 8
def check_login(self):
email = self.email_input.text()
password = self.password_input.text()
if verify_user(email, password):
QMessageBox.information(self, 'Login Success', 'You have successfully logged in.')
# Transition to the next window
else:
QMessageBox.warning(self, 'Login Failed', 'The email or password is incorrect.')
```

So the code so far is:

Front-End PyQt Files

No significant changes needed here, but ensure that you handle transitions and window management properly.

main.py

```
<<<
import sys
from PyQt5.QtWidgets import QApplication, QMainWindow
from login_window import LoginWindow
# Import other windows as needed
class MainWindow(QMainWindow):
def __init__(self):
super().__init__()
self.initUI()
def initUI(self):
self.setWindowTitle('Research Project Management App')
self.setGeometry(100, 100, 800, 600)
self.login_window = LoginWindow(self)
self.setCentralWidget(self.login_window)
def main():
app = QApplication(sys.argv)
main_window = MainWindow()
main_window.show()
sys.exit(app.exec_())
if __name__ == '__main__':
main()
>>>
```

Login_window.py

```
<<<
''' old
from PyQt5.QtWidgets import QWidget, QLabel, QLineEdit, QPushButton, QVBoxLayout
from PyQt5.QtWidgets import QMessageBox #update ver 9 - 25 Dec 2023 20:44
'''

# update ver 9 - 25 Dec 2026 23:55
from PyQt5.QtWidgets import QApplication, QMainWindow, QWidget, QLabel, QLineEdit, QPushButton, QVBoxLayout, QMessageBox
from auth import verify_user
class LoginWindow(QWidget):
def __init__(self, parent=None):
# super().__init__(parent) # not working
# update to correct the error
super(LoginWindow, self).__init__(parent)
# Rest of your code...
```

```python
self.initUI()
def initUI(self):
layout = QVBoxLayout()
self.email_label = QLabel('Email', self)
self.email_input = QLineEdit(self)
self.password_label = QLabel('Password', self)
self.password_input = QLineEdit(self)
self.password_input.setEchoMode(QLineEdit.Password)
self.login_button = QPushButton('Login', self)
self.login_button.clicked.connect(self.check_login)
layout.addWidget(self.email_label)
layout.addWidget(self.email_input)
layout.addWidget(self.password_label)
layout.addWidget(self.password_input)
layout.addWidget(self.login_button)
self.setLayout(layout)
def check_login(self):
email = self.email_input.text()
password = self.password_input.text()
if verify_user(email, password):
''' old
print("Login Successful!")
# Here you should switch to another window or dashboard
'''

# update ver 9 - 25 Dec 2023 20:48
QMessageBox.information(self, 'Login Success', 'You have successfully logged in.')
# Transition to the next window
# end ver 9 - update 25 Dec 2023 20:48
else:
''' old
print("Login Failed!")
'''

# update ver 9 - 25 Dec 2023 20:48
QMessageBox.warning(self, 'Login Failed', 'The email or password is incorrect.')
# end ver 9 - update 25 Dec 2023 20:48
# update ver 8
def check_login(self):
email = self.email_input.text()
password = self.password_input.text()
if verify_user(email, password):
QMessageBox.information(self, 'Login Success', 'You have successfully logged in.')
# Transition to the next window
else:
QMessageBox.warning(self, 'Login Failed', 'The email or password is incorrect.')
```

```
>>>
Registration_window.py
<<<
from PyQt5.QtWidgets import QWidget, QLabel, QLineEdit, QPushButton, QVBoxLayout
from auth import register_user
class RegistrationWindow(QWidget):
def __init__(self, parent=None):
super().__init__(parent)
self.initUI()
def initUI(self):
layout = QVBoxLayout()
self.email_label = QLabel('Email', self)
self.email_input = QLineEdit(self)
self.password_label = QLabel('Password', self)
self.password_input = QLineEdit(self)
self.password_input.setEchoMode(QLineEdit.Password)
self.register_button = QPushButton('Register', self)
self.register_button.clicked.connect(self.register)
layout.addWidget(self.email_label)
layout.addWidget(self.email_input)
layout.addWidget(self.password_label)
layout.addWidget(self.password_input)
layout.addWidget(self.register_button)
self.setLayout(layout)
def register(self):
email = self.email_input.text()
password = self.password_input.text()
# Assuming default role as 'student' and status as 'pending'
register_user(email, password, 'student', 'pending')
print("Registration Request Sent")
# update ver 8
def register(self):
email = self.email_input.text()
password = self.password_input.text()
# Input validation would go here
if not email or not password:
QMessageBox.warning(self, 'Error', 'Email and password are required.')
return
# Assuming default role as 'student' and status as 'pending'
register_user(email, password, 'student', 'pending')
QMessageBox.information(self, 'Registration', 'Registration request sent.')
Project_dashboard.py
<<<
```

```python
from PyQt5.QtWidgets import QWidget, QLabel, QVBoxLayout
class ProjectDashboard(QWidget):
def __init__(self, parent=None):
super().__init__(parent)
self.initUI()
def initUI(self):
layout = QVBoxLayout()
self.title = QLabel('Project Dashboard', self)
# Additional UI elements for project management here
# ...
layout.addWidget(self.title)
# Add other widgets to layout
# ...
self.setLayout(layout)
# Add methods to handle project management tasks
# ...
>>>
```

Admin_panel.py

```
<<<
from PyQt5.QtWidgets import QWidget, QLabel, QVBoxLayout, QPushButton
from user_management import get_all_users, activate_user
class AdminPanel(QWidget):
def __init__(self, parent=None):
super().__init__(parent)
self.initUI()
def initUI(self):
layout = QVBoxLayout()
self.title = QLabel('Admin Panel', self)
self.refresh_button = QPushButton('Refresh User List', self)
self.refresh_button.clicked.connect(self.refresh_user_list)
layout.addWidget(self.title)
layout.addWidget(self.refresh_button)
self.setLayout(layout)
def refresh_user_list(self):
users = get_all_users()
# Display the user list and add buttons or actions for user management
# You might want to use a QTableWidget or QListWidget to display users
print("Users:", users)
# Add more methods for admin functionalities
# ...
>>>
```

Back-End Python Files

Database.py

```
<<<
import sqlite3
from werkzeug.security import generate_password_hash
def get_db_connection():
conn = sqlite3.connect('app.db')
conn.row_factory = sqlite3.Row # Access columns by name
return conn
def setup_database():
conn = get_db_connection()
with conn:
# Users Table
conn.execute('''
CREATE TABLE IF NOT EXISTS users (
id INTEGER PRIMARY KEY,
email TEXT UNIQUE NOT NULL,
password TEXT NOT NULL,
role TEXT NOT NULL,
status TEXT NOT NULL,
supervisor_id INTEGER,
FOREIGN KEY(supervisor_id) REFERENCES users(id)
)
''')
# Add indexing on frequently queried columns
conn.execute('CREATE INDEX IF NOT EXISTS idx_users_email ON users (email)')
# Projects Table
conn.execute('''
CREATE TABLE IF NOT EXISTS projects (
id INTEGER PRIMARY KEY,
title TEXT NOT NULL,
description TEXT,
start_date DATE,
end_date DATE
)
''')
# Tasks Table
conn.execute('''
CREATE TABLE IF NOT EXISTS tasks (
id INTEGER PRIMARY KEY,
project_id INTEGER,
```

```python
title TEXT NOT NULL,
description TEXT,
status TEXT NOT NULL,
due_date DATE,
FOREIGN KEY(project_id) REFERENCES projects(id)
)
''')
# UserProject Table (Many-to-Many Relationship between Users and Projects)
conn.execute('''
CREATE TABLE IF NOT EXISTS user_project (
user_id INTEGER,
project_id INTEGER,
role TEXT,
FOREIGN KEY(user_id) REFERENCES users(id),
FOREIGN KEY(project_id) REFERENCES projects(id),
PRIMARY KEY (user_id, project_id)
)
''')
conn.close()
if __name__ == "__main__":
setup_database()
```

>>>
Auth.py
<<<

```python
import sqlite3
from werkzeug.security import generate_password_hash, check_password_hash
from database import get_db_connection
def register_user(email, password, role, status='pending'):
conn = get_db_connection()
hashed_password = generate_password_hash(password)
with conn:
conn.execute("INSERT INTO users (email, password, role, status) VALUES (?, ?, ?, ?)",
(email, hashed_password, role, status))
def verify_user(email, password):
conn = get_db_connection()
with conn:
user = conn.execute("SELECT password FROM users WHERE email=?", (email,)).fetchone()
return user and check_password_hash(user[0], password)
def change_password(email, new_password):
conn = get_db_connection()
hashed_password = generate_password_hash(new_password)
with conn:
```

```python
conn.execute("UPDATE users SET password=? WHERE email=?", (hashed_password, email))
# update ver 8
def verify_user(email, password):
conn = get_db_connection()
try:
user = conn.execute("SELECT password FROM users WHERE email=?", (email,)).fetchone()
if user and check_password_hash(user['password'], password):
return True
else:
return False
except sqlite3.Error as e:
print(f"An error occurred: {e.args[0]}")
return False
>>>
```

Consider implementing classes that handle the logic here.
Project_management.py
<<<

```python
import sqlite3
from database import get_db_connection
def create_project(title, description, supervisor_id):
conn = get_db_connection()
with conn:
conn.execute("INSERT INTO projects (title, description, supervisor_id) VALUES (?, ?, ?)",
(title, description, supervisor_id))
def get_project(project_id):
conn = get_db_connection()
with conn:
return conn.execute("SELECT * FROM projects WHERE id=?", (project_id,)).fetchone()
>>>
```

Consider implementing classes that handle the logic here.
User_management.py
<<<

```python
import sqlite3
from database import get_db_connection
def get_all_users():
conn = get_db_connection()
with conn:
return conn.execute("SELECT * FROM users").fetchall()
def activate_user(user_id):
conn = get_db_connection()
with conn:
conn.execute("UPDATE users SET status='active' WHERE id=?", (user_id,))
>>>
```

Ensure you follow best practices for interacting with external APIs, such as handling API exceptions and using secure methods to store API credentials.

Communication.py

```
<<<
def send_message(team_id, message):
# Integration with MS Teams API to send a message
# This is a placeholder for actual API integration
pass
def schedule_meeting(team_id, meeting_details):
# Integration with MS Teams API to schedule a meeting
# This is a placeholder for actual API integration
pass
>>>
```

Ensure you follow best practices for interacting with external APIs, such as handling API exceptions and using secure methods to store API credentials.

File_management.py

```
<<<
def upload_file(file_path, onedrive_path):
# Placeholder for method to upload a file to OneDrive
# Actual implementation would use OneDrive API
pass
def download_file(onedrive_path, local_path):
# Placeholder for method to download a file from OneDrive
# Actual implementation would use OneDrive API
pass
>>>
```

Utility Files

utils.py
'''Not yet'''
pass

Resource Files

resources/

- Directory for storing resources like images, icons, stylesheets.

Not yet

Testing Files

tests/
● Test cases for various components of the application.

Not yet

Documentation and Configuration

docs/

● User manuals, developer guides, and API documentation.

Not yet
config.py
"'Not yet'"
pass

Additional Files

requirements.txt

● Python package dependencies.

Not yet
README.md

● Overview of the project, setup instructions, and usage.

Not yet
.gitignore

● Files and directories to be excluded from version control.

Not yet

Not yet
LICENSE

● Project licensing information.

Final Notes

- This structure is designed to be clear and logical, with each file and directory serving a distinct purpose.

- The front-end files are separated based on the major functionalities and interfaces of the application.

- The back-end files are modular, each handling a specific aspect of the application logic.

- Utility, resource, and testing files support the main application by providing common functions, assets, and tests.

- Documentation, configuration, and additional files ensure the application is easy to understand, configure, and use.

This final structure should provide a solid foundation for developing a robust and maintainable research project management application.

Version 10 of implementation (with code):

To update the code for implementing the functionalities as per your application's workflow, we'll focus on enhancing the frontend PyQt files for different windows and ensuring they interact seamlessly with the backend. We'll outline the necessary updates for each window as per your requirements.

Notes for Other Windows

- Student, Supervisor, and Admin Windows: Create separate PyQt widget classes for each of these windows. These classes will handle the respective UI and functionalities for students, supervisors, and admins.

- Switching Between Windows: Use the switch_window method in MainWindow to transition between different windows based on user actions and roles.

- Backend Integration: Ensure that each window interacts appropriately with the backend files (auth.py, project_management.py, etc.) for functionalities like user authentication, project management, and file operations.

Next Steps

- Implement the UI and logic for the Student, Supervisor, and Admin windows.

- Add role-based navigation in the check_login method of LoginWindow.

- Continue building out backend functionalities and integrate them with the frontend windows.

This updated structure provides a clear path for implementing the required functionalities and ensures a smooth user experience with seamless transitions between different windows. Remember to test each part thoroughly as you proceed with the development.

We are stopping here to try different methods considering the coloured background with more suitable windows, start from scratch

An AI Low-code helps (from scratch with code):

We will provide a comprehensive overview of this transformative trend in software development.

The Role of AI in Modern Software Development

AI's Contribution to Software Development

AI is significantly changing the software development landscape. It assists in automating repetitive tasks, optimizing code, and enhancing specific aspects of the development process(Dryka and Pluszczewska, 2023). Researchers are actively applying AI techniques in various stages of software development to improve software quality (Wang, 2017). Generative AI, in particular, is proving to be a game-changer, with tools like GitHub Copilot and ChatGPT offering capabilities such as code generation, software testing, and code optimization(Beres, 2023).

Case Studies: IBM Watson and Google AlphaGo

Two prominent examples of AI in software engineering are IBM Watson and Google AlphaGo. Watson uses AI for decision-making support, learning from man-made resources like papers, while AlphaGo uses neural networks and reinforcement learning, primarily learning from online resources like images (Wang, 2017). These case studies illustrate the diverse applications of AI in solving complex problems and contributing to the development of intelligent systems.

Section 2: Best Practices for Applying AI in Software Development

Embracing Generative AI

Generative AI tools can significantly enhance development processes by automating tasks, thus allowing developers to focus on more creative aspects (Beres, 2023). For instance, GitHub Copilot can assist in code completion, bug detection, and performance optimization (Bennett, 2023). These tools not only save time but also reduce errors and improve the overall efficiency of the software development process (Bennett, 2023).

Ethical Considerations and Scalability

While leveraging AI in software development, it's essential to prioritize ethical considerations like fairness and transparency. Ensuring that AI systems are scalable and adaptable is also crucial. Developers should be cautious of potential drawbacks, such as over-reliance on AI and biased AI decisions.

Section 3: Real-World Applications and Challenges

Applications in Diverse Fields

AI is not just limited to automating tasks but also extends to areas like database optimizations, predictive analytics, image generation, and UX/UI design (Beres, 2023). This versatility showcases AI's potential to contribute significantly across various aspects of software development.

Challenges and Common Mistakes

One of the key challenges in using AI for software development is the quality and availability of training data. The effectiveness of AI tools like GitHub Copilot is contingent on the availability of a large body of publicly available code (Beres, 2023). Developers need to be aware of the limitations of AI tools and ensure thorough testing and validation of AI-generated code.

Conclusion: The Future of Software Development with AI

The integration of AI and low-code platforms in software development heralds a new era of innovation and efficiency. As AI continues to evolve, it's imperative for developers to adapt to these changes, embracing new tools and methodologies while being mindful of their limitations and ethical implications. This holistic approach will enable developers to harness the full potential of AI in creating more sophisticated, user-friendly, and efficient software applications.

Version 11 of Implementation: From Scratch with Code

In transitioning from version 10 to version 11, we embark on a journey of significant refinement and sophistication in our software development process. Version 10 laid a solid foundation with a straightforward PyQt implementation focusing on window management and transitions. However, version 11 marks a pivotal evolution, showcasing a deeper and more intricate engagement with the design and functionality of the application.

Version 11, embodied in login_register_gui.py, represents a substantial leap forward. This version introduces a range of complex features, including global signals for dynamic UI updates, advanced user interface elements, and comprehensive functionalities. The enhancements in this version address the limitations and bugs identified in the previous iteration, culminating in a more robust, user-friendly, and aesthetically pleasing interface.

This progression is a testament to the iterative nature of software development. Each version builds upon the last, integrating new technologies and methodologies to refine and enhance the overall product. Version 11 is not just a continuation but a reinvention that leverages both the lessons learned from past iterations and the capabilities of modern development approaches, underscoring the dynamic and evolving landscape of software creation.

By using the help of low-code apps, with many updates, we reached a point where we can design better login/register windows, they have some bugs that need to be fixed.

The latest version of the app is login_register_gui.py

```python
login_register_gui.py
import sys
import sqlite3
import re
import bcrypt
from PyQt5.QtWidgets import (QApplication, QMainWindow, QPushButton, QLineEdit, QMessageBox, QColorDialog, QLabel,
QInputDialog, QVBoxLayout, QWidget, QCheckBox, QHBoxLayout)
from PyQt5.QtCore import Qt, QSize, QMimeData, QUrl, pyqtSignal, QObject
from PyQt5.QtGui import QImage, QPixmap, QDragEnterEvent, QDropEvent, QPalette, QBrush
from PyQt5.QtGui import QDesktopServices
from PyQt5.QtCore import QUrl


# Global signal class
class GlobalSignals(QObject):
background_image_changed = pyqtSignal(str)
global_signals = GlobalSignals() # Create an instance of the global signals class
global_background_pixmap = None
def set_global_background_image(image_path):
global global_background_pixmap
global_background_pixmap = QPixmap(image_path)
global_signals.background_image_changed.emit(image_path) # Emit the signal through the instance
class CustomWindow(QMainWindow):
def __init__(self, parent=None):
super().__init__(parent)
self.setFixedSize(QSize(800, 400))
global_signals.background_image_changed.connect(self.update_background) # Connect to the global signal
def update_background(self, image_path):
if QPixmap(image_path).isNull():
QMessageBox.warning(self, 'Error', 'The image file is not valid.')
return
palette = QPalette()
brush = QBrush(QPixmap(image_path).scaled(self.size(), Qt.KeepAspectRatioByExpanding,
Qt.SmoothTransformation))
palette.setBrush(QPalette.Window, brush)
self.setPalette(palette)
def create_child_window(self, window_class):
child_window = window_class(self)
global_signals.background_image_changed.connect(child_window.update_background)
child_window.show()
class DraggableLabel(QLabel):
imageDropped = pyqtSignal(str) # Signal to emit the file path
def __init__(self, parent=None):
```

```python
super().__init__(parent)
self.setAcceptDrops(True)
self.setAutoFillBackground(True)
def dragEnterEvent(self, event: QDragEnterEvent):
if event.mimeData().hasUrls():
event.acceptProposedAction()
def dropEvent(self, event: QDropEvent):
mimeData = event.mimeData()
if mimeData.hasUrls():
urls = mimeData.urls()
if len(urls) > 0:
image_path = urls[0].toLocalFile()
self.imageDropped.emit(image_path)
event.acceptProposedAction()
# Continue from Part 1
class LoginWindow(CustomWindow):
def __init__(self, parent=None):
super().__init__(parent)
self.setWindowTitle('Login Window')
self.initUI()
def initUI(self):
# Add layout, labels, line edits, and buttons for login functionality
self.username = QLineEdit(self)
self.password = QLineEdit(self)
self.password.setEchoMode(QLineEdit.Password)
self.login_button = QPushButton('Login', self)
self.login_button.clicked.connect(self.login)
self.show_password_checkbox = QCheckBox('Show Password', self)
self.show_password_checkbox.stateChanged.connect(self.toggle_password_visibility)
# Set placeholder text for the password field
self.password.setPlaceholderText("Enter your password")
# Set the echo mode to hide the password initially
self.password.setEchoMode(QLineEdit.Password)
layout = QVBoxLayout()
layout.addWidget(QLabel('Enter your username:'))
layout.addWidget(self.username)
layout.addWidget(QLabel('Enter your password:'))
layout.addWidget(self.password)
layout.addWidget(self.show_password_checkbox) # Add the checkbox to the layout
layout.addWidget(self.login_button)
# "Forget Password" Button
self.forget_password_button = QPushButton('Forget Password')
self.forget_password_button.clicked.connect(self.forget_password)
layout.addWidget(self.forget_password_button)
```

```python
# Set the central widget with the layout
central_widget = QWidget(self)
central_widget.setLayout(layout)
self.setCentralWidget(central_widget)
def login(self):
# Here you can handle the login logic, for example:
username = self.username.text()
password = self.password.text()
if username and password:
# Perform login (check against database, etc.)
QMessageBox.information(self, 'Success', 'Login successful!')
# Here you would typically also close the login window or open another window upon successful login
else:
QMessageBox.warning(self, 'Error', 'Please enter both username and password.')
def toggle_password_visibility(self, state):
if state == Qt.Checked:
self.password.setEchoMode(QLineEdit.Normal)
else:
self.password.setEchoMode(QLineEdit.Password)
def forget_password(self):
# Open the default email client to send an email
admin_email = "amahir@gmail.com"
subject = "Password Reset Request"
body = "I have forgotten my password and request assistance to reset it."
mailto_link = f"mailto:{admin_email}?subject={subject}&body={body}"
QDesktopServices.openUrl(QUrl(mailto_link))


class RegisterWindow(CustomWindow):
def __init__(self, parent=None):
super().__init__(parent)
self.setWindowTitle('Register Window')
# Initialise all QLineEdit attributes before calling initUI()
self.first_name = QLineEdit(self)
self.last_name = QLineEdit(self)
self.user_id = QLineEdit(self)
self.username = QLineEdit(self)
self.confirm_username = QLineEdit(self)
self.password = QLineEdit(self)
self.confirm_password = QLineEdit(self)
self.initUI()
def initUI(self):
layout = QVBoxLayout()
# Create horizontal layouts for each label-input pair
fields = [
```

```python
    ('First Name:', self.first_name),
    ('Last Name:', self.last_name),
    ('ID:', self.user_id),
    ('Enter your username (email):', self.username),
    ('Re-enter your username (email):', self.confirm_username),
    ('Password:', self.password),
    ('Rewrite Password to validate:', self.confirm_password)
    ]
    for label_text, widget in fields:
        row_layout = QHBoxLayout()
        label = QLabel(label_text)
        label.setAlignment(Qt.AlignRight | Qt.AlignVCenter) # Align right for the label
        row_layout.addWidget(label)
        row_layout.addWidget(widget) # Add the corresponding input field
        layout.addLayout(row_layout) # Add the horizontal layout to the main vertical layout
    # Show Password Checkbox
    self.show_password_checkbox = QCheckBox('Show Password')
    self.show_password_checkbox.stateChanged.connect(self.toggle_password_visibility)
    layout.addWidget(self.show_password_checkbox)
    # Set placeholder text for password fields
    self.password.setPlaceholderText("Password (UpperCase, LowerCase, Special Character, Length > 8)")
    self.confirm_password.setPlaceholderText("Rewrite Password to validate")
    # Set the echo mode to hide the password initially
    self.password.setEchoMode(QLineEdit.Password)
    self.confirm_password.setEchoMode(QLineEdit.Password)
    # "Show Password" Checkbox
    self.show_password_checkbox = QCheckBox('Show Password')
    self.show_password_checkbox.stateChanged.connect(self.toggle_password_visibility)

    # Register Button
    self.register_button = QPushButton('Register')
    self.register_button.clicked.connect(self.register)
    layout.addWidget(self.register_button)
    central_widget = QWidget(self)
    central_widget.setLayout(layout)
    self.setCentralWidget(central_widget)
    def toggle_password_visibility(self, state):
        echo_mode = QLineEdit.Normal if state == Qt.Checked else QLineEdit.Password
        self.password.setEchoMode(echo_mode)
        self.confirm_password.setEchoMode(echo_mode)
    def register(self):
        # Gather all the inputs
        first_name = self.first_name.text().strip()
        last_name = self.last_name.text().strip()
```

```python
        user_id = self.user_id.text().strip()
        email = self.username.text().strip()
        confirm_email = self.confirm_username.text().strip()
        password = self.password.text()
        confirm_password = self.confirm_password.text()
        # Simple email regex for validation
        email_regex = r"^\S+@\S+\.\S+$"
        # Password complexity regex (at least one lowercase, one uppercase, one number, one special char, min length 8)
        password_regex = r"^(?=.*[a-z])(?=.*[A-Z])(?=.*\d)(?=.*[@$!%*?&])[A-Za-z\d@$!%*?&]{8,}$"
        # Check if any field is empty
        if not all([first_name, last_name, user_id, email, confirm_email, password, confirm_password]):
            QMessageBox.warning(self, 'Error', 'All fields are required.')
            return
        # Check if the emails match
        if email != confirm_email:
            QMessageBox.warning(self, 'Error', 'Emails do not match.')
            return
        # Validate the email format
        if not re.match(email_regex, email):
            QMessageBox.warning(self, 'Error', 'Enter a valid email address.')
            return
        # Check if the passwords match
        if password != confirm_password:
            QMessageBox.warning(self, 'Error', 'Passwords do not match.')
            return
        # Validate the password complexity
        if not re.match(password_regex, password):
            QMessageBox.warning(self, 'Error', 'Password must be at least 8 characters long, include an uppercase letter, a
            lowercase letter, a number, and a special character.')
            return
        # If all validations pass, hash the password and store the new user in the database
        # Hashing would be done here with a secure hashing library like bcrypt
        hashed_password = self.hash_password(password)
        # Database logic to store the new user would be done here
        # ...
        QMessageBox.information(self, 'Success', 'Registration successful!')
    def hash_password(self, password):
        # Hash a password with bcrypt
        hashed = bcrypt.hashpw(password.encode('utf-8'), bcrypt.gensalt())
        return hashed


class LoginRegisterWindow(CustomWindow):
    def __init__(self):
        super().__init__()
```

```python
self.setWindowTitle('Login/Register Window')
central_widget = QWidget(self)
self.setCentralWidget(central_widget)
layout = QVBoxLayout(central_widget)
self.background_label = DraggableLabel(self)
self.background_label.resize(self.size())
layout.addWidget(self.background_label)
self.background_label.imageDropped.connect(set_global_background_image)
self.register_button = QPushButton('Register', self)
self.register_button.clicked.connect(lambda: self.create_child_window(RegisterWindow))
layout.addWidget(self.register_button)
self.login_button = QPushButton('Login', self)
self.login_button.clicked.connect(lambda: self.create_child_window(LoginWindow))
layout.addWidget(self.login_button)
self.change_color_button = QPushButton('Change Background Color', self)
self.change_color_button.clicked.connect(self.change_background_color)
layout.addWidget(self.change_color_button)
def create_child_window(self, window_class):
child_window = window_class(self)
child_window.show()
def change_background_color(self):
color = QColorDialog.getColor()
if color.isValid():
palette = QPalette()
palette.setColor(QPalette.Window, color)
self.setPalette(palette)
QApplication.instance().setPalette(palette)
def set_background_image(self, image_path):
set_global_background_image(image_path) # This will trigger the update_background for all windows

# Create or open a database for storing user credentials
db_path = 'users.db'
conn = sqlite3.connect(db_path)
cursor = conn.cursor()
# Create table with new fields
cursor.execute('''
CREATE TABLE IF NOT EXISTS users (
id INTEGER PRIMARY KEY AUTOINCREMENT,
first_name TEXT NOT NULL,
last_name TEXT NOT NULL,
user_id TEXT NOT NULL UNIQUE,
email TEXT NOT NULL UNIQUE,
password TEXT NOT NULL
)
```

```python
""")
conn.commit()
if __name__ == '__main__':
app = QApplication(sys.argv)
win = LoginRegisterWindow()
win.show()
sys.exit(app.exec_())
```

Architecture and design

Login_register_gui.py is quite a comprehensive Python code for a login and registration system using PyQt5, which provides a good starting point for building a desktop application. The code has a main window that handles the login and registration windows and a database setup for storing user credentials.

As for the architecture and design, here are a few professional insights and suggestions:

1. **Modular Design:** Split the code into multiple modules where each module has a single responsibility. For instance, database operations can go into one module, UI components into another, and business logic in a separate one.
2. **Use of OOP:** Define classes not only for UI components but also for handling data (like user information) and business logic (like validation and database interaction).
3. **Global State Management:** Instead of using global variables, consider using a singleton pattern for managing global states or pass references of necessary components.
4. **Database Abstraction:** Abstract the database operations into a class that handles all SQL queries. This will make it easier to manage the database operations and also to switch to a different database system in the future if needed.
5. **Error Handling:** Incorporate comprehensive error handling and logging mechanisms to catch and log errors, especially around database operations.
6. **Security:** When dealing with passwords, ensure that they are not only hashed but also salted. Also, ensure secure communication if this application ever needs to communicate over a network.
7. **UI Responsiveness:** Make sure that long-running operations (like database operations) do not freeze the UI, possibly by using QThreads.
8. **Configuration Management:** Externalize configuration parameters (like database connection strings) to a configuration file or environment variables.
9. **Testing:** Implement unit tests, especially for the business logic and database interaction parts of the application.

Here's a stub of how the code can be organised into different files:

- main.py: Entry point of the application, responsible for starting the application.

- database.py: Contains the database connection and operations.

- user.py: A class that represents a user and its attributes.

- auth.py: Contains authentication and authorization logic.

- ui.py: Contains all the PyQt5 UI classes.

- config.py: Configuration parameters for the application.

- utils.py: Utility functions that can be used across the application.

main.py
Entry point of the application, responsible for starting the application.
<<<

```python
############################################################
## Atheer Work: Research Tracker Project © 2024 A Mahir ###
############################################################
# ****************************************************************
# clear the terminal
from utils import clear_terminal
clear_terminal()
# ****************************************************************
import sys
from PyQt5.QtWidgets import QApplication
from ui import LoginRegisterWindow
if __name__ == '__main__':
app = QApplication(sys.argv)
win = LoginRegisterWindow()
win.show()
sys.exit(app.exec_())
```

>>>
database.py (Database Operations)
Contains the database connection and operations.
<<<

```python
############################################################
## Atheer Work: Research Tracker Project © 2024 A Mahir ###
############################################################
# ****************************************************************
# clear the terminal
# clear the terminal
from utils import clear_terminal
clear_terminal()
# ****************************************************************
# # Path to the SQLite database
# DB_PATH = 'users.db'
from config import DB_PATH
import sqlite3
import bcrypt

def check_and_update_table():
    """Update the table schema while preserving existing data."""
    conn = create_connection()
    cursor = conn.cursor()
```

```python
# Create a new table with the desired schema
cursor.execute('''
CREATE TABLE IF NOT EXISTS new_users (
id INTEGER PRIMARY KEY AUTOINCREMENT,
first_name TEXT NOT NULL,
last_name TEXT NOT NULL,
user_id TEXT NOT NULL UNIQUE,
email TEXT NOT NULL UNIQUE,
password TEXT NOT NULL
)
''')
# Copy the data from the old table to the new table
# Generate unique email for each user based on their existing ID
cursor.execute('''
INSERT INTO new_users (id, password, user_id, first_name, last_name, email)
SELECT id, password, 'defaultUserID', 'DefaultFirstName', 'DefaultLastName', 'user_' || id || '@default.com'
FROM users
''')
# Drop the old table
cursor.execute('DROP TABLE users')
# Rename the new table to the original table name
cursor.execute('ALTER TABLE new_users RENAME TO users')
conn.commit()
conn.close()
def add_admin():
    """Add an admin user to the database with predefined credentials."""
admin_id = '000000'
admin_first_name = 'Admin'
admin_last_name = 'User'
admin_user_id = 'admin'
admin_email = 'amahir@bedford.ac.uk' # Replace with the desired admin email if needed
admin_password = 'Bedford@2024' # The predetermined admin password
# Hash the admin password
hashed_admin_password = bcrypt.hashpw(admin_password.encode('utf-8'), bcrypt.gensalt())
# Add the admin user to the database
conn = create_connection()
cursor = conn.cursor()
cursor.execute('''
INSERT OR IGNORE INTO users(first_name, last_name, user_id, email, password)
VALUES(?, ?, ?, ?, ?)
''', (admin_first_name, admin_last_name, admin_user_id, admin_email, hashed_admin_password))
conn.commit()
conn.close()
def create_connection():
```

```python
"""Create a database connection to the SQLite database specified by DB_PATH."""
conn = None
try:
    conn = sqlite3.connect(DB_PATH)
    return conn
except sqlite3.Error as e:
    print(e)
return conn
def create_table():
    """Create a table (if not exists) for storing user credentials."""
    conn = create_connection()
    cursor = conn.cursor()
    cursor.execute('''
    CREATE TABLE IF NOT EXISTS users (
    id INTEGER PRIMARY KEY AUTOINCREMENT,
    first_name TEXT NOT NULL,
    last_name TEXT NOT NULL,
    user_id TEXT NOT NULL UNIQUE,
    email TEXT NOT NULL UNIQUE,
    password TEXT NOT NULL
    )
    ''')
    conn.commit()
    conn.close()


# Initialise the database and table
if __name__ == '__main__':
    create_table()
    check_and_update_table() # Make sure the table schema is up to date
    add_admin() # This will add the admin user when the script is run standalone
```

>>>

user.py (User Class)

A class that represents a user and its attributes.

<<<

```python
from auth import add_user, validate_user, hash_password
class User:
    def __init__(self, first_name, last_name, user_id, email, password):
        self.first_name = first_name
        self.last_name = last_name
        self.user_id = user_id
        self.email = email
        self.password = password
```

```python
def register(self):
# Here you can include any additional validation if necessary
add_user(self.first_name, self.last_name, self.user_id, self.email, self.password)
return True
def check_credentials(self):
# This method would be used to validate the user's login credentials
return validate_user(self.email, self.password)
>>>
```

auth.py (Authentication Logic)

Contains authentication and authorization logic.

```python
<<<
import bcrypt
import sqlite3
from database import create_connection
def hash_password(password):
"""Hash a password with bcrypt."""
return bcrypt.hashpw(password.encode('utf-8'), bcrypt.gensalt())
def validate_user(username, password):
"""Validate a user's login credentials."""
conn = create_connection()
cursor = conn.cursor()
cursor.execute('''
SELECT password FROM users WHERE user_id=? OR email=?
''', (username, username,))
user_data = cursor.fetchone()
conn.close()
if user_data:
stored_password = user_data[0]
return bcrypt.checkpw(password.encode('utf-8'), stored_password)
return False
def add_user(first_name, last_name, user_id, email, password):
"""Add a new user to the database."""
conn = create_connection()
cursor = conn.cursor()
hashed_password = hash_password(password)
cursor.execute('''
INSERT INTO users(first_name, last_name, user_id, email, password)
VALUES(?, ?, ?, ?, ?)
''', (first_name, last_name, user_id, email, hashed_password))
conn.commit()
conn.close()
>>>
```

ui.py (User Interface)

113

Contains all the PyQt5 UI classes.
<<<

```python
##########################################################
## Atheer Work: Research Tracker Project © 2024 A Mahir ###
##########################################################
# ********************************************************************
import os
import sys
import sqlite3
import re
import bcrypt
from PyQt5.QtWidgets import (QApplication, QMainWindow, QPushButton, QLineEdit, QMessageBox, QColorDialog, QLabel,
QInputDialog, QVBoxLayout, QWidget, QCheckBox, QHBoxLayout)
from PyQt5.QtCore import Qt, QSize, QMimeData, QUrl, pyqtSignal, QObject
from PyQt5.QtGui import QImage, QPixmap, QDragEnterEvent, QDropEvent, QPalette, QBrush
from PyQt5.QtGui import QDesktopServices
from PyQt5.QtCore import QUrl
from auth import validate_user, add_user
os.system('cls||clear') # clear the terminal
# Global signal class
class GlobalSignals(QObject):
background_image_changed = pyqtSignal(str)
global_signals = GlobalSignals() # Create an instance of the global signals class
global_background_pixmap = None
def set_global_background_image(image_path):
global global_background_pixmap
global_background_pixmap = QPixmap(image_path)
global_signals.background_image_changed.emit(image_path) # Emit the signal through the instance
class CustomWindow(QMainWindow):
def __init__(self, parent=None):
super().__init__(parent)
self.setFixedSize(QSize(800, 400))
global_signals.background_image_changed.connect(self.update_background) # Connect to the global signal
def update_background(self, image_path):
if QPixmap(image_path).isNull():
QMessageBox.warning(self, 'Error', 'The image file is not valid.')
return
palette = QPalette()
brush = QBrush(QPixmap(image_path).scaled(self.size(), Qt.KeepAspectRatioByExpanding,
Qt.SmoothTransformation))
palette.setBrush(QPalette.Window, brush)
self.setPalette(palette)
```

```python
def create_child_window(self, window_class):
child_window = window_class(self)
global_signals.background_image_changed.connect(child_window.update_background)
child_window.show()
class DraggableLabel(QLabel):
imageDropped = pyqtSignal(str) # Signal to emit the file path
def __init__(self, parent=None):
super().__init__(parent)
self.setAcceptDrops(True)
self.setAutoFillBackground(True)
def dragEnterEvent(self, event: QDragEnterEvent):
if event.mimeData().hasUrls():
event.acceptProposedAction()
def dropEvent(self, event: QDropEvent):
mimeData = event.mimeData()
if mimeData.hasUrls():
urls = mimeData.urls()
if len(urls) > 0:
image_path = urls[0].toLocalFile()
self.imageDropped.emit(image_path)
event.acceptProposedAction()
# Continue from Part 1
class LoginWindow(CustomWindow):
def __init__(self, parent=None):
super().__init__(parent)
self.setWindowTitle('Login Window')
self.initUI()
def initUI(self):
# Add layout, labels, line edits, and buttons for login functionality
self.username = QLineEdit(self)
self.password = QLineEdit(self)
self.password.setEchoMode(QLineEdit.Password)
self.login_button = QPushButton('Login', self)
self.login_button.clicked.connect(self.login)
self.show_password_checkbox = QCheckBox('Show Password', self)
self.show_password_checkbox.stateChanged.connect(self.toggle_password_visibility)
# Set placeholder text for the password field
self.password.setPlaceholderText("Enter your password")
# Set the echo mode to hide the password initially
self.password.setEchoMode(QLineEdit.Password)
layout = QVBoxLayout()
layout.addWidget(QLabel('Enter your username:'))
layout.addWidget(self.username)
layout.addWidget(QLabel('Enter your password:'))
```

```python
layout.addWidget(self.password)
layout.addWidget(self.show_password_checkbox) # Add the checkbox to the layout
layout.addWidget(self.login_button)
# "Forget Password" Button
self.forget_password_button = QPushButton('Forget Password')
self.forget_password_button.clicked.connect(self.forget_password)
layout.addWidget(self.forget_password_button)
# Set the central widget with the layout
central_widget = QWidget(self)
central_widget.setLayout(layout)
self.setCentralWidget(central_widget)
def login(self):
username = self.username.text() # Retrieve the text from the username input
password = self.password.text() # Retrieve the text from the password input
if username and password: # Check if both username and password fields are not empty
if validate_user(username, password): # Use the validate_user function from # Now using the auth module
QMessageBox.information(self, 'Success', 'Login successful!')
else:
QMessageBox.warning(self, 'Error', 'Invalid username or password.')
else:
QMessageBox.warning(self, 'Error', 'Please enter both username and password.')
def toggle_password_visibility(self, state):
if state == Qt.Checked:
self.password.setEchoMode(QLineEdit.Normal)
else:
self.password.setEchoMode(QLineEdit.Password)
def forget_password(self):
# Open the default email client to send an email
admin_email = "amahir@gmail.com"
subject = "Password Reset Request"
body = "I have forgotten my password and request assistance to reset it."
mailto_link = f"mailto:{admin_email}?subject={subject}&body={body}"
QDesktopServices.openUrl(QUrl(mailto_link))


class RegisterWindow(CustomWindow):
def __init__(self, parent=None):
super().__init__(parent)
self.setWindowTitle('Register Window')
# Initialise all QLineEdit attributes before calling initUI()
self.first_name = QLineEdit(self)
self.last_name = QLineEdit(self)
self.user_id = QLineEdit(self)
self.username = QLineEdit(self)
self.confirm_username = QLineEdit(self)
```

```python
self.password = QLineEdit(self)
self.confirm_password = QLineEdit(self)
self.initUI()
def initUI(self):
layout = QVBoxLayout()
# Create horizontal layouts for each label-input pair
fields = [
('First Name:', self.first_name),
('Last Name:', self.last_name),
('ID:', self.user_id),
('Enter your username (email):', self.username),
('Re-enter your username (email):', self.confirm_username),
('Password:', self.password),
('Rewrite Password to validate:', self.confirm_password)
]
for label_text, widget in fields:
row_layout = QHBoxLayout()
label = QLabel(label_text)
label.setAlignment(Qt.AlignRight | Qt.AlignVCenter) # Align right for the label
row_layout.addWidget(label)
row_layout.addWidget(widget) # Add the corresponding input field
layout.addLayout(row_layout) # Add the horizontal layout to the main vertical layout
# Show Password Checkbox
self.show_password_checkbox = QCheckBox('Show Password')
self.show_password_checkbox.stateChanged.connect(self.toggle_password_visibility)
layout.addWidget(self.show_password_checkbox)
# Set placeholder text for password fields
self.password.setPlaceholderText("Password (UpperCase, LowerCase, Special Character, Length > 8)")
self.confirm_password.setPlaceholderText("Rewrite Password to validate")
# Set the echo mode to hide the password initially
self.password.setEchoMode(QLineEdit.Password)
self.confirm_password.setEchoMode(QLineEdit.Password)
# "Show Password" Checkbox
self.show_password_checkbox = QCheckBox('Show Password')
self.show_password_checkbox.stateChanged.connect(self.toggle_password_visibility)

# Register Button
self.register_button = QPushButton('Register')
self.register_button.clicked.connect(self.register)
layout.addWidget(self.register_button)
central_widget = QWidget(self)
central_widget.setLayout(layout)
self.setCentralWidget(central_widget)
def toggle_password_visibility(self, state):
```

```python
echo_mode = QLineEdit.Normal if state == Qt.Checked else QLineEdit.Password
self.password.setEchoMode(echo_mode)
self.confirm_password.setEchoMode(echo_mode)
def register(self):
# Gather all the inputs
first_name = self.first_name.text().strip()
last_name = self.last_name.text().strip()
user_id = self.user_id.text().strip()
email = self.username.text().strip()
confirm_email = self.confirm_username.text().strip()
password = self.password.text()
confirm_password = self.confirm_password.text()
add_user(first_name, last_name, user_id, email, password) # Now using the auth module
QMessageBox.information(self, 'Success', 'Registration successful!')

def hash_password(self, password):
# Hash a password with bcrypt
hashed = bcrypt.hashpw(password.encode('utf-8'), bcrypt.gensalt())
return hashed

class LoginRegisterWindow(CustomWindow):
def __init__(self):
super().__init__()
self.setWindowTitle('Login/Register Window')
central_widget = QWidget(self)
self.setCentralWidget(central_widget)
layout = QVBoxLayout(central_widget)
self.background_label = DraggableLabel(self)
self.background_label.resize(self.size())
layout.addWidget(self.background_label)
self.background_label.imageDropped.connect(set_global_background_image)
self.register_button = QPushButton('Register', self)
self.register_button.clicked.connect(lambda: self.create_child_window(RegisterWindow))
layout.addWidget(self.register_button)
self.login_button = QPushButton('Login', self)
self.login_button.clicked.connect(lambda: self.create_child_window(LoginWindow))
layout.addWidget(self.login_button)
self.change_color_button = QPushButton('Change Background Color', self)
self.change_color_button.clicked.connect(self.change_background_color)
layout.addWidget(self.change_color_button)
def create_child_window(self, window_class):
child_window = window_class(self)
child_window.show()
def change_background_color(self):
```

120

```python
color = QColorDialog.getColor()
if color.isValid():
palette = QPalette()
palette.setColor(QPalette.Window, color)
self.setPalette(palette)
QApplication.instance().setPalette(palette)
def set_background_image(self, image_path):
set_global_background_image(image_path) # This will trigger the update_background for all windows
>>>
```

config.py

Configuration parameters for the application.

<<<

```python
# config.py
DB_PATH = 'users.db'
ADMIN_EMAIL = 'amahir@bedford.ac.uk'
ADMIN_PASSWORD = 'Bedford@2024'
>>>
```

utils.py

Utility functions that can be used across the application.

<<<

```python
# utils.py
import os
def clear_terminal():
os.system('cls||clear')
>>>
```

Here's a textual description of what the diagram could look like:

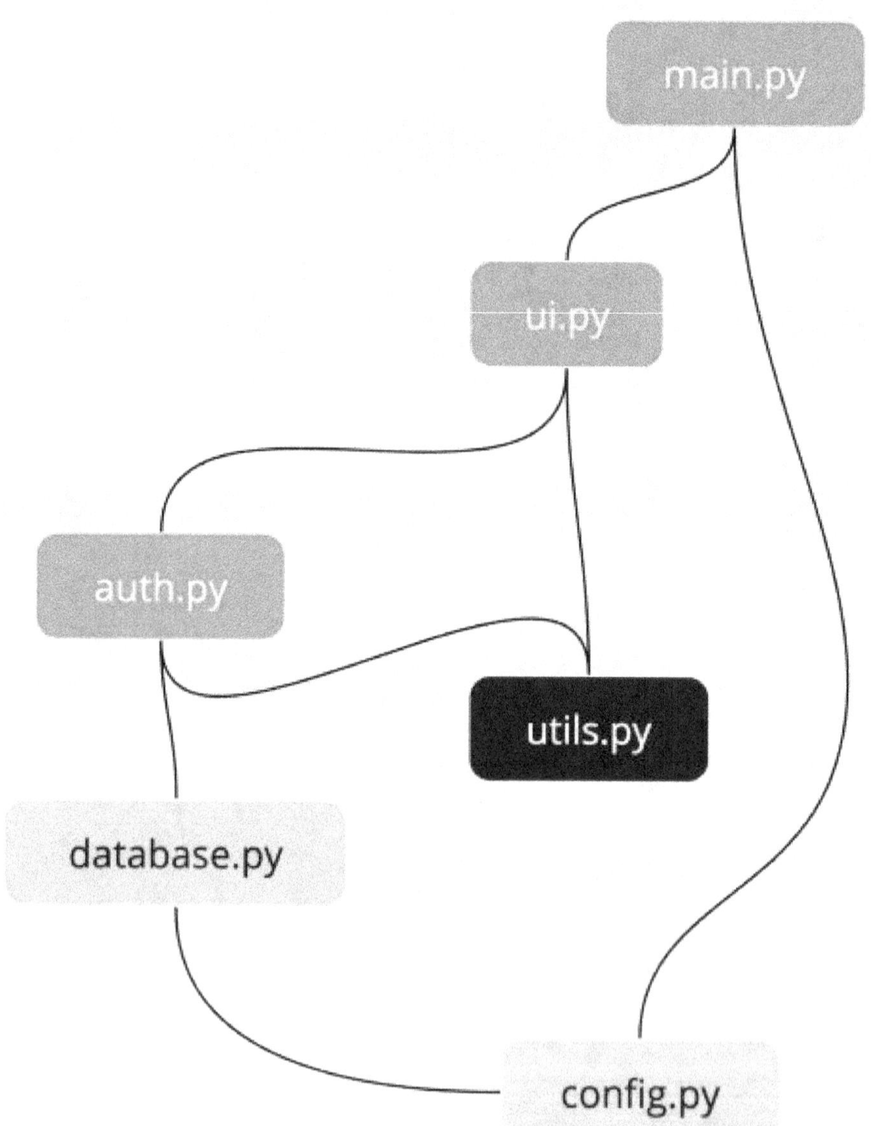

● main.py - This is the entry point of the application. It would be represented as a rectangle labelled "main.py". From this rectangle, arrows would point to ui.py and config.py.

● ui.py - This module contains all user interface components. It would be another rectangle labelled "ui.py". It would have arrows coming from main.py and pointing towards auth.py and utils.py to indicate the use of these modules within the UI.

● auth.py - Handles authentication logic. A rectangle labelled "auth.py" would have arrows pointing from ui.py and towards database.py and utils.py, indicating that it uses functions from both of these modules.

● database.py - Manages database operations. A rectangle for "database.py" would have arrows coming from auth.py to show that auth.py makes calls to the database operations defined here.

- config.py - Contains configuration settings. It would be a rectangle with arrows pointing towards both main.py and database.py, indicating that these modules read configuration settings.

- utils.py - A collection of utility functions. A rectangle for "utils.py" with arrows pointing from ui.py and auth.py, since these modules would use the utility functions.

https://miro.com/app/board/uXjVN-q6qb8=/

Version 12 of implementation (Refine Ver11):

121

Analysis from professional POV:

The integration between the files looks conceptually correct, and the division of responsibilities is well-aligned with good software architecture principles. However, I'll point out a few things you might need to consider and update for consistency and correctness:

1. config.py: This file is correctly holding the configuration constants that might be used across the application. You've done well to use these constants in database.py.
2. utils.py: The clear_terminal() function is a utility that's used in both main.py and database.py. This is a good use of a utility function.
3. database.py: You're using DB_PATH from config.py which is good. However, there's a section where you're creating a new table new_users and copying data from an old table users. This seems like a one-time migration script rather than something that should be in your main database operations file. Make sure this is intentional and appropriate for your use case.
4. auth.py: It's using functions from database.py to interact with the database, which is a good separation of concerns. It also correctly uses bcrypt for password hashing.
5. user.py: This class is a representation of a user and utilises auth.py for adding a user and validating credentials. This is a good example of object-oriented design.
6. ui.py: It seems to be well-integrated, using functions from auth.py. It also utilises the global signals for background changes, which is a nice touch for a dynamic UI.
7. LoginWindow and RegisterWindow: These are classes within ui.py that handle the user interface for login and registration. They correctly use the auth.py module to interact with the authentication logic.
8. LoginRegisterWindow: This is the main window that allows navigation between the login and registration windows. It uses the CustomWindow class and the DraggableLabel class for the background functionality.

To further ensure the integration is seamless, you would need to test the application extensively. Unit tests for individual components (like User, CustomWindow, etc.) and integration tests for the application as a whole would be beneficial to catch any issues that could arise from the interaction between these components.

A final note: Make sure you handle database connection closing properly. In database.py, you have a create_connection function that could potentially leave connections open if an exception occurs. It's usually a good practice to use context managers (with statements) to ensure that resources are properly closed after use.

Lastly, remember to follow the security best practices for password handling and database operations, especially if this application is intended for real-world use.

main.py

Entry point of the application, responsible for starting the application.

<<<

```python
###########################################################
## Atheer Work: Research Tracker Project © 2024 A Mahir ###
###########################################################
# *****************************************************************
# clear the terminal
from utils import clear_terminal
clear_terminal()
# *****************************************************************
import sys
from PyQt5.QtWidgets import QApplication
from ui import LoginRegisterWindow
if __name__ == '__main__':
app = QApplication(sys.argv)
win = LoginRegisterWindow()
win.show()
sys.exit(app.exec_())
```

>>>

database.py (Database Operations)

Contains the database connection and operations.

<<<

```python
###########################################################
## Atheer Work: Research Tracker Project © 2024 A Mahir ###
###########################################################
# *****************************************************************
# clear the terminal
# clear the terminal
from utils import clear_terminal
clear_terminal()
# *****************************************************************
import sqlite3
import bcrypt
from config import DB_PATH, ADMIN_EMAIL, ADMIN_PASSWORD
def create_connection():
"""Create a database connection to the SQLite database specified by DB_PATH."""
conn = sqlite3.connect(DB_PATH)
return conn
def create_table():
"""Create a table (if not exists) for storing user credentials."""
with create_connection() as conn:
```

```python
cursor = conn.cursor()
cursor.execute('''
CREATE TABLE IF NOT EXISTS users (
id INTEGER PRIMARY KEY AUTOINCREMENT,
first_name TEXT NOT NULL,
last_name TEXT NOT NULL,
user_id TEXT NOT NULL UNIQUE,
email TEXT NOT NULL UNIQUE,
password TEXT NOT NULL
)
''')
conn.commit()
def add_user(first_name, last_name, user_id, email, password):
"""Add a new user to the database."""
hashed_password = bcrypt.hashpw(password.encode('utf-8'), bcrypt.gensalt())
with create_connection() as conn:
cursor = conn.cursor()
cursor.execute('''
INSERT INTO users(first_name, last_name, user_id, email, password)
VALUES(?, ?, ?, ?, ?)
''', (first_name, last_name, user_id, email, hashed_password))
conn.commit()
def add_admin():
"""Add an admin user to the database with predefined credentials."""
admin_first_name = 'Admin'
admin_last_name = 'User'
admin_user_id = 'admin'
admin_email = ADMIN_EMAIL # Corrected to use the standalone variable
admin_password = ADMIN_PASSWORD # Corrected to use the standalone variable
add_user(admin_first_name, admin_last_name, admin_user_id, admin_email, admin_password)
def check_and_update_table():
"""Update the table schema while preserving existing data."""
with create_connection() as conn:
cursor = conn.cursor()
# Create a new table with the desired schema
cursor.execute('''
CREATE TABLE IF NOT EXISTS new_users (
id INTEGER PRIMARY KEY AUTOINCREMENT,
first_name TEXT NOT NULL,
last_name TEXT NOT NULL,
user_id TEXT NOT NULL UNIQUE,
email TEXT NOT NULL UNIQUE,
password TEXT NOT NULL
)
```

```python
''')
# Copy the data from the old table to the new table
cursor.execute('''
INSERT INTO new_users (id, first_name, last_name, user_id, email, password)
SELECT id, first_name, last_name, user_id, email, password FROM users
''')
# Drop the old table
cursor.execute('DROP TABLE IF EXISTS users')
# Rename the new table to the original table name
cursor.execute('ALTER TABLE new_users RENAME TO users')
conn.commit()
# Initialise the database and table
if __name__ == '__main__':
create_table()
check_and_update_table()
add_admin() # Add an admin user with predefined credentials
>>>
```

user.py (User Class)

A class that represents a user and its attributes.

<<<

```python
from auth import add_user, validate_user, hash_password
class User:
def __init__(self, first_name, last_name, user_id, email, password):
self.first_name = first_name
self.last_name = last_name
self.user_id = user_id
self.email = email
self.password = password
def register(self):
# Here you can include any additional validation if necessary
add_user(self.first_name, self.last_name, self.user_id, self.email, self.password)
return True
def check_credentials(self):
# This method would be used to validate the user's login credentials
return validate_user(self.email, self.password)
>>>
```

auth.py (Authentication Logic)

Contains authentication and authorization logic.

<<<

```python
import bcrypt
import sqlite3
from database import create_connection
def hash_password(password):
```

```python
    """Hash a password with bcrypt."""
    return bcrypt.hashpw(password.encode('utf-8'), bcrypt.gensalt())
def validate_user(username, password):
    """Validate a user's login credentials."""
    conn = create_connection()
    cursor = conn.cursor()
    cursor.execute('''
SELECT password FROM users WHERE user_id=? OR email=?
''', (username, username,))
    user_data = cursor.fetchone()
    conn.close()
    if user_data:
        stored_password = user_data[0]
        return bcrypt.checkpw(password.encode('utf-8'), stored_password)
    return False
def add_user(first_name, last_name, user_id, email, password):
    """Add a new user to the database."""
    conn = create_connection()
    cursor = conn.cursor()
    hashed_password = hash_password(password)
    cursor.execute('''
INSERT INTO users(first_name, last_name, user_id, email, password)
VALUES(?, ?, ?, ?, ?)
''', (first_name, last_name, user_id, email, hashed_password))
    conn.commit()
    conn.close()
```

\>\>\>

ui.py (User Interface)
Contains all the PyQt5 UI classes.

\<\<\<

```python
##############################################################
## Atheer Work: Research Tracker Project © 2024 A Mahir ###
##############################################################
# ****************************************************************
import os
import sys
import sqlite3
import re
import bcrypt
from PyQt5.QtWidgets import (QApplication, QMainWindow, QPushButton, QLineEdit, QMessageBox, QColorDialog, QLabel,
QInputDialog, QVBoxLayout, QWidget, QCheckBox, QHBoxLayout)
from PyQt5.QtCore import Qt, QSize, QMimeData, QUrl, pyqtSignal, QObject
```

```python
from PyQt5.QtGui import QImage, QPixmap, QDragEnterEvent, QDropEvent, QPalette, QBrush
from PyQt5.QtGui import QDesktopServices
from PyQt5.QtCore import QUrl
from auth import validate_user, add_user
os.system('cls||clear') # clear the terminal
# Global signal class
class GlobalSignals(QObject):
background_image_changed = pyqtSignal(str)
global_signals = GlobalSignals() # Create an instance of the global signals class
global_background_pixmap = None
def set_global_background_image(image_path):
global global_background_pixmap
global_background_pixmap = QPixmap(image_path)
global_signals.background_image_changed.emit(image_path) # Emit the signal through the instance
class CustomWindow(QMainWindow):
def __init__(self, parent=None):
super().__init__(parent)
self.setFixedSize(QSize(800, 400))
global_signals.background_image_changed.connect(self.update_background) # Connect to the global signal
def update_background(self, image_path):
if QPixmap(image_path).isNull():
QMessageBox.warning(self, 'Error', 'The image file is not valid.')
return
palette = QPalette()
brush = QBrush(QPixmap(image_path).scaled(self.size(), Qt.KeepAspectRatioByExpanding,
Qt.SmoothTransformation))
palette.setBrush(QPalette.Window, brush)
self.setPalette(palette)
def create_child_window(self, window_class):
child_window = window_class(self)
global_signals.background_image_changed.connect(child_window.update_background)
child_window.show()
class DraggableLabel(QLabel):
imageDropped = pyqtSignal(str) # Signal to emit the file path
def __init__(self, parent=None):
super().__init__(parent)
self.setAcceptDrops(True)
self.setAutoFillBackground(True)
def dragEnterEvent(self, event: QDragEnterEvent):
if event.mimeData().hasUrls():
event.acceptProposedAction()
def dropEvent(self, event: QDropEvent):
mimeData = event.mimeData()
if mimeData.hasUrls():
```

```python
urls = mimeData.urls()
if len(urls) > 0:
image_path = urls[0].toLocalFile()
self.imageDropped.emit(image_path)
event.acceptProposedAction()
# Continue from Part 1
class LoginWindow(CustomWindow):
def __init__(self, parent=None):
super().__init__(parent)
self.setWindowTitle('Login Window')
self.initUI()
def initUI(self):
# Add layout, labels, line edits, and buttons for login functionality
self.username = QLineEdit(self)
self.password = QLineEdit(self)
self.password.setEchoMode(QLineEdit.Password)
self.login_button = QPushButton('Login', self)
self.login_button.clicked.connect(self.login)
self.show_password_checkbox = QCheckBox('Show Password', self)
self.show_password_checkbox.stateChanged.connect(self.toggle_password_visibility)
# Set placeholder text for the password field
self.password.setPlaceholderText("Enter your password")
# Set the echo mode to hide the password initially
self.password.setEchoMode(QLineEdit.Password)
layout = QVBoxLayout()
layout.addWidget(QLabel('Enter your username:'))
layout.addWidget(self.username)
layout.addWidget(QLabel('Enter your password:'))
layout.addWidget(self.password)
layout.addWidget(self.show_password_checkbox) # Add the checkbox to the layout
layout.addWidget(self.login_button)
# "Forget Password" Button
self.forget_password_button = QPushButton('Forget Password')
self.forget_password_button.clicked.connect(self.forget_password)
layout.addWidget(self.forget_password_button)
# Set the central widget with the layout
central_widget = QWidget(self)
central_widget.setLayout(layout)
self.setCentralWidget(central_widget)
def login(self):
username = self.username.text() # Retrieve the text from the username input
password = self.password.text() # Retrieve the text from the password input
if username and password: # Check if both username and password fields are not empty
if validate_user(username, password): # Use the validate_user function from # Now using the auth module
```

```python
            QMessageBox.information(self, 'Success', 'Login successful!')
        else:
            QMessageBox.warning(self, 'Error', 'Invalid username or password.')
    else:
        QMessageBox.warning(self, 'Error', 'Please enter both username and password.')
def toggle_password_visibility(self, state):
    if state == Qt.Checked:
        self.password.setEchoMode(QLineEdit.Normal)
    else:
        self.password.setEchoMode(QLineEdit.Password)
def forget_password(self):
    # Open the default email client to send an email
    admin_email = "amahir@gmail.com"
    subject = "Password Reset Request"
    body = "I have forgotten my password and request assistance to reset it."
    mailto_link = f"mailto:{admin_email}?subject={subject}&body={body}"
    QDesktopServices.openUrl(QUrl(mailto_link))


class RegisterWindow(CustomWindow):
    def __init__(self, parent=None):
        super().__init__(parent)
        self.setWindowTitle('Register Window')
        # Initialise all QLineEdit attributes before calling initUI()
        self.first_name = QLineEdit(self)
        self.last_name = QLineEdit(self)
        self.user_id = QLineEdit(self)
        self.username = QLineEdit(self)
        self.confirm_username = QLineEdit(self)
        self.password = QLineEdit(self)
        self.confirm_password = QLineEdit(self)
        self.initUI()
    def initUI(self):
        layout = QVBoxLayout()
        # Create horizontal layouts for each label-input pair
        fields = [
            ('First Name:', self.first_name),
            ('Last Name:', self.last_name),
            ('ID:', self.user_id),
            ('Enter your username (email):', self.username),
            ('Re-enter your username (email):', self.confirm_username),
            ('Password:', self.password),
            ('Rewrite Password to validate:', self.confirm_password)
        ]
        for label_text, widget in fields:
```

```python
row_layout = QHBoxLayout()
label = QLabel(label_text)
label.setAlignment(Qt.AlignRight | Qt.AlignVCenter) # Align right for the label
row_layout.addWidget(label)
row_layout.addWidget(widget) # Add the corresponding input field
layout.addLayout(row_layout) # Add the horizontal layout to the main vertical layout
# Show Password Checkbox
self.show_password_checkbox = QCheckBox('Show Password')
self.show_password_checkbox.stateChanged.connect(self.toggle_password_visibility)
layout.addWidget(self.show_password_checkbox)
# Set placeholder text for password fields
self.password.setPlaceholderText("Password (UpperCase, LowerCase, Special Character, Length > 8)")
self.confirm_password.setPlaceholderText("Rewrite Password to validate")
# Set the echo mode to hide the password initially
self.password.setEchoMode(QLineEdit.Password)
self.confirm_password.setEchoMode(QLineEdit.Password)
# "Show Password" Checkbox
self.show_password_checkbox = QCheckBox('Show Password')
self.show_password_checkbox.stateChanged.connect(self.toggle_password_visibility)

# Register Button
self.register_button = QPushButton('Register')
self.register_button.clicked.connect(self.register)
layout.addWidget(self.register_button)
central_widget = QWidget(self)
central_widget.setLayout(layout)
self.setCentralWidget(central_widget)
def toggle_password_visibility(self, state):
echo_mode = QLineEdit.Normal if state == Qt.Checked else QLineEdit.Password
self.password.setEchoMode(echo_mode)
self.confirm_password.setEchoMode(echo_mode)
def register(self):
# Gather all the inputs
first_name = self.first_name.text().strip()
last_name = self.last_name.text().strip()
user_id = self.user_id.text().strip()
email = self.username.text().strip()
confirm_email = self.confirm_username.text().strip()
password = self.password.text()
confirm_password = self.confirm_password.text()
add_user(first_name, last_name, user_id, email, password) # Now using the auth module
QMessageBox.information(self, 'Success', 'Registration successful!')

def hash_password(self, password):
```

```python
# Hash a password with bcrypt
hashed = bcrypt.hashpw(password.encode('utf-8'), bcrypt.gensalt())
return hashed

class LoginRegisterWindow(CustomWindow):
def __init__(self):
super().__init__()
self.setWindowTitle('Login/Register Window')
central_widget = QWidget(self)
self.setCentralWidget(central_widget)
layout = QVBoxLayout(central_widget)
self.background_label = DraggableLabel(self)
self.background_label.resize(self.size())
layout.addWidget(self.background_label)
self.background_label.imageDropped.connect(set_global_background_image)
self.register_button = QPushButton('Register', self)
self.register_button.clicked.connect(lambda: self.create_child_window(RegisterWindow))
layout.addWidget(self.register_button)
self.login_button = QPushButton('Login', self)
self.login_button.clicked.connect(lambda: self.create_child_window(LoginWindow))
layout.addWidget(self.login_button)
self.change_color_button = QPushButton('Change Background Color', self)
self.change_color_button.clicked.connect(self.change_background_color)
layout.addWidget(self.change_color_button)
def create_child_window(self, window_class):
child_window = window_class(self)
child_window.show()
def change_background_color(self):
color = QColorDialog.getColor()
if color.isValid():
palette = QPalette()
palette.setColor(QPalette.Window, color)
self.setPalette(palette)
QApplication.instance().setPalette(palette)
def set_background_image(self, image_path):
set_global_background_image(image_path) # This will trigger the update_background for all windows
>>>
```

config.py

Configuration parameters for the application.

```
<<<
# config.py
DB_PATH = 'users.db'
ADMIN_EMAIL = 'amahir@bedford.ac.uk'
```

```
ADMIN_PASSWORD = 'Bedford@2024'
```

>>>

utils.py

Utility functions that can be used across the application.

<<<

```
# utils.py
import os
def clear_terminal():
os.system('cls||clear')
```

>>>

Version 13 of implementation (Refine Ver12):

The application is currently operating as anticipated. However, there is a need to implement the following enhancements:

1. Incorporate two updates into the system:
   a. Introduce a new column in the user table labelled 'Role,' encompassing three distinct roles for users: Administrator, Supervisor, and Student.
   b. During the registration process, inform users that the default role assigned will be 'Student' unless modified by an Administrator or Supervisor.
2. If a user selects the 'Student' role during registration, they must seek approval from either a Supervisor or Administrator to finalise their role assignment.
3. If a user initially selects the 'Student' role but is identified as a Supervisor, the role designation should be adjusted and validated by a Supervisor or Administrator.
4. In the event that a user initially selects the 'Student' role but is recognized as an Administrator, the role must be modified and validated exclusively by an Administrator.
5. It is important to note that new users will be unable to access the system until their role designation has been approved.

Implementation

To implement these updates, you will need to modify the database schema, update the registration logic, and implement a role approval system. Here's how you can approach each development:

1. Update the database schema to include a role column.

You will need to update the create_table function in database.py to include the 'Role' column and modify the add_user function to accept a role parameter.

database.py:

```python
from utils import clear_terminal
clear_terminal()
import sqlite3
import bcrypt
from config import DB_PATH, ADMIN_EMAIL, ADMIN_PASSWORD
def create_connection():
"""Create a database connection to the SQLite database specified by DB_PATH."""
conn = sqlite3.connect(DB_PATH)
return conn
# update 202312272031 start
#**********************************************************************#
def ensure_table_schema():
with create_connection() as conn:
cursor = conn.cursor()
# Create table if it doesn't exist
cursor.execute('''
CREATE TABLE IF NOT EXISTS users (
id INTEGER PRIMARY KEY AUTOINCREMENT,
first_name TEXT NOT NULL,
last_name TEXT NOT NULL,
user_id TEXT NOT NULL UNIQUE,
email TEXT NOT NULL UNIQUE,
password TEXT NOT NULL
)
''')
# Check if 'role' column exists and add if not
cursor.execute("PRAGMA table_info(users)")
columns = [info[1] for info in cursor.fetchall()]
if 'role' not in columns:
cursor.execute('ALTER TABLE users ADD COLUMN role TEXT DEFAULT "Student"')
# Check if 'role_approved' column exists and add if not
if 'role_approved' not in columns:
cursor.execute('ALTER TABLE users ADD COLUMN role_approved INTEGER DEFAULT 0')
conn.commit()
#**********************************************************************#
# update 202312272031 end
# update 2023122719:29 start
#**********************************************************************#
def add_user(first_name, last_name, user_id, email, password, role='Student', role_approved=0):
"""Add a new user to the database with a specified role and approval status."""
hashed_password = bcrypt.hashpw(password.encode('utf-8'), bcrypt.gensalt())
with create_connection() as conn:
cursor = conn.cursor()
cursor.execute('''
```

```python
INSERT INTO users(first_name, last_name, user_id, email, password, role, role_approved)
VALUES(?, ?, ?, ?, ?, ?, ?)
''', (first_name, last_name, user_id, email, hashed_password, role, role_approved))
conn.commit()
def add_admin():
    """Add an admin user to the database with predefined credentials and role."""
    admin_first_name = 'Admin'
    admin_last_name = 'User'
    admin_user_id = 'admin'
    admin_email = ADMIN_EMAIL # Corrected to use the standalone variable
    admin_password = ADMIN_PASSWORD # Corrected to use the standalone variable
    # Set the role as 'Administrator' and role_approved as 1 for the admin user
    add_user(admin_first_name, admin_last_name, admin_user_id, admin_email, admin_password, 'Administrator', 1)
#************************************************************************#
# update 2023122719:29 end
# update 2023122719:42 start for testing
#************************************************************************#
def add_test_users():
    # Add 3 random students (role-approved)
    for i in range(1, 4):
        add_user(f'Student{i}', 'Approved', f'student{i}', f'student{i}@example.com', 'password', 'Student', 1)
    # Add 3 random students (role not approved yet)
    for i in range(4, 7):
        add_user(f'Student{i}', 'NotApproved', f'student{i}', f'student{i}@example.com', 'password', 'Student', 0)
    # Add 2 random supervisors (role-approved)
    for i in range(1, 3):
        add_user(f'Supervisor{i}', 'Approved', f'supervisor{i}', f'supervisor{i}@example.com', 'password', 'Supervisor', 1)
    # Add 2 random admins (role-approved)
    for i in range(1, 3):
        add_user(f'Admin{i}', 'Approved', f'admin{i}', f'admin{i}@example.com', 'password', 'Administrator', 1)
#************************************************************************#
# update 2023122719:42 end
# update 2023122719:05 start
#************************************************************************#
# Add a function to update the user's role and approval status
def update_user_role(user_id, role, role_approved):
    with create_connection() as conn:
        cursor = conn.cursor()
        cursor.execute('''
UPDATE users SET role = ?, role_approved = ? WHERE user_id = ?
''', (role, role_approved, user_id))
        conn.commit()
#************************************************************************#
```

```python
# update 2023122719:05 end
# update 2023122719:51 start
#*************************************************************************#
def add_test_users():
    test_users = [
        # Students (role-approved)
        {"first_name": "Student1", "last_name": "Approved", "user_id": "student1", "email": "student1@example.com",
         "password": "password1", "role": "Student", "role_approved": 1},
        {"first_name": "Student2", "last_name": "Approved", "user_id": "student2", "email": "student2@example.com",
         "password": "password2", "role": "Student", "role_approved": 1},
        {"first_name": "Student3", "last_name": "Approved", "user_id": "student3", "email": "student3@example.com",
         "password": "password3", "role": "Student", "role_approved": 1},
        # Students (role not approved yet)
        {"first_name": "Student4", "last_name": "NotApproved", "user_id": "student4", "email": "student4@example.com",
         "password": "password4", "role": "Student", "role_approved": 0},
        {"first_name": "Student5", "last_name": "NotApproved", "user_id": "student5", "email": "student5@example.com",
         "password": "password5", "role": "Student", "role_approved": 0},
        {"first_name": "Student6", "last_name": "NotApproved", "user_id": "student6", "email": "student6@example.com",
         "password": "password6", "role": "Student", "role_approved": 0},
        # Supervisors (role-approved)
        {"first_name": "Supervisor1", "last_name": "Approved", "user_id": "supervisor1", "email": "supervisor1@example.com",
         "password": "password7", "role": "Supervisor", "role_approved": 1},
        {"first_name": "Supervisor2", "last_name": "Approved", "user_id": "supervisor2", "email": "supervisor2@example.com",
         "password": "password8", "role": "Supervisor", "role_approved": 1},
        # Admins (role-approved)
        {"first_name": "Admin1", "last_name": "Approved", "user_id": "admin1", "email": "admin1@example.com",
         "password": "password9", "role": "Administrator", "role_approved": 1},
        {"first_name": "Admin2", "last_name": "Approved", "user_id": "admin2", "email": "admin2@example.com",
         "password": "password10", "role": "Administrator", "role_approved": 1}
    ]
    for user in test_users:
        print(f"Adding user: {user['user_id']}, Role: {user['role']}, Password: {user['password']}")
        add_user(user["first_name"], user["last_name"], user["user_id"], user["email"], user["password"], user["role"],
                 user["role_approved"])
def display_users():
    """Display users with their roles and hashed passwords."""
    with create_connection() as conn:
        cursor = conn.cursor()
        cursor.execute('''
        SELECT id, first_name, last_name, user_id, email, role, role_approved, password FROM users
        ''')
        users = cursor.fetchall()
        for user in users:
            print(f"ID: {user[0]}, Name: {user[1]} {user[2]}, UserID: {user[3]}, Email: {user[4]}, Role: {user[5]}, Approved:
```

```python
{'Yes' if user[6] == 1 else 'No'}, Hashed Password: {user[7]}")
#*********************************************************************#
# update 2023122719:51 end
# update 202312272046 start
#*********************************************************************#
def user_exists(email):
"""Check if a user already exists in the database based on their email."""
with create_connection() as conn:
cursor = conn.cursor()
cursor.execute('SELECT id FROM users WHERE email = ?', (email,))
return cursor.fetchone() is not None
#*********************************************************************#
# update 202312272046 end

# update 202312272046 start
#*********************************************************************#
def main():
ensure_table_schema()
# Check if the admin user already exists before attempting to add
if not user_exists(ADMIN_EMAIL):
add_admin() # Add an admin user with the Administrator role and approved status
else:
print("Admin user already exists.")
# Similarly, check for other test users before adding
test_users_emails = [f'student{i}@example.com' for i in range(1, 7)] + \
[f'supervisor{i}@example.com' for i in range(1, 3)] + \
[f'admin{i}@example.com' for i in range(1, 3)]
for email in test_users_emails:
if not user_exists(email):
print(f"Adding test user with email: {email}")
# Logic to add the user
# Note: You need to pass the appropriate parameters to the add_user function based on the email
else:
print(f"User with email {email} already exists.")
display_users() # Display the list of users
if __name__ == '__main__':
main()
#*********************************************************************#
# update 202312272046 end
```

2. Update the other files (suggestions):

auth.py:

Here you will need to add the logic for role approval. This could be a set of functions that check and update the role approval status.

ui.py:

Adjust your registration UI to include role selection and display information about the default role being 'Student'. After registration, display a message informing the user that their role needs approval.

user.py:

In the User class, add an attribute for the role and modify the register method to handle the default role. You might also want to add methods for role adjustment and checking approval status.

These enhancements will require careful planning, especially regarding how users interact with the system and how roles are validated and approved. You'll need to ensure that your UI clearly communicates the role approval process to the users and that you have appropriate mechanisms in place for Administrators and Supervisors to approve roles.

Remember to secure the process for role adjustment and approval, possibly requiring re-authentication of the approving user, to prevent unauthorised role changes.

Version 14 of implementation (updating Ver13):

The following development document outlines the specific features and behaviour modifications to be implemented in the login process and the admin tools section of the application for admin users.

Login Window Behavior for Admin Users

Scenario 1: Admin Role Not Activated

- Condition: When an admin user logs in and their role is marked as "admin" in the system, but their role activation status (role_approved) is not yet activated (indicated by role_approved being 0 or false).

- Functionality:

- Provide an option within the login window to trigger the default email client on the user's system.

- The email should be pre-populated to send to all active admin users (users with role as "admin" and role_approved as 1 or true) with a request to activate the logged-in admin's role.

- The subject and body of the email should be appropriately crafted to convey the request for role activation.

Scenario 2: Admin Role Activated

- Condition: An admin user with an activated role (indicated by role_approved being 1 or true) logs into the system.

- Functionality: Open a new window titled "Admin Tools" which provides the following functionalities:

Admin Tools Window Features

Display All Users:

- A table view that lists all users in the system.

- The table should provide sorting options for the following attributes:

- First Name

- Last Name

- Username

- ID

- Email

- Roles

- Activation Status (tickbox)

Delete User:

- A table view similar to the Display All Users feature but with an additional "Delete" column containing checkboxes.

- Admin users can select multiple users for deletion by ticking the checkboxes beside their names.

- The admin cannot select themselves for deletion (self-deletion prevention).

- The table view should include sorting options as described in the Display All Users feature.

Update User:

- A table view that allows the admin to mark users for updates via checkboxes.

- It should be clarified what user attributes can be updated through this interface.

- The table view should provide the same sorting options as mentioned previously.

Reset Password:

- A feature within the table view that allows the admin to select users for password resets using checkboxes.

- When a user's password is reset, a mechanism should be in place for the user to be notified and prompted to change their password upon their next login.

- The table should also allow sorting by the various user attributes as mentioned above.

Additional Development Notes

- Implement appropriate error handling and user feedback mechanisms to ensure a smooth user experience.

- Ensure all email functionality adheres to security and privacy standards.

- Security measures must be in place to protect user data, especially when performing sensitive operations like password resets.

- Any changes to the user's status or credentials should be logged for audit purposes.

```
main.py
Entry point of the application, responsible for starting the application.
<<<
############################################################
## Atheer Work: Research Tracker Project © 2024 A Mahir ###
############################################################
# ******************************************************************
# clear the terminal
from utils import clear_terminal
clear_terminal()
# ******************************************************************
import sys
from PyQt5.QtWidgets import QApplication
from ui import LoginRegisterWindow
if __name__ == '__main__':
app = QApplication(sys.argv)
win = LoginRegisterWindow()
win.show()
sys.exit(app.exec_())
>>>
database.py (Database Operations)
Contains the database connection and operations.
<<<
############################################################
## Atheer Work: Research Tracker Project © 2024 A Mahir ###
############################################################
# ******************************************************************
# clear the terminal
# clear the terminal
from utils import clear_terminal
clear_terminal()
# ******************************************************************
import sqlite3
import bcrypt
from config import DB_PATH, ADMIN_EMAIL, ADMIN_PASSWORD
def create_connection():
    """Create a database connection to the SQLite database specified by DB_PATH."""
conn = sqlite3.connect(DB_PATH)
return conn
# update 202312272031 start
#******************************************************************#
def ensure_table_schema():
with create_connection() as conn:
```

```python
cursor = conn.cursor()
# Create table if it doesn't exist
cursor.execute('''
CREATE TABLE IF NOT EXISTS users (
id INTEGER PRIMARY KEY AUTOINCREMENT,
first_name TEXT NOT NULL,
last_name TEXT NOT NULL,
user_id TEXT NOT NULL UNIQUE,
email TEXT NOT NULL UNIQUE,
password TEXT NOT NULL
)
''')
# Check if 'role' column exists and add if not
cursor.execute("PRAGMA table_info(users)")
columns = [info[1] for info in cursor.fetchall()]
if 'role' not in columns:
cursor.execute('ALTER TABLE users ADD COLUMN role TEXT DEFAULT "Student"')
# Check if 'role_approved' column exists and add if not
if 'role_approved' not in columns:
cursor.execute('ALTER TABLE users ADD COLUMN role_approved INTEGER DEFAULT 0')
conn.commit()
#**********************************************************************#
# update 202312272031 end

# update 2023122719:29 start
#**********************************************************************#
def add_user(first_name, last_name, user_id, email, password, role='Student', role_approved=0):
    """Add a new user to the database with a specified role and approval status."""
    hashed_password = bcrypt.hashpw(password.encode('utf-8'), bcrypt.gensalt())
    with create_connection() as conn:
        cursor = conn.cursor()
        cursor.execute('''
        INSERT INTO users(first_name, last_name, user_id, email, password, role, role_approved)
        VALUES(?, ?, ?, ?, ?, ?, ?)
        ''', (first_name, last_name, user_id, email, hashed_password, role, role_approved))
        conn.commit()
def add_admin():
    """Add an admin user to the database with predefined credentials and role."""
    admin_first_name = 'Admin'
    admin_last_name = 'User'
    admin_user_id = 'admin'
    admin_email = ADMIN_EMAIL # Corrected to use the standalone variable
    admin_password = ADMIN_PASSWORD # Corrected to use the standalone variable
    # Set the role as 'Administrator' and role_approved as 1 for the admin user
```

```python
add_user(admin_first_name, admin_last_name, admin_user_id, admin_email, admin_password, 'Administrator',
1)
#*********************************************************************#
# update 2023122719:29 end
# update 2023122719:42 start for testing
#*********************************************************************#
def add_test_users():
# Add 3 random students (role-approved)
for i in range(1, 4):
add_user(f'Student{i}', 'Approved', f'student{i}', f'student{i}@example.com', 'password', 'Student', 1)
# Add 3 random students (role not approved yet)
for i in range(4, 7):
add_user(f'Student{i}', 'NotApproved', f'student{i}', f'student{i}@example.com', 'password', 'Student', 0)
# Add 2 random supervisors (role-approved)
for i in range(1, 3):
add_user(f'Supervisor{i}', 'Approved', f'supervisor{i}', f'supervisor{i}@example.com', 'password', 'Supervisor', 1)
# Add 2 random admins (role-approved)
for i in range(1, 3):
add_user(f'Admin{i}', 'Approved', f'admin{i}', f'admin{i}@example.com', 'password', 'Administrator', 1)
#*********************************************************************#
# update 2023122719:42 end

# update 2023122719:05 start
#*********************************************************************#
# Add a function to update the user's role and approval status
def update_user_role(user_id, role, role_approved):
with create_connection() as conn:
cursor = conn.cursor()
cursor.execute('''
UPDATE users SET role = ?, role_approved = ? WHERE user_id = ?
''', (role, role_approved, user_id))
conn.commit()
#*********************************************************************#
# update 2023122719:05 end
# update 2023122719:51 start
#*********************************************************************#
def add_test_users():
test_users = [
# Students (role-approved)
{"first_name": "Student1", "last_name": "Approved", "user_id": "student1", "email": "student1@example.com",
"password": "password1", "role": "Student", "role_approved": 1},
{"first_name": "Student2", "last_name": "Approved", "user_id": "student2", "email": "student2@example.com",
"password": "password2", "role": "Student", "role_approved": 1},
{"first_name": "Student3", "last_name": "Approved", "user_id": "student3", "email": "student3@example.com",
```

```python
    "password": "password3", "role": "Student", "role_approved": 1},
    # Students (role not approved yet)
    {"first_name": "Student4", "last_name": "NotApproved", "user_id": "student4", "email": "student4@example.com",
    "password": "password4", "role": "Student", "role_approved": 0},
    {"first_name": "Student5", "last_name": "NotApproved", "user_id": "student5", "email": "student5@example.com",
    "password": "password5", "role": "Student", "role_approved": 0},
    {"first_name": "Student6", "last_name": "NotApproved", "user_id": "student6", "email": "student6@example.com",
    "password": "password6", "role": "Student", "role_approved": 0},
    # Supervisors (role-approved)
    {"first_name": "Supervisor1", "last_name": "Approved", "user_id": "supervisor1", "email": "supervisor1@example.com",
    "password": "password7", "role": "Supervisor", "role_approved": 1},
    {"first_name": "Supervisor2", "last_name": "Approved", "user_id": "supervisor2", "email": "supervisor2@example.com",
    "password": "password8", "role": "Supervisor", "role_approved": 1},
    # Admins (role-approved)
    {"first_name": "Admin1", "last_name": "Approved", "user_id": "admin1", "email": "admin1@example.com",
    "password": "password9", "role": "Administrator", "role_approved": 1},
    {"first_name": "Admin2", "last_name": "Approved", "user_id": "admin2", "email": "admin2@example.com",
    "password": "password10", "role": "Administrator", "role_approved": 1}
]
for user in test_users:
    print(f"Adding user: {user['user_id']}, Role: {user['role']}, Password: {user['password']}")
    add_user(user["first_name"], user["last_name"], user["user_id"], user["email"], user["password"], user["role"],
    user["role_approved"])
def display_users():
    """Display users with their roles and hashed passwords."""
    with create_connection() as conn:
        cursor = conn.cursor()
        cursor.execute('''
SELECT id, first_name, last_name, user_id, email, role, role_approved, password FROM users
''')
    users = cursor.fetchall()
    for user in users:
        print(f"ID: {user[0]}, Name: {user[1]} {user[2]}, UserID: {user[3]}, Email: {user[4]}, Role: {user[5]}, Approved:
{'Yes' if user[6] == 1 else 'No'}, Hashed Password: {user[7]}")
#************************************************************************#
# update 2023122719:51 end
# update 202312272046 start
#************************************************************************#
def user_exists(email):
    """Check if a user already exists in the database based on their email."""
    with create_connection() as conn:
        cursor = conn.cursor()
        cursor.execute('SELECT id FROM users WHERE email = ?', (email,))
        return cursor.fetchone() is not None
```

```python
#********************************************************************#
# update 202312272046 end
# update 202312272046 start
#********************************************************************#
def main():
ensure_table_schema()
# Check if the admin user already exists before attempting to add
if not user_exists(ADMIN_EMAIL):
add_admin() # Add an admin user with the Administrator role and approved status
else:
print("Admin user already exists.")
# Similarly, check for other test users before adding
test_users_emails = [f'student{i}@example.com' for i in range(1, 7)] + \
[f'supervisor{i}@example.com' for i in range(1, 3)] + \
[f'admin{i}@example.com' for i in range(1, 3)]
for email in test_users_emails:
if not user_exists(email):
print(f"Adding test user with email: {email}")
# Logic to add the user
# Note: You need to pass the appropriate parameters to the add_user function based on the email
else:
print(f"User with email {email} already exists.")
display_users() # Display the list of users
if __name__ == '__main__':
main()
#********************************************************************#
# update 202312272046 end
```

>>>

user.py (User Class)

A class that represents a user and its attributes.

<<<

```python
from auth import add_user, validate_user, hash_password
class User:
def __init__(self, first_name, last_name, user_id, email, password):
self.first_name = first_name
self.last_name = last_name
self.user_id = user_id
self.email = email
self.password = password
def register(self):
# Here you can include any additional validation if necessary
add_user(self.first_name, self.last_name, self.user_id, self.email, self.password)
return True
```

```python
def check_credentials(self):
# This method would be used to validate the user's login credentials
return validate_user(self.email, self.password)
>>>
```

auth.py (Authentication Logic)

Contains authentication and authorization logic.

```
<<<
```

```python
import bcrypt
import sqlite3
from database import create_connection
def hash_password(password):
"""Hash a password with bcrypt."""
return bcrypt.hashpw(password.encode('utf-8'), bcrypt.gensalt())
def validate_user(username, password):
"""Validate a user's login credentials."""
conn = create_connection()
cursor = conn.cursor()
cursor.execute('''
SELECT password FROM users WHERE user_id=? OR email=?
''', (username, username,))
user_data = cursor.fetchone()
conn.close()
if user_data:
stored_password = user_data[0]
return bcrypt.checkpw(password.encode('utf-8'), stored_password)
return False
def add_user(first_name, last_name, user_id, email, password):
"""Add a new user to the database."""
conn = create_connection()
cursor = conn.cursor()
hashed_password = hash_password(password)
cursor.execute('''
INSERT INTO users(first_name, last_name, user_id, email, password)
VALUES(?, ?, ?, ?, ?)
''', (first_name, last_name, user_id, email, hashed_password))
conn.commit()
conn.close()
def get_user_role_and_status(username):
"""Retrieve the role and role approval status for a user."""
with create_connection() as conn:
cursor = conn.cursor()
cursor.execute('''
SELECT role, role_approved FROM users WHERE user_id=? OR email=?
```

```python
''', (username, username,))
user_data = cursor.fetchone()
if user_data:
return user_data
else:
return None, None
>>>
ui.py (User Interface)
Contains all the PyQt5 UI classes.
<<<
###############################################################
## Atheer Work: Research Tracker Project © 2024 A Mahir ###
###############################################################
# ****************************************************************
import os
import sys
import sqlite3
import re
import bcrypt
from PyQt5.QtWidgets import (QApplication, QMainWindow, QPushButton, QLineEdit, QMessageBox,
QColorDialog, QLabel,
QInputDialog, QVBoxLayout, QWidget, QCheckBox, QHBoxLayout)
from PyQt5.QtCore import Qt, QSize, QMimeData, QUrl, pyqtSignal, QObject
from PyQt5.QtGui import QImage, QPixmap, QDragEnterEvent, QDropEvent, QPalette, QBrush
from PyQt5.QtGui import QDesktopServices
from PyQt5.QtCore import QUrl
# from auth import validate_user, add_user
from auth import validate_user, add_user, get_user_role_and_status # update 202312272338
from database import ensure_table_schema


os.system('cls||clear') # clear the terminal
# Global signal class
class GlobalSignals(QObject):
background_image_changed = pyqtSignal(str)
global_signals = GlobalSignals() # Create an instance of the global signals class
global_background_pixmap = None
def set_global_background_image(image_path):
global global_background_pixmap
global_background_pixmap = QPixmap(image_path)
global_signals.background_image_changed.emit(image_path) # Emit the signal through the instance
class CustomWindow(QMainWindow):
def __init__(self, parent=None):
super().__init__(parent)
```

```python
self.setFixedSize(QSize(800, 400))
global_signals.background_image_changed.connect(self.update_background) # Connect to the global signal
def update_background(self, image_path):
if QPixmap(image_path).isNull():
QMessageBox.warning(self, 'Error', 'The image file is not valid.')
return
palette = QPalette()
brush = QBrush(QPixmap(image_path).scaled(self.size(), Qt.KeepAspectRatioByExpanding,
Qt.SmoothTransformation))
palette.setBrush(QPalette.Window, brush)
self.setPalette(palette)
def create_child_window(self, window_class):
child_window = window_class(self)
global_signals.background_image_changed.connect(child_window.update_background)
child_window.show()
class DraggableLabel(QLabel):
imageDropped = pyqtSignal(str) # Signal to emit the file path
def __init__(self, parent=None):
super().__init__(parent)
self.setAcceptDrops(True)
self.setAutoFillBackground(True)
def dragEnterEvent(self, event: QDragEnterEvent):
if event.mimeData().hasUrls():
event.acceptProposedAction()
def dropEvent(self, event: QDropEvent):
mimeData = event.mimeData()
if mimeData.hasUrls():
urls = mimeData.urls()
if len(urls) > 0:
image_path = urls[0].toLocalFile()
self.imageDropped.emit(image_path)
event.acceptProposedAction()
# Continue from Part 1
class LoginWindow(CustomWindow):
def __init__(self, parent=None):
super().__init__(parent)
self.setWindowTitle('Login Window')
self.initUI()
def initUI(self):
# Add layout, labels, line edits, and buttons for login functionality
self.username = QLineEdit(self)
self.password = QLineEdit(self)
self.password.setEchoMode(QLineEdit.Password)
self.login_button = QPushButton('Login', self)
```

```python
self.login_button.clicked.connect(self.login)
self.show_password_checkbox = QCheckBox('Show Password', self)
self.show_password_checkbox.stateChanged.connect(self.toggle_password_visibility)
# Set placeholder text for the password field
self.password.setPlaceholderText("Enter your password")
# Set the echo mode to hide the password initially
self.password.setEchoMode(QLineEdit.Password)
layout = QVBoxLayout()
layout.addWidget(QLabel('Enter your username:'))
layout.addWidget(self.username)
layout.addWidget(QLabel('Enter your password:'))
layout.addWidget(self.password)
layout.addWidget(self.show_password_checkbox) # Add the checkbox to the layout
layout.addWidget(self.login_button)
# "Forget Password" Button
self.forget_password_button = QPushButton('Forget Password')
self.forget_password_button.clicked.connect(self.forget_password)
layout.addWidget(self.forget_password_button)
# Set the central widget with the layout
central_widget = QWidget(self)
central_widget.setLayout(layout)
self.setCentralWidget(central_widget)
# update 202312272338 start
#*********************************************************************#
def login(self):
username = self.username.text()
password = self.password.text()
if username and password:
if validate_user(username, password):
user_role, role_approved = get_user_role_and_status(username)
if user_role == 'Administrator':
if role_approved:
self.open_admin_tools()
else:
self.email_activated_admins()
else:
QMessageBox.information(self, 'Success', 'Login successful!')
else:
QMessageBox.warning(self, 'Error', 'Invalid username or password.')
else:
QMessageBox.warning(self, 'Error', 'Please enter both username and password.')
def email_activated_admins(self):
# Open default email client to email all activated admins
# You would need to implement get_activated_admin_emails to retrieve the emails
```

```python
admin_emails = ";".join(get_activated_admin_emails())
subject = "Activation Request"
body = "I am an admin and require my role to be activated."
mailto_link = f"mailto:{admin_emails}?subject={subject}&body={body}"
QDesktopServices.openUrl(QUrl(mailto_link))
def open_admin_tools(self):
self.admin_tools_window = AdminToolsWindow()
self.admin_tools_window.show()
#****************************************************************************#
# update 202312272338 end

def toggle_password_visibility(self, state):
if state == Qt.Checked:
self.password.setEchoMode(QLineEdit.Normal)
else:
self.password.setEchoMode(QLineEdit.Password)
def forget_password(self):
# Open the default email client to send an email
admin_email = "amahir@gmail.com"
subject = "Password Reset Request"
body = "I have forgotten my password and request assistance to reset it."
mailto_link = f"mailto:{admin_email}?subject={subject}&body={body}"
QDesktopServices.openUrl(QUrl(mailto_link))

class RegisterWindow(CustomWindow):
def __init__(self, parent=None):
super().__init__(parent)
self.setWindowTitle('Register Window')
# Initialise all QLineEdit attributes before calling initUI()
self.first_name = QLineEdit(self)
self.last_name = QLineEdit(self)
self.user_id = QLineEdit(self)
self.username = QLineEdit(self)
self.confirm_username = QLineEdit(self)
self.password = QLineEdit(self)
self.confirm_password = QLineEdit(self)
self.initUI()
def initUI(self):
layout = QVBoxLayout()
# Create horizontal layouts for each label-input pair
fields = [
('First Name:', self.first_name),
('Last Name:', self.last_name),
('ID:', self.user_id),
```

```python
    ('Enter your username (email):', self.username),
    ('Re-enter your username (email):', self.confirm_username),
    ('Password:', self.password),
    ('Rewrite Password to validate:', self.confirm_password)
    ]
    for label_text, widget in fields:
        row_layout = QHBoxLayout()
        label = QLabel(label_text)
        label.setAlignment(Qt.AlignRight | Qt.AlignVCenter) # Align right for the label
        row_layout.addWidget(label)
        row_layout.addWidget(widget) # Add the corresponding input field
        layout.addLayout(row_layout) # Add the horizontal layout to the main vertical layout
    # Show Password Checkbox
    self.show_password_checkbox = QCheckBox('Show Password')
    self.show_password_checkbox.stateChanged.connect(self.toggle_password_visibility)
    layout.addWidget(self.show_password_checkbox)
    # Set placeholder text for password fields
    self.password.setPlaceholderText("Password (UpperCase, LowerCase, Special Character, Length > 8)")
    self.confirm_password.setPlaceholderText("Rewrite Password to validate")
    # Set the echo mode to hide the password initially
    self.password.setEchoMode(QLineEdit.Password)
    self.confirm_password.setEchoMode(QLineEdit.Password)
    # "Show Password" Checkbox
    self.show_password_checkbox = QCheckBox('Show Password')
    self.show_password_checkbox.stateChanged.connect(self.toggle_password_visibility)

    # Register Button
    self.register_button = QPushButton('Register')
    self.register_button.clicked.connect(self.register)
    layout.addWidget(self.register_button)
    central_widget = QWidget(self)
    central_widget.setLayout(layout)
    self.setCentralWidget(central_widget)
def toggle_password_visibility(self, state):
    echo_mode = QLineEdit.Normal if state == Qt.Checked else QLineEdit.Password
    self.password.setEchoMode(echo_mode)
    self.confirm_password.setEchoMode(echo_mode)
def register(self):
    # Gather all the inputs
    first_name = self.first_name.text().strip()
    last_name = self.last_name.text().strip()
    user_id = self.user_id.text().strip()
    email = self.username.text().strip()
    confirm_email = self.confirm_username.text().strip()
```

```python
password = self.password.text()
confirm_password = self.confirm_password.text()
add_user(first_name, last_name, user_id, email, password) # Now using the auth module
QMessageBox.information(self, 'Success', 'Registration successful!')

def hash_password(self, password):
# Hash a password with bcrypt
hashed = bcrypt.hashpw(password.encode('utf-8'), bcrypt.gensalt())
return hashed

class LoginRegisterWindow(CustomWindow):
def __init__(self):
super().__init__()
self.setWindowTitle('Login/Register Window')
central_widget = QWidget(self)
self.setCentralWidget(central_widget)
layout = QVBoxLayout(central_widget)
self.background_label = DraggableLabel(self)
self.background_label.resize(self.size())
layout.addWidget(self.background_label)
self.background_label.imageDropped.connect(set_global_background_image)
self.register_button = QPushButton('Register', self)
self.register_button.clicked.connect(lambda: self.create_child_window(RegisterWindow))
layout.addWidget(self.register_button)
self.login_button = QPushButton('Login', self)
self.login_button.clicked.connect(lambda: self.create_child_window(LoginWindow))
layout.addWidget(self.login_button)
self.change_color_button = QPushButton('Change Background Color', self)
self.change_color_button.clicked.connect(self.change_background_color)
layout.addWidget(self.change_color_button)
def create_child_window(self, window_class):
child_window = window_class(self)
child_window.show()
def change_background_color(self):
color = QColorDialog.getColor()
if color.isValid():
palette = QPalette()
palette.setColor(QPalette.Window, color)
self.setPalette(palette)
QApplication.instance().setPalette(palette)
def set_background_image(self, image_path):
set_global_background_image(image_path) # This will trigger the update_background for all windows
# update 202312272338 start
#*******************************************************************#
```

```python
class AdminToolsWindow(QMainWindow):
def __init__(self, parent=None):
super().__init__(parent)
self.setWindowTitle('Admin Tools')
self.initUI()
def initUI(self):
# Layout and buttons go here
layout = QVBoxLayout()
self.display_users_button = QPushButton('Display Users')
self.display_users_button.clicked.connect(self.display_users)
layout.addWidget(self.display_users_button)
self.delete_user_button = QPushButton('Delete User')
self.delete_user_button.clicked.connect(self.delete_user)
layout.addWidget(self.delete_user_button)
self.update_user_button = QPushButton('Update User')
self.update_user_button.clicked.connect(self.update_user)
layout.addWidget(self.update_user_button)
self.reset_password_button = QPushButton('Reset Password')
self.reset_password_button.clicked.connect(self.reset_password)
layout.addWidget(self.reset_password_button)
# Set central widget and layout
central_widget = QWidget()
central_widget.setLayout(layout)
self.setCentralWidget(central_widget)
def display_users(self):
# Implement user display logic
pass
def delete_user(self):
# Implement user deletion logic
pass
def update_user(self):
# Implement user update logic
pass
def reset_password(self):
# Implement password reset logic
pass
#************************************************************************#
# update 202312272338 end
>>>
config.py
Configuration parameters for the application.
<<<
# config.py
```

```python
DB_PATH = 'users.db'
ADMIN_EMAIL = 'amahir@bedford.ac.uk'
ADMIN_PASSWORD = 'Bedford@2024'
```

>>>

utils.py

Utility functions that can be used across the application.

<<<

```python
# utils.py
import os
def clear_terminal():
    os.system('cls||clear')
```

>>>

Results are as expected but not enough.

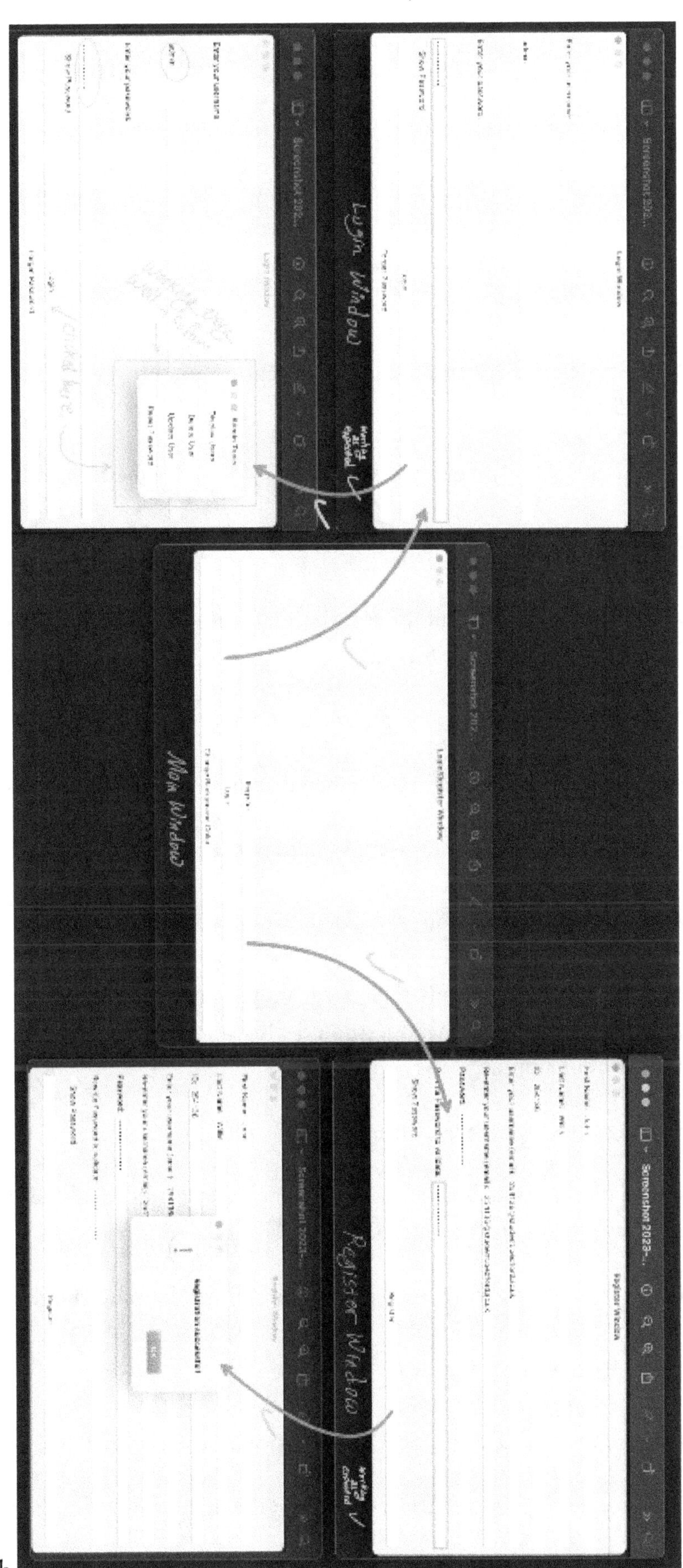

Results are as expected but not enough.

Version 15 of Development Instructions:

Overview

Version 15 introduces an enhanced user registration flow with additional validation and confirmation steps to ensure data accuracy and inform the user about the account activation process.

Registration Validation

- Implement a check at the start of the registration process to determine if the user's details already exist in the database.

- If a user is already registered, display an informative message and redirect them to the main menu.

Data Confirmation

- After a new user fills out the registration form and submits it, present a confirmation window displaying all entered data in a table format.

- Provide two options in the confirmation window:

- Confirm: If clicked, register the user as an unactivated user in the database.

- Edit: If clicked, allow the user to return to the registration form to edit their details.

Post-Registration Notification

- Once the user confirms their data, show a message indicating that they have been registered as an unactivated user. The message should also inform them that their account requires activation by a supervisor or admin.

- Along with the message, include two buttons:

- Send Notification Email: This should open the default email client, ready to send a pre-formulated email to all supervisors and admins to request account activation.

- OK: This button will close the confirmation window and end the registration process.

Closing the Registration Window

- Configure the 'OK' and 'Send Notification Email' buttons to close the registration window upon click.

- Ensure the application navigates back to the main menu after the registration window is closed.

Return to Main Menu

- After closing the registration confirmation window, the user should be taken back to the main interface of the application.

Implementation Notes

- Utilise context management for database interactions to prevent resource leaks.

- Ensure all user messages are clear and informative to improve the user experience.

- Handle potential exceptions gracefully, particularly during database operations.

Testing

- Test the new registration flow thoroughly to catch any edge cases or potential bugs.

- Ensure that the email functionality opens the default email client across different operating systems.

By following these instructions, the development of Version 15 should result in a user-friendly registration process that verifies user data and clearly communicates the next steps to the users regarding their account activation.

Implementation:

To implement the requested registration flow updates, we'll need to modify the RegisterWindow class in the ui.py file and add some new methods for showing the confirmation window, handling the unactivated user notification, and integrating these with the existing user registration logic. Let's go through the ui.py file to make the necessary updates, step by step.

Here are the steps we will take:

1. Check if the user already exists during registration.
2. After the user submits the form, show a confirmation window with the details they entered.
3. Allow the user to confirm or edit the information.
4. If the user confirms, add them as an unactivated user to the database.
5. Display a message about the need for activation and provide options to send a notification email or just acknowledge the message (OK).
6. Close the registration window after the user clicks 'OK' or sends an email and returns to the main menu.

Let's start by implementing the first step: User Registration Validation. We'll add logic to the RegisterWindow class to check if the user is already registered before proceeding with the registration.

```
ui.py
# ui.py
# ... (other imports remain unchanged)
from database import user_exists # We need to import the user_exists function to check for existing users
# ... (rest of the file remains unchanged until the RegisterWindow class)
class RegisterWindow(CustomWindow):
def __init__(self, parent=None):
super().__init__(parent)
self.setWindowTitle('Register Window')
# ... (rest of the initialization remains unchanged)
# ... (rest of the methods remain unchanged)
# Update the register method to include user existence check
def register(self):
# Gather all the inputs
first_name = self.first_name.text().strip()
last_name = self.last_name.text().strip()
user_id = self.user_id.text().strip()
email = self.username.text().strip()
confirm_email = self.confirm_username.text().strip()
password = self.password.text()
confirm_password = self.confirm_password.text()
# Check if the email or user ID already exists in the database
if user_exists(email) or user_exists(user_id):
QMessageBox.warning(self, 'Error', 'A user with this email or user ID already exists.')
return
# Here we would call a method to show the confirmation window with the details
# For now, let's assume the user confirms and we add them as an unactivated user
# The logic for showing the confirmation window and handling the response will be added later
add_user(first_name, last_name, user_id, email, password) # Now using the auth module
QMessageBox.information(self, 'Success', 'Registration successful!')
# ... (rest of the methods remain unchanged)
# ... (rest of the file remains unchanged)
```

In the code above, I added a call to user_exists() before proceeding with the registration. If the user already exists, a warning message is shown, and the function returns early, stopping the registration process.

Next, we would need to implement the confirmation window and integrate it into the registration process. This will involve creating a new class or method to show the user's details and confirm or edit them. Shall I proceed with this next step?

Testing: I tried to register a registered user , but I got this error message:

Traceback (most recent call last): line 253, in register
add_user(first_name, last_name, user_id, email, password) # Now using the auth module
File ".../auth.py", line 29, in add_user
cursor.execute("'
sqlite3.IntegrityError: UNIQUE constraint failed: users.email
zsh: abort /Users/atheermahir/opt/anaconda3/bin/python

Fixing:

The error message indicates that there is a UNIQUE constraint on the email column in the users table of your database, and an attempt to insert a new user with an email that already exists has been made. This triggers a sqlite3.IntegrityError.

To handle this, we should enhance the user_exists function to check for both the email and user_id to ensure we're not attempting to insert a duplicate record. Then, we should call this function before trying to add a new user and handle any potential exceptions that might arise from the insert operation.

I'll provide you with the updated register method in the RegisterWindow class that includes these checks and proper error handling:

```python
ui.py
# ui.py
# ... (other imports remain unchanged)
from database import user_exists # We need to import the user_exists function to check for existing users
# ... (rest of the file remains unchanged until the RegisterWindow class)
class RegisterWindow(CustomWindow):
def __init__(self, parent=None):
super().__init__(parent)
self.setWindowTitle('Register Window')
# ... (rest of the initialization remains unchanged)
# ... (rest of the methods remain unchanged)
# Update the register method to include user existence check
def register(self):
# Gather all the inputs
first_name = self.first_name.text().strip()
last_name = self.last_name.text().strip()
user_id = self.user_id.text().strip()
email = self.username.text().strip()
confirm_email = self.confirm_username.text().strip()
password = self.password.text()
confirm_password = self.confirm_password.text()
# Check if the email or user ID already exists in the database
if user_exists(email) or user_exists(user_id):
QMessageBox.warning(self, 'Error', 'A user with this email or user ID already exists.')
return
# Proceed only if the password and confirmation match
if password != confirm_password or email != confirm_email:
QMessageBox.warning(self, 'Error', 'Email addresses or passwords do not match.')
return
try:
# Here we would call a method to show the confirmation window with the details
# For now, let's assume the user confirms and we add them as an unactivated user
# The logic for showing the confirmation window and handling the response will be added later
add_user(first_name, last_name, user_id, email, password) # Now using the auth module
QMessageBox.information(self, 'Success', 'Registration successful!')
except sqlite3.IntegrityError as e:
QMessageBox.warning(self, 'Error', 'A user with this email or user ID already exists in the database.')
# ... (rest of the methods remain unchanged)

# ... (rest of the file remains unchanged)
```

Testing: I tried to register a registered user , the message came to me as expected .. Passed

let us save what we got so far:

main.py
Entry point of the application, responsible for starting the application.
<<<

```python
#############################################################
## Atheer Work: Research Tracker Project © 2024 A Mahir ###
#############################################################
# ******************************************************************
# clear the terminal
from utils import clear_terminal
clear_terminal()
# ******************************************************************
import sys
from PyQt5.QtWidgets import QApplication
from ui import LoginRegisterWindow
if __name__ == '__main__':
app = QApplication(sys.argv)
win = LoginRegisterWindow()
win.show()
sys.exit(app.exec_())
```

>>>

database.py **(Database Operations)**
Contains the database connection and operations.
<<<

```python
#############################################################
## Atheer Work: Research Tracker Project © 2024 A Mahir ###
#############################################################
# ******************************************************************
# clear the terminal
# clear the terminal
from utils import clear_terminal
clear_terminal()
# ******************************************************************
import sqlite3
import bcrypt
from config import DB_PATH, ADMIN_EMAIL, ADMIN_PASSWORD
def create_connection():
"""Create a database connection to the SQLite database specified by DB_PATH."""
conn = sqlite3.connect(DB_PATH)
return conn
# update 202312272031 start
#*****************************************************************#
def ensure_table_schema():
with create_connection() as conn:
cursor = conn.cursor()
# Create table if it doesn't exist
cursor.execute('''
CREATE TABLE IF NOT EXISTS users (
```

```
id INTEGER PRIMARY KEY AUTOINCREMENT,
first_name TEXT NOT NULL,
last_name TEXT NOT NULL,
user_id TEXT NOT NULL UNIQUE,
email TEXT NOT NULL UNIQUE,
password TEXT NOT NULL
)
''')
# Check if 'role' column exists and add if not
cursor.execute("PRAGMA table_info(users)")
columns = [info[1] for info in cursor.fetchall()]
if 'role' not in columns:
cursor.execute('ALTER TABLE users ADD COLUMN role TEXT DEFAULT "Student"')
# Check if 'role_approved' column exists and add if not
if 'role_approved' not in columns:
cursor.execute('ALTER TABLE users ADD COLUMN role_approved INTEGER
DEFAULT 0')
conn.commit()
#*********************************************************************#
# update 202312272031 end


# update 2023122719:29 start
#*********************************************************************#
def add_user(first_name, last_name, user_id, email, password, role='Student',
role_approved=0):
"""Add a new user to the database with a specified role and approval status."""
hashed_password = bcrypt.hashpw(password.encode('utf-8'), bcrypt.gensalt())
with create_connection() as conn:
cursor = conn.cursor()
cursor.execute('''
INSERT INTO users(first_name, last_name, user_id, email, password, role,
role_approved)
VALUES(?, ?, ?, ?, ?, ?, ?)
''', (first_name, last_name, user_id, email, hashed_password, role, role_approved))
conn.commit()
def add_admin():
"""Add an admin user to the database with predefined credentials and role."""
admin_first_name = 'Admin'
admin_last_name = 'User'
admin_user_id = 'admin'
admin_email = ADMIN_EMAIL # Corrected to use the standalone variable
admin_password = ADMIN_PASSWORD # Corrected to use the standalone variable
# Set the role as 'Administrator' and role_approved as 1 for the admin user
add_user(admin_first_name, admin_last_name, admin_user_id, admin_email,
admin_password, 'Administrator', 1)
#*********************************************************************#
# update 2023122719:29 end
```

```python
# update 2023122719:42 start for testing
#*********************************************************************#
def add_test_users():
# Add 3 random students (role-approved)
for i in range(1, 4):
add_user(f'Student{i}', 'Approved', f'student{i}', f'student{i}@example.com', 'password',
'Student', 1)
# Add 3 random students (role not approved yet)
for i in range(4, 7):
add_user(f'Student{i}', 'NotApproved', f'student{i}', f'student{i}@example.com',
'password', 'Student', 0)
# Add 2 random supervisors (role-approved)
for i in range(1, 3):
add_user(f'Supervisor{i}', 'Approved', f'supervisor{i}', f'supervisor{i}@example.com',
'password', 'Supervisor', 1)
# Add 2 random admins (role-approved)
for i in range(1, 3):
add_user(f'Admin{i}', 'Approved', f'admin{i}', f'admin{i}@example.com', 'password',
'Administrator', 1)
#*********************************************************************#
# update 2023122719:42 end


# update 2023122719:05 start
#*********************************************************************#
# Add a function to update the user's role and approval status
def update_user_role(user_id, role, role_approved):
with create_connection() as conn:
cursor = conn.cursor()
cursor.execute('''
UPDATE users SET role = ?, role_approved = ? WHERE user_id = ?
''', (role, role_approved, user_id))
conn.commit()
#*********************************************************************#
# update 2023122719:05 end
# update 2023122719:51 start
#*********************************************************************#
def add_test_users():
test_users = [
# Students (role-approved)
{"first_name": "Student1", "last_name": "Approved", "user_id": "student1", "email":
"student1@example.com", "password": "password1", "role": "Student", "role_approved": 1},
{"first_name": "Student2", "last_name": "Approved", "user_id": "student2", "email":
"student2@example.com", "password": "password2", "role": "Student", "role_approved": 1},
{"first_name": "Student3", "last_name": "Approved", "user_id": "student3", "email":
"student3@example.com", "password": "password3", "role": "Student", "role_approved": 1},
# Students (role not approved yet)
{"first_name": "Student4", "last_name": "NotApproved", "user_id": "student4", "email":
```

```python
    "student4@example.com", "password": "password4", "role": "Student", "role_approved": 0},
    {"first_name": "Student5", "last_name": "NotApproved", "user_id": "student5", "email":
    "student5@example.com", "password": "password5", "role": "Student", "role_approved": 0},
    {"first_name": "Student6", "last_name": "NotApproved", "user_id": "student6", "email":
    "student6@example.com", "password": "password6", "role": "Student", "role_approved": 0},
    # Supervisors (role-approved)
    {"first_name": "Supervisor1", "last_name": "Approved", "user_id": "supervisor1", "email":
    "supervisor1@example.com", "password": "password7", "role": "Supervisor",
    "role_approved": 1},
    {"first_name": "Supervisor2", "last_name": "Approved", "user_id": "supervisor2", "email":
    "supervisor2@example.com", "password": "password8", "role": "Supervisor",
    "role_approved": 1},
    # Admins (role-approved)
    {"first_name": "Admin1", "last_name": "Approved", "user_id": "admin1", "email":
    "admin1@example.com", "password": "password9", "role": "Administrator",
    "role_approved": 1},
    {"first_name": "Admin2", "last_name": "Approved", "user_id": "admin2", "email":
    "admin2@example.com", "password": "password10", "role": "Administrator",
    "role_approved": 1}
]
for user in test_users:
    print(f"Adding user: {user['user_id']}, Role: {user['role']}, Password: {user['password']}")
    add_user(user["first_name"], user["last_name"], user["user_id"], user["email"],
    user["password"], user["role"], user["role_approved"])
def display_users():
    """Display users with their roles and hashed passwords."""
    with create_connection() as conn:
        cursor = conn.cursor()
        cursor.execute('''
SELECT id, first_name, last_name, user_id, email, role, role_approved, password FROM
users
''')
        users = cursor.fetchall()
        for user in users:
            print(f"ID: {user[0]}, Name: {user[1]} {user[2]}, UserID: {user[3]}, Email: {user[4]}, Role:
{user[5]}, Approved: {'Yes' if user[6] == 1 else 'No'}, Hashed Password: {user[7]}")
#*********************************************************************#
# update 2023122719:51 end
# update 202312272046 start
#*********************************************************************#
def user_exists(email):
    """Check if a user already exists in the database based on their email."""
    with create_connection() as conn:
        cursor = conn.cursor()
        cursor.execute('SELECT id FROM users WHERE email = ?', (email,))
        return cursor.fetchone() is not None
#*********************************************************************#
```

```python
# update 202312272046 end

# update 20231228626 start
#*********************************************************************#
def get_activated_admin_emails():
    """Retrieve email addresses of all activated admins."""
    with create_connection() as conn:
        cursor = conn.cursor()
        cursor.execute('''
            SELECT email FROM users WHERE role='Administrator' AND role_approved=1
        ''')
        emails = cursor.fetchall()
        return [email[0] for email in emails] if emails else []
#*********************************************************************#
# update 20231228626 end
# update 202312272046 start
#*********************************************************************#
def main():
    ensure_table_schema()
    # Check if the admin user already exists before attempting to add
    if not user_exists(ADMIN_EMAIL):
        add_admin() # Add an admin user with the Administrator role and approved status
    else:
        print("Admin user already exists.")
    # Similarly, check for other test users before adding
    test_users_emails = [f'student{i}@example.com' for i in range(1, 7)] + \
        [f'supervisor{i}@example.com' for i in range(1, 3)] + \
        [f'admin{i}@example.com' for i in range(1, 3)]
    for email in test_users_emails:
        if not user_exists(email):
            print(f"Adding test user with email: {email}")
            # Logic to add the user
            # Note: You need to pass the appropriate parameters to the add_user function based on the email
        else:
            print(f"User with email {email} already exists.")
    display_users() # Display the list of users
    if __name__ == '__main__':
        main()
#*********************************************************************#
# update 202312272046 end
```

>>>

user.py (User Class)

A class that represents a user and its attributes.

<<<

```python
from auth import add_user, validate_user, hash_password
class User:
```

```python
def __init__(self, first_name, last_name, user_id, email, password):
self.first_name = first_name
self.last_name = last_name
self.user_id = user_id
self.email = email
self.password = password
def register(self):
# Here you can include any additional validation if necessary
add_user(self.first_name, self.last_name, self.user_id, self.email, self.password)
return True
def check_credentials(self):
# This method would be used to validate the user's login credentials
return validate_user(self.email, self.password)
```

>>>

auth.py (Authentication Logic)

Contains authentication and authorization logic.

<<<

```python
import bcrypt
import sqlite3
from database import create_connection
def hash_password(password):
    """Hash a password with bcrypt."""
return bcrypt.hashpw(password.encode('utf-8'), bcrypt.gensalt())
def validate_user(username, password):
    """Validate a user's login credentials."""
conn = create_connection()
cursor = conn.cursor()
cursor.execute('''
SELECT password FROM users WHERE user_id=? OR email=?
''', (username, username,))
user_data = cursor.fetchone()
conn.close()
if user_data:
stored_password = user_data[0]
return bcrypt.checkpw(password.encode('utf-8'), stored_password)
return False
def add_user(first_name, last_name, user_id, email, password):
    """Add a new user to the database."""
conn = create_connection()
cursor = conn.cursor()
hashed_password = hash_password(password)
cursor.execute('''
INSERT INTO users(first_name, last_name, user_id, email, password)
VALUES(?, ?, ?, ?, ?)
''', (first_name, last_name, user_id, email, hashed_password))
conn.commit()
conn.close()
```

```python
def get_user_role_and_status(username):
    """Retrieve the role and role approval status for a user."""
    with create_connection() as conn:
        cursor = conn.cursor()
        cursor.execute('''
        SELECT role, role_approved FROM users WHERE user_id=? OR email=?
        ''', (username, username,))
        user_data = cursor.fetchone()
        if user_data:
            return user_data
        else:
            return None, Non
>>>
```

ui.py (User Interface)

Contains all the PyQt5 UI classes.

<<<

```python
###################################################################
## Atheer Work: Research Tracker Project © 2024 A Mahir ###
###################################################################
# *********************************************************************
import os
import sys
import sqlite3
import re
import bcrypt
from PyQt5.QtWidgets import (QApplication, QMainWindow, QPushButton,
QLineEdit, QMessageBox, QColorDialog, QLabel,
QInputDialog, QVBoxLayout, QWidget, QCheckBox, QHBoxLayout)
from PyQt5.QtCore import Qt, QSize, QMimeData, QUrl, pyqtSignal, QObject
from PyQt5.QtGui import QImage, QPixmap, QDragEnterEvent, QDropEvent,
QPalette, QBrush
from PyQt5.QtGui import QDesktopServices
from PyQt5.QtCore import QUrl
# from auth import validate_user, add_user
from auth import validate_user, add_user, get_user_role_and_status # update
202312272338
from database import ensure_table_schema
from database import user_exists # We need to import the user_exists function to check for
existing users
from database import get_activated_admin_emails # Add this import to get the activated
admin emails # update 20231228626


os.system('cls||clear') # clear the terminal
# Global signal class
class GlobalSignals(QObject):
    background_image_changed = pyqtSignal(str)
global_signals = GlobalSignals() # Create an instance of the global signals class
```

```python
global_background_pixmap = None
def set_global_background_image(image_path):
global global_background_pixmap
global_background_pixmap = QPixmap(image_path)
global_signals.background_image_changed.emit(image_path) # Emit the signal through
the instance
class CustomWindow(QMainWindow):
def __init__(self, parent=None):
super().__init__(parent)
self.setFixedSize(QSize(800, 400))
global_signals.background_image_changed.connect(self.update_background) # Connect
to the global signal
def update_background(self, image_path):
if QPixmap(image_path).isNull():
QMessageBox.warning(self, 'Error', 'The image file is not valid.')
return
palette = QPalette()
brush = QBrush(QPixmap(image_path).scaled(self.size(),
Qt.KeepAspectRatioByExpanding, Qt.SmoothTransformation))
palette.setBrush(QPalette.Window, brush)
self.setPalette(palette)
def create_child_window(self, window_class):
child_window = window_class(self)
global_signals.background_image_changed.connect(child_window.update_background)
child_window.show()
class DraggableLabel(QLabel):
imageDropped = pyqtSignal(str) # Signal to emit the file path
def __init__(self, parent=None):
super().__init__(parent)
self.setAcceptDrops(True)
self.setAutoFillBackground(True)
def dragEnterEvent(self, event: QDragEnterEvent):
if event.mimeData().hasUrls():
event.acceptProposedAction()
def dropEvent(self, event: QDropEvent):
mimeData = event.mimeData()
if mimeData.hasUrls():
urls = mimeData.urls()
if len(urls) > 0:
image_path = urls[0].toLocalFile()
self.imageDropped.emit(image_path)
event.acceptProposedAction()
# Continue from Part 1
class LoginWindow(CustomWindow):
def __init__(self, parent=None):
super().__init__(parent)
self.setWindowTitle('Login Window')
```

```python
        self.initUI()
    def initUI(self):
        # Add layout, labels, line edits, and buttons for login functionality
        self.username = QLineEdit(self)
        self.password = QLineEdit(self)
        self.password.setEchoMode(QLineEdit.Password)
        self.login_button = QPushButton('Login', self)
        self.login_button.clicked.connect(self.login)
        self.show_password_checkbox = QCheckBox('Show Password', self)
        self.show_password_checkbox.stateChanged.connect(self.toggle_password_visibility)
        # Set placeholder text for the password field
        self.password.setPlaceholderText("Enter your password")
        # Set the echo mode to hide the password initially
        self.password.setEchoMode(QLineEdit.Password)
        layout = QVBoxLayout()
        layout.addWidget(QLabel('Enter your username:'))
        layout.addWidget(self.username)
        layout.addWidget(QLabel('Enter your password:'))
        layout.addWidget(self.password)
        layout.addWidget(self.show_password_checkbox) # Add the checkbox to the layout
        layout.addWidget(self.login_button)
        # "Forget Password" Button
        self.forget_password_button = QPushButton('Forget Password')
        self.forget_password_button.clicked.connect(self.forget_password)
        layout.addWidget(self.forget_password_button)
        # Set the central widget with the layout
        central_widget = QWidget(self)
        central_widget.setLayout(layout)
        self.setCentralWidget(central_widget)
        # old as of 202312272338
        # def login(self):
        # username = self.username.text() # Retrieve the text from the username input
        # password = self.password.text() # Retrieve the text from the password input
        # if username and password: # Check if both username and password fields are not empty
        # if validate_user(username, password): # Use the validate_user function from # Now using the auth module
        # QMessageBox.information(self, 'Success', 'Login successful!')
        # else:
        # QMessageBox.warning(self, 'Error', 'Invalid username or password.')
        # else:
        # QMessageBox.warning(self, 'Error', 'Please enter both username and password.')

        # update 202312272338 start
        #***********************************************************************#
        def login(self):
            username = self.username.text()
            password = self.password.text()
```

```python
if username and password:
if validate_user(username, password):
user_role, role_approved = get_user_role_and_status(username)
if user_role == 'Administrator':
if role_approved:
self.open_admin_tools()
else:
self.email_activated_admins()
else:
QMessageBox.information(self, 'Success', 'Login successful!')
else:
QMessageBox.warning(self, 'Error', 'Invalid username or password.')
else:
QMessageBox.warning(self, 'Error', 'Please enter both username and password.')
def email_activated_admins(self):
# Open default email client to email all activated admins
# You would need to implement get_activated_admin_emails to retrieve the emails
admin_emails = ";".join(get_activated_admin_emails())
subject = "Activation Request"
body = "I am an admin and require my role to be activated."
mailto_link = f"mailto:{admin_emails}?subject={subject}&body={body}"
QDesktopServices.openUrl(QUrl(mailto_link))
def open_admin_tools(self):
self.admin_tools_window = AdminToolsWindow()
self.admin_tools_window.show()
#*********************************************************************#
# update 202312272338 end

def toggle_password_visibility(self, state):
if state == Qt.Checked:
self.password.setEchoMode(QLineEdit.Normal)
else:
self.password.setEchoMode(QLineEdit.Password)
def forget_password(self):
# Open the default email client to send an email
admin_email = "amahir@gmail.com"
subject = "Password Reset Request"
body = "I have forgotten my password and request assistance to reset it."
mailto_link = f"mailto:{admin_email}?subject={subject}&body={body}"
QDesktopServices.openUrl(QUrl(mailto_link))

class RegisterWindow(CustomWindow):
def __init__(self, parent=None):
super().__init__(parent)
self.setWindowTitle('Register Window')
# Initialize all QLineEdit attributes before calling initUI()
self.first_name = QLineEdit(self)
```

```python
self.last_name = QLineEdit(self)
self.user_id = QLineEdit(self)
self.username = QLineEdit(self)
self.confirm_username = QLineEdit(self)
self.password = QLineEdit(self)
self.confirm_password = QLineEdit(self)
self.initUI()
def initUI(self):
layout = QVBoxLayout()
# Create horizontal layouts for each label-input pair
fields = [
('First Name:', self.first_name),
('Last Name:', self.last_name),
('ID:', self.user_id),
('Enter your username (email):', self.username),
('Re-enter your username (email):', self.confirm_username),
('Password:', self.password),
('Rewrite Password to validate:', self.confirm_password)
]
for label_text, widget in fields:
row_layout = QHBoxLayout()
label = QLabel(label_text)
label.setAlignment(Qt.AlignRight | Qt.AlignVCenter) # Align right for the label
row_layout.addWidget(label)
row_layout.addWidget(widget) # Add the corresponding input field
layout.addLayout(row_layout) # Add the horizontal layout to the main vertical layout
# Show Password Checkbox
self.show_password_checkbox = QCheckBox('Show Password')
self.show_password_checkbox.stateChanged.connect(self.toggle_password_visibility)
layout.addWidget(self.show_password_checkbox)
# Set placeholder text for password fields
self.password.setPlaceholderText("Password (UpperCase, LowerCase, Special Character,
Length > 8)")
self.confirm_password.setPlaceholderText("Rewrite Password to validate")
# Set the echo mode to hide the password initially
self.password.setEchoMode(QLineEdit.Password)
self.confirm_password.setEchoMode(QLineEdit.Password)
# "Show Password" Checkbox
self.show_password_checkbox = QCheckBox('Show Password')
self.show_password_checkbox.stateChanged.connect(self.toggle_password_visibility)

# Register Button
self.register_button = QPushButton('Register')
self.register_button.clicked.connect(self.register)
layout.addWidget(self.register_button)
central_widget = QWidget(self)
central_widget.setLayout(layout)
```

```python
self.setCentralWidget(central_widget)
def toggle_password_visibility(self, state):
echo_mode = QLineEdit.Normal if state == Qt.Checked else QLineEdit.Password
self.password.setEchoMode(echo_mode)
self.confirm_password.setEchoMode(echo_mode)
def register(self):
# Gather all the inputs
first_name = self.first_name.text().strip()
last_name = self.last_name.text().strip()
user_id = self.user_id.text().strip()
email = self.username.text().strip()
confirm_email = self.confirm_username.text().strip()
password = self.password.text()
confirm_password = self.confirm_password.text()
# Check if the email or user ID already exists in the database
if user_exists(email) or user_exists(user_id):
QMessageBox.warning(self, 'Error', 'A user with this email or user ID already exists.')
return
# Proceed only if the password and confirmation match
if password != confirm_password or email != confirm_email:
QMessageBox.warning(self, 'Error', 'Email addresses or passwords do not match.')
return
try:
# Here we would call a method to show the confirmation window with the details
# For now, let's assume the user confirms and we add them as an unactivated user
# The logic for showing the confirmation window and handling the response will be added
later
add_user(first_name, last_name, user_id, email, password) # Now using the auth module
QMessageBox.information(self, 'Success', 'Registration successful!')
except sqlite3.IntegrityError as e:
QMessageBox.warning(self, 'Error', 'A user with this email or user ID already exists in the
database.')

def hash_password(self, password):
# Hash a password with bcrypt
hashed = bcrypt.hashpw(password.encode('utf-8'), bcrypt.gensalt())
return hashed

class LoginRegisterWindow(CustomWindow):
def __init__(self):
super().__init__()
self.setWindowTitle('Login/Register Window')
central_widget = QWidget(self)
self.setCentralWidget(central_widget)
layout = QVBoxLayout(central_widget)
self.background_label = DraggableLabel(self)
self.background_label.resize(self.size())
```

```python
layout.addWidget(self.background_label)
self.background_label.imageDropped.connect(set_global_background_image)
self.register_button = QPushButton('Register', self)
self.register_button.clicked.connect(lambda:
self.create_child_window(RegisterWindow))
layout.addWidget(self.register_button)
self.login_button = QPushButton('Login', self)
self.login_button.clicked.connect(lambda: self.create_child_window(LoginWindow))
layout.addWidget(self.login_button)
self.change_color_button = QPushButton('Change Background Color', self)
self.change_color_button.clicked.connect(self.change_background_color)
layout.addWidget(self.change_color_button)
def create_child_window(self, window_class):
child_window = window_class(self)
child_window.show()
def change_background_color(self):
color = QColorDialog.getColor()
if color.isValid():
palette = QPalette()
palette.setColor(QPalette.Window, color)
self.setPalette(palette)
QApplication.instance().setPalette(palette)
def set_background_image(self, image_path):
set_global_background_image(image_path) # This will trigger the update_background for
all windows
# update 202312272338 start
#****************************************************************#
class AdminToolsWindow(QMainWindow):
def __init__(self, parent=None):
super().__init__(parent)
self.setWindowTitle('Admin Tools')
self.initUI()
def initUI(self):
# Layout and buttons go here
layout = QVBoxLayout()
self.display_users_button = QPushButton('Display Users')
self.display_users_button.clicked.connect(self.display_users)
layout.addWidget(self.display_users_button)
self.delete_user_button = QPushButton('Delete User')
self.delete_user_button.clicked.connect(self.delete_user)
layout.addWidget(self.delete_user_button)
self.update_user_button = QPushButton('Update User')
self.update_user_button.clicked.connect(self.update_user)
layout.addWidget(self.update_user_button)
self.reset_password_button = QPushButton('Reset Password')
self.reset_password_button.clicked.connect(self.reset_password)
layout.addWidget(self.reset_password_button)
```

```python
# Set central widget and layout
central_widget = QWidget()
central_widget.setLayout(layout)
self.setCentralWidget(central_widget)
def display_users(self):
# Implement user display logic
pass
def delete_user(self):
# Implement user deletion logic
pass
def update_user(self):
# Implement user update logic
pass
def reset_password(self):
# Implement password reset logic
pass
#*************************************************************************#
# update 202312272338 end
>>>
```

config.py

Configuration parameters for the application.

```
<<<
# config.py
DB_PATH = 'users.db'
ADMIN_EMAIL = 'amahir@bedford.ac.uk'
ADMIN_PASSWORD = 'Bedford@2024'
>>>
```

utils.py

Utility functions that can be used across the application.

```
<<<
# utils.py
import os
def clear_terminal():
os.system('cls||clear')
>>>
```

Version 16

We will implement the data confirmation step where we display the user's entered data in a new window for confirmation. If the user confirms, we will register them as an unactivated user and inform them that their account needs to be activated by a supervisor or admin. We will also provide the functionality to send a notification email or end the registration process.

Implementation:

To implement the data confirmation step and the subsequent registration flow, we will need to make several changes. We will create a new confirmation window and modify the register method in the RegisterWindow class to launch this confirmation window. Let's update the ui.py file with the necessary changes.

Here's the updated code:

```python
ui.py
# ... (previous imports remain unchanged)
from PyQt5.QtWidgets import QTableWidget, QTableWidgetItem, QHeaderView
# ... (other parts of the file remain unchanged)
class ConfirmationWindow(CustomWindow):
def __init__(self, user_data, parent=None):
super().__init__(parent)
self.user_data = user_data
self.setWindowTitle('Confirm Registration Details')
self.initUI()
def initUI(self):
layout = QVBoxLayout()
# Create a read-only table to display user data for confirmation
self.table = QTableWidget(6, 2, self)
self.table.setHorizontalHeaderLabels(['Field', 'Value'])
self.table.verticalHeader().setVisible(False)
self.table.setEditTriggers(QTableWidget.NoEditTriggers)
self.table.horizontalHeader().setSectionResizeMode(QHeaderView.Stretch)
fields = ['First Name', 'Last Name', 'User ID', 'Email', 'Password', 'Confirm Password']
for i, field in enumerate(fields):
self.table.setItem(i, 0, QTableWidgetItem(field))
self.table.setItem(i, 1, QTableWidgetItem(self.user_data[field]))
layout.addWidget(self.table)
# Confirm and Edit buttons
self.confirm_button = QPushButton('Confirm')
self.confirm_button.clicked.connect(self.confirm)
layout.addWidget(self.confirm_button)
self.edit_button = QPushButton('Edit')
self.edit_button.clicked.connect(self.edit)
layout.addWidget(self.edit_button)
central_widget = QWidget(self)
central_widget.setLayout(layout)
self.setCentralWidget(central_widget)
def confirm(self):
# Here you would add the user to the database as an unactivated user
# Then, display the message that the user needs to be activated by an admin
# For now, let's print the confirmation to the console
print("User confirmed the details. Proceeding with registration.")
self.close()
def edit(self):
# Here you would allow the user to edit their details
# For now, let's print the edit action to the console
print("User chose to edit their details.")
```

```python
self.close()
class RegisterWindow(CustomWindow):
# ... (rest of the class remains unchanged)
def register(self):
# ... (previous registration logic remains unchanged)
# Gather all the inputs into a dictionary for easy passing to the confirmation window
user_data = {
'First Name': self.first_name.text().strip(),
'Last Name': self.last_name.text().strip(),
'User ID': self.user_id.text().strip(),
'Email': self.username.text().strip(),
'Password': self.password.text(),
'Confirm Password': self.confirm_password.text()
}
# Check if passwords and emails match before proceeding
if user_data['Password'] != user_data['Confirm Password']:
QMessageBox.warning(self, 'Error', 'Passwords do not match.')
return
if user_data['Email'] != self.confirm_username.text().strip():
QMessageBox.warning(self, 'Error', 'Email addresses do not match.')
return
# Open the confirmation window with the user's data
self.confirmation_window = ConfirmationWindow(user_data)
self.confirmation_window.show()
# ... (rest of the methods remain unchanged)
# ... (rest of the file remains unchanged)
```

After many updates and fixing many bugs , we've addressed the following conditions from the requirements:

1. Check if the user already exists during registration: The register method in the RegisterWindow class checks if the user's email or user ID already exists in the database using the user_exists function.
2. After the user submits the form, show a confirmation window with the details they entered: We have created a ConfirmationWindow class that displays all the entered details except for the password.
3. Allow the user to confirm or edit the information: In the ConfirmationWindow, there are 'Confirm' and 'Edit' buttons. The 'Edit' button closes the confirmation window and brings the user back to the registration form with their details still intact.

This is the working ui.py code so far

```python
ui.py
###########################################################
## Atheer Work: Research Tracker Project © 2024 A Mahir ###
###########################################################
# ****************************************************************
import os
import sys
import sqlite3
import re
import bcrypt
from PyQt5.QtWidgets import (QApplication, QMainWindow, QPushButton, QLineEdit, QMessageBox,
QColorDialog, QLabel,
QInputDialog, QVBoxLayout, QWidget, QCheckBox, QHBoxLayout)
from PyQt5.QtCore import Qt, QSize, QMimeData, QUrl, pyqtSignal, QObject
from PyQt5.QtGui import QImage, QPixmap, QDragEnterEvent, QDropEvent, QPalette, QBrush
from PyQt5.QtGui import QDesktopServices
from PyQt5.QtCore import QUrl
# from auth import validate_user, add_user
from auth import validate_user, add_user, get_user_role_and_status # update 202312272338
from database import ensure_table_schema
from database import user_exists # We need to import the user_exists function to check for existing users
from database import get_activated_admin_emails # Add this import to get the activated admin emails # update
20231228626

os.system('cls||clear') # clear the terminal
# Global signal class
class GlobalSignals(QObject):
background_image_changed = pyqtSignal(str)
global_signals = GlobalSignals() # Create an instance of the global signals class
global_background_pixmap = None
def set_global_background_image(image_path):
global global_background_pixmap
global_background_pixmap = QPixmap(image_path)
global_signals.background_image_changed.emit(image_path) # Emit the signal through the instance
class CustomWindow(QMainWindow):
def __init__(self, parent=None):
super().__init__(parent)
self.setFixedSize(QSize(800, 400))
global_signals.background_image_changed.connect(self.update_background) # Connect to the global signal
def update_background(self, image_path):
if QPixmap(image_path).isNull():
QMessageBox.warning(self, 'Error', 'The image file is not valid.')
return
```

```python
palette = QPalette()
brush = QBrush(QPixmap(image_path).scaled(self.size(), Qt.KeepAspectRatioByExpanding,
Qt.SmoothTransformation))
palette.setBrush(QPalette.Window, brush)
self.setPalette(palette)
def create_child_window(self, window_class):
child_window = window_class(self)
global_signals.background_image_changed.connect(child_window.update_background)
child_window.show()
class DraggableLabel(QLabel):
imageDropped = pyqtSignal(str) # Signal to emit the file path
def __init__(self, parent=None):
super().__init__(parent)
self.setAcceptDrops(True)
self.setAutoFillBackground(True)
def dragEnterEvent(self, event: QDragEnterEvent):
if event.mimeData().hasUrls():
event.acceptProposedAction()
def dropEvent(self, event: QDropEvent):
mimeData = event.mimeData()
if mimeData.hasUrls():
urls = mimeData.urls()
if len(urls) > 0:
image_path = urls[0].toLocalFile()
self.imageDropped.emit(image_path)
event.acceptProposedAction()
# Continue from Part 1
class LoginWindow(CustomWindow):
def __init__(self, parent=None):
super().__init__(parent)
self.setWindowTitle('Login Window')
self.initUI()
def initUI(self):
# Add layout, labels, line edits, and buttons for login functionality
self.username = QLineEdit(self)
self.password = QLineEdit(self)
self.password.setEchoMode(QLineEdit.Password)
self.login_button = QPushButton('Login', self)
self.login_button.clicked.connect(self.login)
self.show_password_checkbox = QCheckBox('Show Password', self)
self.show_password_checkbox.stateChanged.connect(self.toggle_password_visibility)
# Set placeholder text for the password field
self.password.setPlaceholderText("Enter your password")
# Set the echo mode to hide the password initially
```

```python
self.password.setEchoMode(QLineEdit.Password)
layout = QVBoxLayout()
layout.addWidget(QLabel('Enter your username:'))
layout.addWidget(self.username)
layout.addWidget(QLabel('Enter your password:'))
layout.addWidget(self.password)
layout.addWidget(self.show_password_checkbox) # Add the checkbox to the layout
layout.addWidget(self.login_button)
# "Forget Password" Button
self.forget_password_button = QPushButton('Forget Password')
self.forget_password_button.clicked.connect(self.forget_password)
layout.addWidget(self.forget_password_button)
# Set the central widget with the layout
central_widget = QWidget(self)
central_widget.setLayout(layout)
self.setCentralWidget(central_widget)

# update 202312272338 start
#*************************************************************************#
def login(self):
username = self.username.text()
password = self.password.text()
if username and password:
if validate_user(username, password):
user_role, role_approved = get_user_role_and_status(username)
if user_role == 'Administrator':
if role_approved:
self.open_admin_tools()
else:
self.email_activated_admins()
else:
QMessageBox.information(self, 'Success', 'Login successful!')
else:
QMessageBox.warning(self, 'Error', 'Invalid username or password.')
else:
QMessageBox.warning(self, 'Error', 'Please enter both username and password.')
def email_activated_admins(self):
# Open default email client to email all activated admins
# You would need to implement get_activated_admin_emails to retrieve the emails
admin_emails = ";".join(get_activated_admin_emails())
subject = "Activation Request"
body = "I am an admin and require my role to be activated."
mailto_link = f"mailto:{admin_emails}?subject={subject}&body={body}"
QDesktopServices.openUrl(QUrl(mailto_link))
```

```python
def open_admin_tools(self):
self.admin_tools_window = AdminToolsWindow()
self.admin_tools_window.show()
#************************************************************************#
# update 202312272338 end

def toggle_password_visibility(self, state):
if state == Qt.Checked:
self.password.setEchoMode(QLineEdit.Normal)
else:
self.password.setEchoMode(QLineEdit.Password)
def forget_password(self):
# Open the default email client to send an email
admin_email = "amahir@gmail.com"
subject = "Password Reset Request"
body = "I have forgotten my password and request assistance to reset it."
mailto_link = f"mailto:{admin_email}?subject={subject}&body={body}"
QDesktopServices.openUrl(QUrl(mailto_link))

class RegisterWindow(CustomWindow):
def __init__(self, parent=None):
super().__init__(parent)
self.setWindowTitle('Register Window')
# Initialise all QLineEdit attributes before calling initUI()
self.first_name = QLineEdit(self)
self.last_name = QLineEdit(self)
self.user_id = QLineEdit(self)
self.username = QLineEdit(self)
self.confirm_username = QLineEdit(self)
self.password = QLineEdit(self)
self.confirm_password = QLineEdit(self)
self.initUI()
def initUI(self):
layout = QVBoxLayout()
# Create horizontal layouts for each label-input pair
fields = [
('First Name:', self.first_name),
('Last Name:', self.last_name),
('ID:', self.user_id),
('Enter your username (email):', self.username),
('Re-enter your username (email):', self.confirm_username),
('Password:', self.password),
('Rewrite Password to validate:', self.confirm_password)
]
```

```python
for label_text, widget in fields:
row_layout = QHBoxLayout()
label = QLabel(label_text)
label.setAlignment(Qt.AlignRight | Qt.AlignVCenter) # Align right for the label
row_layout.addWidget(label)
row_layout.addWidget(widget) # Add the corresponding input field
layout.addLayout(row_layout) # Add the horizontal layout to the main vertical layout
# Show Password Checkbox
self.show_password_checkbox = QCheckBox('Show Password')
self.show_password_checkbox.stateChanged.connect(self.toggle_password_visibility)
layout.addWidget(self.show_password_checkbox)
# Set placeholder text for password fields
self.password.setPlaceholderText("Password (UpperCase, LowerCase, Special Character, Length > 8)")
self.confirm_password.setPlaceholderText("Rewrite Password to validate")
# Set the echo mode to hide the password initially
self.password.setEchoMode(QLineEdit.Password)
self.confirm_password.setEchoMode(QLineEdit.Password)
# "Show Password" Checkbox
self.show_password_checkbox = QCheckBox('Show Password')
self.show_password_checkbox.stateChanged.connect(self.toggle_password_visibility)

# Register Button
self.register_button = QPushButton('Register')
self.register_button.clicked.connect(self.register)
layout.addWidget(self.register_button)
central_widget = QWidget(self)
central_widget.setLayout(layout)
self.setCentralWidget(central_widget)
def toggle_password_visibility(self, state):
echo_mode = QLineEdit.Normal if state == Qt.Checked else QLineEdit.Password
self.password.setEchoMode(echo_mode)
self.confirm_password.setEchoMode(echo_mode)
def register(self):
# Gather all the inputs
first_name = self.first_name.text().strip()
last_name = self.last_name.text().strip()
user_id = self.user_id.text().strip()
email = self.username.text().strip()
confirm_email = self.confirm_username.text().strip()
password = self.password.text()
confirm_password = self.confirm_password.text()
# Check if the email or user ID already exists in the database
if user_exists(email) or user_exists(user_id):
QMessageBox.warning(self, 'Error', 'A user with this email or user ID already exists.')
```

```python
return
# Proceed only if the password and confirmation match
if password != confirm_password or email != confirm_email:
QMessageBox.warning(self, 'Error', 'Email addresses or passwords do not match.')
return
try:
# Here we would call a method to show the confirmation window with the details
# For now, let's assume the user confirms and we add them as an unactivated user
# The logic for showing the confirmation window and handling the response will be added later
add_user(first_name, last_name, user_id, email, password) # Now using the auth module
QMessageBox.information(self, 'Success', 'Registration successful!')
except sqlite3.IntegrityError as e:
QMessageBox.warning(self, 'Error', 'A user with this email or user ID already exists in the database.')

def hash_password(self, password):
# Hash a password with bcrypt
hashed = bcrypt.hashpw(password.encode('utf-8'), bcrypt.gensalt())
return hashed

class LoginRegisterWindow(CustomWindow):
def __init__(self):
super().__init__()
self.setWindowTitle('Login/Register Window')
central_widget = QWidget(self)
self.setCentralWidget(central_widget)
layout = QVBoxLayout(central_widget)
self.background_label = DraggableLabel(self)
self.background_label.resize(self.size())
layout.addWidget(self.background_label)
self.background_label.imageDropped.connect(set_global_background_image)
self.register_button = QPushButton('Register', self)
self.register_button.clicked.connect(lambda: self.create_child_window(RegisterWindow))
layout.addWidget(self.register_button)
self.login_button = QPushButton('Login', self)
self.login_button.clicked.connect(lambda: self.create_child_window(LoginWindow))
layout.addWidget(self.login_button)
self.change_color_button = QPushButton('Change Background Color', self)
self.change_color_button.clicked.connect(self.change_background_color)
layout.addWidget(self.change_color_button)
def create_child_window(self, window_class):
child_window = window_class(self)
child_window.show()
def change_background_color(self):
color = QColorDialog.getColor()
```

```python
if color.isValid():
palette = QPalette()
palette.setColor(QPalette.Window, color)
self.setPalette(palette)
QApplication.instance().setPalette(palette)
def set_background_image(self, image_path):
set_global_background_image(image_path) # This will trigger the update_background for all windows
# update 202312272338 start
#*************************************************************************#
class AdminToolsWindow(QMainWindow):
def __init__(self, parent=None):
super().__init__(parent)
self.setWindowTitle('Admin Tools')
self.initUI()
def initUI(self):
# Layout and buttons go here
layout = QVBoxLayout()
self.display_users_button = QPushButton('Display Users')
self.display_users_button.clicked.connect(self.display_users)
layout.addWidget(self.display_users_button)
self.delete_user_button = QPushButton('Delete User')
self.delete_user_button.clicked.connect(self.delete_user)
layout.addWidget(self.delete_user_button)
self.update_user_button = QPushButton('Update User')
self.update_user_button.clicked.connect(self.update_user)
layout.addWidget(self.update_user_button)
self.reset_password_button = QPushButton('Reset Password')
self.reset_password_button.clicked.connect(self.reset_password)
layout.addWidget(self.reset_password_button)
# Set central widget and layout
central_widget = QWidget()
central_widget.setLayout(layout)
self.setCentralWidget(central_widget)
def display_users(self):
# Implement user display logic
pass
def delete_user(self):
# Implement user deletion logic
pass
def update_user(self):
# Implement user update logic
pass
def reset_password(self):
# Implement password reset logic
```

```
pass
#**********************************************************************#
# update 202312272338 end
```

We still need to implement the following steps:

1. **If the user confirms, add them as an unactivated user to the database**: After the user confirms their details in the ConfirmationWindow, we need to actually add them to the database as an unactivated user. This requires calling an appropriate function, likely add_user, with a parameter or flag indicating that the user's account is not yet activated.
2. **Display a message about the need for activation and provide options to send a notification email or just acknowledge the message (OK)**: After adding the user as unactivated, we should display a message box to inform them that their account needs to be activated. This message box should include a button to send an email to an admin or supervisor requesting activation.
3. **Close the registration window after the user clicks 'OK' or sends an email and return to the main menu**: The current implementation closes the confirmation window upon clicking 'Confirm' but does not yet handle the email sending functionality or ensure that the application returns to the main menu.

Implementation:

For step 1, we'll implement the functionality to add the user as an unactivated user in the ConfirmationWindow class. We'll assume that the add_user function from the auth.py file can take an additional argument that specifies whether the user is activated or not.

For step 2, we'll add a message box that informs the user that their account needs to be activated. This message box will also have a button for sending a notification email.

For step 3, we'll make sure that after the user confirms their information, or sends the email, they are returned to the main menu.

```python
# Inside the ConfirmationWindow class:
def confirm(self):
# Add the user to the database as an unactivated user here
try:
# Assuming add_user function accepts a 'role_approved' parameter indicating activation status
# Here we set 'role_approved' to 0 indicating the user is not activated
add_user(
self.user_data['First Name'],
self.user_data['Last Name'],
self.user_data['User ID'],
self.user_data['Email'],
self.user_data['Password'],
role_approved=0
)
QMessageBox.information(self, 'Registration Confirmed', 'Your details have been confirmed. You will be notified once your account is activated.')
self.close()
# Now close the main registration window as well
self.register_window_ref.close()
except Exception as e:
QMessageBox.warning(self, 'Registration Failed', f'An error occurred during registration: {e}')
def edit(self):
# Close the confirmation window and bring the registration window to the front for editing
self.close()
self.register_window_ref.show()
```

For step 2 and 3, we'll need to add the email sending functionality. For simplicity, we'll just show how to launch the default email client with a pre-filled compose window:

```python
# At the end of the confirm method in the ConfirmationWindow class:
def confirm(self):
# ... (existing code)
# After confirming the user details
QMessageBox.information(self, 'Registration Confirmed', 'Your details have been confirmed. Please wait for an admin to activate your account.')
# Prompt to send an activation request email
reply = QMessageBox.question(self, 'Activation Request', 'Do you want to send an activation request now?',
QMessageBox.Yes | QMessageBox.No, QMessageBox.No)
if reply == QMessageBox.Yes:
# Here you would construct the mailto link with the appropriate details
subject = "Account Activation Request"
body = f"Hello,\n\nPlease activate my account.\n\nUser ID: {self.user_data['User ID']}"
mailto_link = f"mailto:admin@example.com?subject={subject}&body={body}"
QDesktopServices.openUrl(QUrl(mailto_link))
self.register_window_ref.close() # Close the registration window as well
```

Now, when the user confirms their details, they are added as an unactivated user to the database. Then they are informed about the activation process and given an option to send an email to request activation. After this process, the registration window is closed, and the application should return to the main menu, which may involve showing the LoginRegisterWindow or another appropriate window.

Please integrate these changes into your ui.py file, and adjust the add_user function in your auth.py or equivalent file to handle the role_approved parameter as needed. If there's any other specific functionality or detail you need assistance with, let me know!

Test: Register a new user is not working as expected after confirmation, I got this error box message:

"An error occurred during registration: add_user() got an unexpected keyword argument 'role_approved'"

Fixing:

The error message you're seeing indicates that the add_user function does not recognize the role_approved keyword argument. This suggests that the add_user function needs to be updated to accept this new argument or that the argument is not being passed correctly.

Here's what you need to do:

1. Update the add_user function in your auth.py (or wherever this function is located) to accept a role_approved argument.
2. Ensure that the add_user function properly handles this new argument when inserting data into the database.

The updated add_user function might look something like this:

```python
# In auth.py or the relevant file where add_user is defined
def add_user(first_name, last_name, user_id, email, password, role_approved):
    """Add a new user to the database with a specified approval status."""
    hashed_password = bcrypt.hashpw(password.encode('utf-8'), bcrypt.gensalt())
    with create_connection() as conn:
        cursor = conn.cursor()
        cursor.execute('''
        INSERT INTO users (first_name, last_name, user_id, email, password, role_approved)
        VALUES (?, ?, ?, ?, ?, ?)
        ''', (first_name, last_name, user_id, email, hashed_password, role_approved))
        conn.commit()
```

Once you have updated the add_user function to handle the role_approved argument, the error should be resolved, and you should be able to register new users without encountering this error.

Test: Working, but we have issues

1. After this message "Your details have been confirmed. Please wait for an admin to activate your account." , then press 'OK' on that message, this should be close the confirm/edit window (not happened)

2. After clicking OK, the message box comes with "Do you want to send an activation request now?", when it is selected 'Yes', the app should search the database for any admin role or supervisor role, get their email and prepare an email of all of those people, you have to get these emails from the database (not happened)

Fixing:

To address these issues, we'll make the following changes:

Closing the Confirmation/Edit Window: We will ensure the confirmation window closes immediately after the user acknowledges the message stating their details have been confirmed.

Sending Activation Request to Admins/Supervisors: We will query the database for users with the role of admin or supervisor and collect their emails. Then, we will prepare an email with all those email addresses filled in the recipient field.

Here's the updated confirm method to address issue 1:

```python
def confirm(self):
try:
# ... (existing add_user code)
# Show confirmation message to the user
QMessageBox.information(self, 'Registration Confirmed', 'Your details have been confirmed. Please wait for an admin to activate your account.')
# Prompt to send an activation request email
reply = QMessageBox.question(self, 'Activation Request', 'Do you want to send an activation request now?',
QMessageBox.Yes | QMessageBox.No, QMessageBox.No)
if reply == QMessageBox.Yes:
# Function to retrieve admin and supervisor emails from the database
admin_and_supervisor_emails = self.get_admin_and_supervisor_emails()
if admin_and_supervisor_emails:
# Prepare the mailto link with all the retrieved emails
emails_string = ";".join(admin_and_supervisor_emails)
subject = "Account Activation Request"
body = f"Hello,\n\nPlease activate my account.\n\nUser ID: {self.user_data['User ID']}"
mailto_link = f"mailto:{emails_string}?subject={subject}&body={body}"
QDesktopServices.openUrl(QUrl(mailto_link))
# Close the confirmation window after user interaction
self.close()
self.register_window_ref.close()
except Exception as e:
QMessageBox.warning(self, 'Registration Failed', f'An error occurred during registration: {e}')
```

Now for issue 2, we need a new method get_admin_and_supervisor_emails that retrieves the emails of admins and supervisors:

```python
# Inside the ConfirmationWindow class:
from database import create_connection # Make sure to import the database connection function
# ...
def get_admin_and_supervisor_emails(self):
"""Retrieve email addresses of all admins and supervisors."""
emails = []
with create_connection() as conn:
cursor = conn.cursor()
# Adjust the query to match your database schema
cursor.execute("SELECT email FROM users WHERE role='Admin' OR role='Supervisor'")
for row in cursor.fetchall():
emails.append(row[0])
return emails
```

Define the get_admin_and_supervisor_emails function in database.py.

```python
# In database.py
def get_admin_and_supervisor_emails():
"""Retrieve email addresses of all admins and supervisors."""
emails = []
with create_connection() as conn:
cursor = conn.cursor()
# Adjust the query to match your database schema
cursor.execute("SELECT email FROM users WHERE role='Administrator' OR role='Supervisor'")
emails = [row[0] for row in cursor.fetchall()]
return emails
```

Update the confirm method in the ConfirmationWindow class within ui.py to call this function.

```python
# In ui.py, within the ConfirmationWindow class
from database import get_admin_and_supervisor_emails # Import the function
class ConfirmationWindow(CustomWindow):
# ... (rest of the ConfirmationWindow class)
def confirm(self):
# ... (existing code before the QMessageBox)
reply = QMessageBox.question(self, 'Activation Request', 'Do you want to send an activation request now?',
QMessageBox.Yes | QMessageBox.No, QMessageBox.No)
if reply == QMessageBox.Yes:
admin_and_supervisor_emails = get_admin_and_supervisor_emails()
if admin_and_supervisor_emails:
# Prepare the mailto link with all the retrieved emails
emails_string = ";".join(admin_and_supervisor_emails)
subject = "Account Activation Request"
body = f"Hello,\n\nPlease activate my account.\n\nUser ID: {self.user_data['User ID']}"
mailto_link = f"mailto:{emails_string}?subject={subject}&body={body}"
QDesktopServices.openUrl(QUrl(mailto_link))
self.close()
self.register_window_ref.close()
# ... (rest of the confirm method)
```

Testing: create a new Python file, draft.py, that displays a list of users and their details in a table within a scrollable window.

you can use PyQt5. This file will create a simple GUI application with a table to show user data fetched from your database.

Here's an example code for draft.py. This script assumes that you have PyQt5 installed and a function in your database.py module to fetch user data:

```python
import sys
from PyQt5.QtWidgets import QApplication, QMainWindow, QTableWidget, QTableWidgetItem,
QVBoxLayout, QWidget, QScrollArea
from database import fetch_all_users # Make sure this function exists in your database module
class UserTableWindow(QMainWindow):
def __init__(self):
super().__init__()
self.setWindowTitle("User List")
self.setGeometry(100, 100, 800, 600)
self.initUI()
def initUI(self):
# Create a central widget
central_widget = QWidget(self)
self.setCentralWidget(central_widget)
# Create a vertical layout
layout = QVBoxLayout(central_widget)
# Create a table widget
self.table = QTableWidget(self)
self.table.setColumnCount(6) # Adjust the number of columns based on your user data
self.table.setHorizontalHeaderLabels(["First Name", "Last Name", "User ID", "Email", "Role","activated"]) # Set your
headers here
# Populate the table with data
self.populate_table()
# Add the table to a scroll area
scroll_area = QScrollArea(self)
scroll_area.setWidgetResizable(True)
scroll_area.setWidget(self.table)
layout.addWidget(scroll_area)
def populate_table(self):
# Fetch user data
users = fetch_all_users() # This function should now return the role_approved data as well
self.table.setRowCount(len(users))
for row_num, user in enumerate(users):
for col_num, data in enumerate(user):
# Convert boolean or integer role_approved to a readable format if needed
if col_num == 5: # Assuming role_approved is the 6th column
data = 'Yes' if data else 'No'
self.table.setItem(row_num, col_num, QTableWidgetItem(str(data)))


def main():
app = QApplication(sys.argv)
main_window = UserTableWindow()
main_window.show()
sys.exit(app.exec_())
```

```
if __name__ == "__main__":
main()
```

To run this , you need implement the fetch_all_users function

```
# In your database.py file
def fetch_all_users():
"""Fetch all user data from the database."""
users = []
with create_connection() as conn:
cursor = conn.cursor()
cursor.execute("SELECT first_name, last_name, user_id, email, role FROM users") # Adjust the columns based on
your database schema
users = cursor.fetchall()
return users
```

This function opens a connection to the database, executes a SQL query to fetch specific columns from the users table, and then returns all the rows as a list of tuples.

Finally after checking deeply the code and fix bugs , we reach to this current good codes:

main.py
Entry point of the application, responsible for starting the application.
<<<

```python
#############################################################
## Atheer Work: Research Tracker Project © 2024 A Mahir ###
#############################################################
# ******************************************************************
# clear the terminal
from utils import clear_terminal
clear_terminal()
# ******************************************************************
import sys
from PyQt5.QtWidgets import QApplication
from ui import LoginRegisterWindow
if __name__ == '__main__':
app = QApplication(sys.argv)
win = LoginRegisterWindow()
win.show()
sys.exit(app.exec_())
```

>>>

database.py (Database Operations)
Contains the database connection and operations.
<<<

```python
#############################################################
## Atheer Work: Research Tracker Project © 2024 A Mahir ###
#############################################################
# ******************************************************************
# clear the terminal
from utils import clear_terminal
clear_terminal()
# ******************************************************************
import sqlite3
import bcrypt
from config import DB_PATH, ADMIN_EMAIL, ADMIN_PASSWORD
def create_connection():
"""Create a database connection to the SQLite database specified by DB_PATH."""
conn = sqlite3.connect(DB_PATH)
return conn
# update 202312272031 start
#******************************************************************#
def ensure_table_schema():
with create_connection() as conn:
cursor = conn.cursor()
```

```python
# Create table if it doesn't exist
cursor.execute('''
CREATE TABLE IF NOT EXISTS users (
id INTEGER PRIMARY KEY AUTOINCREMENT,
first_name TEXT NOT NULL,
last_name TEXT NOT NULL,
user_id TEXT NOT NULL UNIQUE,
email TEXT NOT NULL UNIQUE,
password TEXT NOT NULL
)
''')
# Check if 'role' column exists and add if not
cursor.execute("PRAGMA table_info(users)")
columns = [info[1] for info in cursor.fetchall()]
if 'role' not in columns:
cursor.execute('ALTER TABLE users ADD COLUMN role TEXT DEFAULT "Student"')
# Check if 'role_approved' column exists and add if not
if 'role_approved' not in columns:
cursor.execute('ALTER TABLE users ADD COLUMN role_approved INTEGER DEFAULT 0')
conn.commit()
#**********************************************************************#
# update 202312272031 end

# update 2023122719:29 start
#**********************************************************************#
def add_user(first_name, last_name, user_id, email, password, role='Student', role_approved=0):
"""Add a new user to the database with a specified role and approval status."""
hashed_password = bcrypt.hashpw(password.encode('utf-8'), bcrypt.gensalt())
with create_connection() as conn:
cursor = conn.cursor()
cursor.execute('''
INSERT INTO users(first_name, last_name, user_id, email, password, role, role_approved)
VALUES(?, ?, ?, ?, ?, ?, ?)
''', (first_name, last_name, user_id, email, hashed_password, role, role_approved))
conn.commit()
def add_admin():
"""Add an admin user to the database with predefined credentials and role."""
admin_first_name = 'Admin'
admin_last_name = 'User'
admin_user_id = 'admin'
admin_email = ADMIN_EMAIL # Corrected to use the standalone variable
admin_password = ADMIN_PASSWORD # Corrected to use the standalone variable
# Set the role as 'Administrator' and role_approved as 1 for the admin user
add_user(admin_first_name, admin_last_name, admin_user_id, admin_email, admin_password, 'Administrator',
```

```
1)
#*********************************************************#
# update 2023122719:29 end
# # update 2023122719:42 start for testing
# #*********************************************************#
# def add_test_users():
# # Add 3 random students (role-approved)
# for i in range(1, 4):
# add_user(f'Student{i}', 'Approved', f'student{i}', f'student{i}@example.com', 'password', 'Student', 1)
# # Add 3 random students (role not approved yet)
# for i in range(4, 7):
# add_user(f'Student{i}', 'NotApproved', f'student{i}', f'student{i}@example.com', 'password', 'Student', 0)
# # Add 2 random supervisors (role-approved)
# for i in range(1, 3):
# add_user(f'Supervisor{i}', 'Approved', f'supervisor{i}', f'supervisor{i}@example.com', 'password', 'Supervisor', 1)
# # Add 2 random admins (role-approved)
# for i in range(1, 3):
# add_user(f'Admin{i}', 'Approved', f'admin{i}', f'admin{i}@example.com', 'password', 'Administrator', 1)
# #*********************************************************#
# # update 2023122719:42 end

# update 2023122719:05 start
#*********************************************************#
# Add a function to update the user's role and approval status
def update_user_role(user_id, role, role_approved):
with create_connection() as conn:
cursor = conn.cursor()
cursor.execute('''
UPDATE users SET role = ?, role_approved = ? WHERE user_id = ?
''', (role, role_approved, user_id))
conn.commit()
#*********************************************************#
# update 2023122719:05 end
# update 2023122719:51 start
#*********************************************************#
def add_test_users():
test_users = [
# Students (role-approved)
{"first_name": "Student1", "last_name": "Approved", "user_id": "student1", "email": "student1@example.com",
"password": "password1", "role": "Student", "role_approved": 1},
{"first_name": "Student2", "last_name": "Approved", "user_id": "student2", "email": "student2@example.com",
"password": "password2", "role": "Student", "role_approved": 1},
{"first_name": "Student3", "last_name": "Approved", "user_id": "student3", "email": "student3@example.com",
"password": "password3", "role": "Student", "role_approved": 1},
```

```python
# Students (role not approved yet)
{"first_name": "Student4", "last_name": "NotApproved", "user_id": "student4", "email": "student4@example.com",
"password": "password4", "role": "Student", "role_approved": 0},
{"first_name": "Student5", "last_name": "NotApproved", "user_id": "student5", "email": "student5@example.com",
"password": "password5", "role": "Student", "role_approved": 0},
{"first_name": "Student6", "last_name": "NotApproved", "user_id": "student6", "email": "student6@example.com",
"password": "password6", "role": "Student", "role_approved": 0},
# Supervisors (role-approved)
{"first_name": "Supervisor1", "last_name": "Approved", "user_id": "supervisor1", "email": "supervisor1@example.com",
"password": "password7", "role": "Supervisor", "role_approved": 1},
{"first_name": "Supervisor2", "last_name": "Approved", "user_id": "supervisor2", "email": "supervisor2@example.com",
"password": "password8", "role": "Supervisor", "role_approved": 1},
# Admins (role-approved)
{"first_name": "Admin1", "last_name": "Approved", "user_id": "admin1", "email": "admin1@example.com",
"password": "password9", "role": "Administrator", "role_approved": 1},
{"first_name": "Admin2", "last_name": "Approved", "user_id": "admin2", "email": "admin2@example.com",
"password": "password10", "role": "Administrator", "role_approved": 1}
]
for user in test_users:
    print(f"Adding user: {user['user_id']}, Role: {user['role']}, Password: {user['password']}")
    # Check if the user already exists before attempting to add
    if not user_exists(user["email"]):
        add_user(user["first_name"], user["last_name"], user["user_id"], user["email"], user["password"], user["role"],
user["role_approved"])
    else:
        print(user["email"], " Test user already exists.")
def display_users():
    """Display users with their roles and hashed passwords."""
    with create_connection() as conn:
        cursor = conn.cursor()
        cursor.execute('''
SELECT id, first_name, last_name, user_id, email, role, role_approved, password FROM users
''')
        users = cursor.fetchall()
        for user in users:
            print(f"ID: {user[0]}, Name: {user[1]} {user[2]}, UserID: {user[3]}, Email: {user[4]}, Role: {user[5]}, Approved:
{'Yes' if user[6] == 1 else 'No'}, Hashed Password: {user[7]}")
#********************************************************************#
# update 2023122719:51 end
# update 202312272046 start
#********************************************************************#
def user_exists(email):
    """Check if a user already exists in the database based on their email."""
    with create_connection() as conn:
```

```python
cursor = conn.cursor()
cursor.execute('SELECT id FROM users WHERE email = ?', (email,))
return cursor.fetchone() is not None
#**********************************************************************#
# update 202312272046 end

# update 20231228626 start
#**********************************************************************#
def get_activated_admin_emails():
    """Retrieve email addresses of all activated admins."""
    with create_connection() as conn:
        cursor = conn.cursor()
        cursor.execute('''
        SELECT email FROM users WHERE role='Administrator' AND role_approved=1
        ''')
        emails = cursor.fetchall()
        return [email[0] for email in emails] if emails else []
#**********************************************************************#
# update 20231228626 end
# update 2023281004 start
#**********************************************************************#
def get_admin_and_supervisor_emails():
    """Retrieve email addresses of all admins and supervisors."""
    emails = []
    with create_connection() as conn:
        cursor = conn.cursor()
        # Adjust the query to match your database schema
        cursor.execute("SELECT email FROM users WHERE role='Administrator' OR role='Supervisor'")
        emails = [row[0] for row in cursor.fetchall()]
    return emails
#**********************************************************************#
# update 2023281004 end

# update 2023281054 start
#**********************************************************************#
def fetch_all_users():
    """Fetch all user data from the database."""
    users = []
    with create_connection() as conn:
        cursor = conn.cursor()
        cursor.execute("SELECT first_name, last_name, user_id, email, role, role_approved FROM users") # Adjust the
        columns based on your database schema
        users = cursor.fetchall()
    return users
```

```python
#**********************************************************************#
# update 2023281054 end
# update 202312272046 start
#**********************************************************************#
def main():
ensure_table_schema()
# Check if the admin user already exists before attempting to add
if not user_exists(ADMIN_EMAIL):
add_admin() # Add an admin user with the Administrator role and approved status
else:
print("Admin user already exists.")
add_test_users()
display_users() # Display the list of users
if __name__ == '__main__':
main()
#**********************************************************************#
# update 202312272046 end
```

> > >

user.py (User Class)

A class that represents a user and its attributes.

< < <

```python
from auth import add_user, validate_user, hash_password
class User:
def __init__(self, first_name, last_name, user_id, email, password):
self.first_name = first_name
self.last_name = last_name
self.user_id = user_id
self.email = email
self.password = password
def register(self):
# Here you can include any additional validation if necessary
add_user(self.first_name, self.last_name, self.user_id, self.email, self.password)
return True
def check_credentials(self):
# This method would be used to validate the user's login credentials
return validate_user(self.email, self.password)
```

> > >

auth.py (Authentication Logic)

Contains authentication and authorization logic.

< < <

```python
import bcrypt
import sqlite3
from database import create_connection
```

```python
def hash_password(password):
    """Hash a password with bcrypt."""
    return bcrypt.hashpw(password.encode('utf-8'), bcrypt.gensalt())
def validate_user(username, password):
    """Validate a user's login credentials."""
    conn = create_connection()
    cursor = conn.cursor()
    cursor.execute('''
    SELECT password FROM users WHERE user_id=? OR email=?
    ''', (username, username,))
    user_data = cursor.fetchone()
    conn.close()
    if user_data:
        stored_password = user_data[0]
        return bcrypt.checkpw(password.encode('utf-8'), stored_password)
    return False


# update 2023280934 start
#*********************************************************************#
def add_user(first_name, last_name, user_id, email, password, role_approved):
    """Add a new user to the database with a specified approval status."""
    hashed_password = bcrypt.hashpw(password.encode('utf-8'), bcrypt.gensalt())
    with create_connection() as conn:
        cursor = conn.cursor()
        cursor.execute('''
        INSERT INTO users (first_name, last_name, user_id, email, password, role_approved)
        VALUES (?, ?, ?, ?, ?, ?)
        ''', (first_name, last_name, user_id, email, hashed_password, role_approved))
        conn.commit()
#*********************************************************************#
# update 2023280934 end


def get_user_role_and_status(username):
    """Retrieve the role and role approval status for a user."""
    with create_connection() as conn:
        cursor = conn.cursor()
        cursor.execute('''
        SELECT role, role_approved FROM users WHERE user_id=? OR email=?
        ''', (username, username,))
        user_data = cursor.fetchone()
        if user_data:
            return user_data
        else:
            return None, None
```

```
>>>
ui.py (User Interface)
Contains all the PyQt5 UI classes.
<<<

##############################################################
## Atheer Work: Research Tracker Project © 2024 A Mahir ###
##############################################################
# ****************************************************************
import os
import sys
import sqlite3
import re
import bcrypt
from PyQt5.QtWidgets import (QApplication, QMainWindow, QPushButton, QLineEdit, QMessageBox, QColorDialog, QLabel,
QInputDialog, QVBoxLayout, QWidget, QCheckBox, QHBoxLayout)
from PyQt5.QtCore import Qt, QSize, QMimeData, QUrl, pyqtSignal, QObject
from PyQt5.QtGui import QImage, QPixmap, QDragEnterEvent, QDropEvent, QPalette, QBrush
from PyQt5.QtGui import QDesktopServices
from PyQt5.QtCore import QUrl
# from auth import validate_user, add_user
from auth import validate_user, add_user, get_user_role_and_status # update 202312272338
from database import ensure_table_schema
from database import user_exists # We need to import the user_exists function to check for existing users
from database import get_activated_admin_emails # Add this import to get the activated admin emails # update 20231228626


os.system('cls||clear') # clear the terminal
# Global signal class
class GlobalSignals(QObject):
background_image_changed = pyqtSignal(str)
global_signals = GlobalSignals() # Create an instance of the global signals class
global_background_pixmap = None
def set_global_background_image(image_path):
global global_background_pixmap
global_background_pixmap = QPixmap(image_path)
global_signals.background_image_changed.emit(image_path) # Emit the signal through the instance
class CustomWindow(QMainWindow):
def __init__(self, parent=None):
super().__init__(parent)
self.setFixedSize(QSize(800, 400))
global_signals.background_image_changed.connect(self.update_background) # Connect to the global signal
def update_background(self, image_path):
```

```python
if QPixmap(image_path).isNull():
QMessageBox.warning(self, 'Error', 'The image file is not valid.')
return
palette = QPalette()
brush = QBrush(QPixmap(image_path).scaled(self.size(), Qt.KeepAspectRatioByExpanding,
Qt.SmoothTransformation))
palette.setBrush(QPalette.Window, brush)
self.setPalette(palette)
def create_child_window(self, window_class):
child_window = window_class(self)
global_signals.background_image_changed.connect(child_window.update_background)
child_window.show()
class DraggableLabel(QLabel):
imageDropped = pyqtSignal(str) # Signal to emit the file path
def __init__(self, parent=None):
super().__init__(parent)
self.setAcceptDrops(True)
self.setAutoFillBackground(True)
def dragEnterEvent(self, event: QDragEnterEvent):
if event.mimeData().hasUrls():
event.acceptProposedAction()
def dropEvent(self, event: QDropEvent):
mimeData = event.mimeData()
if mimeData.hasUrls():
urls = mimeData.urls()
if len(urls) > 0:
image_path = urls[0].toLocalFile()
self.imageDropped.emit(image_path)
event.acceptProposedAction()
# Continue from Part 1
class LoginWindow(CustomWindow):
def __init__(self, parent=None):
super().__init__(parent)
self.setWindowTitle('Login Window')
self.initUI()
def initUI(self):
# Add layout, labels, line edits, and buttons for login functionality
self.username = QLineEdit(self)
self.password = QLineEdit(self)
self.password.setEchoMode(QLineEdit.Password)
self.login_button = QPushButton('Login', self)
self.login_button.clicked.connect(self.login)
self.show_password_checkbox = QCheckBox('Show Password', self)
self.show_password_checkbox.stateChanged.connect(self.toggle_password_visibility)
```

```python
# Set placeholder text for the password field
self.password.setPlaceholderText("Enter your password")
# Set the echo mode to hide the password initially
self.password.setEchoMode(QLineEdit.Password)
layout = QVBoxLayout()
layout.addWidget(QLabel('Enter your username:'))
layout.addWidget(self.username)
layout.addWidget(QLabel('Enter your password:'))
layout.addWidget(self.password)
layout.addWidget(self.show_password_checkbox) # Add the checkbox to the layout
layout.addWidget(self.login_button)
# "Forget Password" Button
self.forget_password_button = QPushButton('Forget Password')
self.forget_password_button.clicked.connect(self.forget_password)
layout.addWidget(self.forget_password_button)
# Set the central widget with the layout
central_widget = QWidget(self)
central_widget.setLayout(layout)
self.setCentralWidget(central_widget)
# update 202312272338 start
#************************************************************************#
def login(self):
username = self.username.text()
password = self.password.text()
if username and password:
if validate_user(username, password):
user_role, role_approved = get_user_role_and_status(username)
if user_role == 'Administrator':
if role_approved:
self.open_admin_tools()
else:
self.email_activated_admins()
else:
QMessageBox.information(self, 'Success', 'Login successful!')
else:
QMessageBox.warning(self, 'Error', 'Invalid username or password.')
else:
QMessageBox.warning(self, 'Error', 'Please enter both username and password.')
def email_activated_admins(self):
# Open default email client to email all activated admins
# You would need to implement get_activated_admin_emails to retrieve the emails
admin_emails = ";".join(get_activated_admin_emails())
subject = "Activation Request"
body = "I am an admin and require my role to be activated."
```

```python
        mailto_link = f"mailto:{admin_emails}?subject={subject}&body={body}"
        QDesktopServices.openUrl(QUrl(mailto_link))
    def open_admin_tools(self):
        self.admin_tools_window = AdminToolsWindow()
        self.admin_tools_window.show()
#*************************************************************************#
# update 202312272338 end

    def toggle_password_visibility(self, state):
        if state == Qt.Checked:
            self.password.setEchoMode(QLineEdit.Normal)
        else:
            self.password.setEchoMode(QLineEdit.Password)
    def forget_password(self):
        # Open the default email client to send an email
        admin_email = "amahir@gmail.com"
        subject = "Password Reset Request"
        body = "I have forgotten my password and request assistance to reset it."
        mailto_link = f"mailto:{admin_email}?subject={subject}&body={body}"
        QDesktopServices.openUrl(QUrl(mailto_link))


class RegisterWindow(CustomWindow):
    def __init__(self, parent=None):
        super().__init__(parent)
        self.setWindowTitle('Register Window')
        # Initialise all QLineEdit attributes before calling initUI()
        self.first_name = QLineEdit(self)
        self.last_name = QLineEdit(self)
        self.user_id = QLineEdit(self)
        self.username = QLineEdit(self)
        self.confirm_username = QLineEdit(self)
        self.password = QLineEdit(self)
        self.confirm_password = QLineEdit(self)
        self.initUI()
    def initUI(self):
        layout = QVBoxLayout()
        # Create horizontal layouts for each label-input pair
        fields = [
            ('First Name:', self.first_name),
            ('Last Name:', self.last_name),
            ('ID:', self.user_id),
            ('Enter your username (email):', self.username),
            ('Re-enter your username (email):', self.confirm_username),
            ('Password:', self.password),
```

```python
('Rewrite Password to validate:', self.confirm_password)
]
for label_text, widget in fields:
row_layout = QHBoxLayout()
label = QLabel(label_text)
label.setAlignment(Qt.AlignRight | Qt.AlignVCenter) # Align right for the label
row_layout.addWidget(label)
row_layout.addWidget(widget) # Add the corresponding input field
layout.addLayout(row_layout) # Add the horizontal layout to the main vertical layout
# Show Password Checkbox
self.show_password_checkbox = QCheckBox('Show Password')
self.show_password_checkbox.stateChanged.connect(self.toggle_password_visibility)
layout.addWidget(self.show_password_checkbox)
# Set placeholder text for password fields
self.password.setPlaceholderText("Password (UpperCase, LowerCase, Special Character, Length > 8)")
self.confirm_password.setPlaceholderText("Rewrite Password to validate")
# Set the echo mode to hide the password initially
self.password.setEchoMode(QLineEdit.Password)
self.confirm_password.setEchoMode(QLineEdit.Password)
# "Show Password" Checkbox
self.show_password_checkbox = QCheckBox('Show Password')
self.show_password_checkbox.stateChanged.connect(self.toggle_password_visibility)

# Register Button
self.register_button = QPushButton('Register')
self.register_button.clicked.connect(self.register)
layout.addWidget(self.register_button)
central_widget = QWidget(self)
central_widget.setLayout(layout)
self.setCentralWidget(central_widget)
def toggle_password_visibility(self, state):
echo_mode = QLineEdit.Normal if state == Qt.Checked else QLineEdit.Password
self.password.setEchoMode(echo_mode)
self.confirm_password.setEchoMode(echo_mode)
def register(self):
# Gather all the inputs
first_name = self.first_name.text().strip()
last_name = self.last_name.text().strip()
user_id = self.user_id.text().strip()
email = self.username.text().strip()
confirm_email = self.confirm_username.text().strip()
password = self.password.text()
confirm_password = self.confirm_password.text()
# Check if the email or user ID already exists in the database
```

```python
if user_exists(email) or user_exists(user_id):
QMessageBox.warning(self, 'Error', 'A user with this email or user ID already exists.')
return
# Proceed only if the password and confirmation match
if password != confirm_password or email != confirm_email:
QMessageBox.warning(self, 'Error', 'Email addresses or passwords do not match.')
return
try:
# Here we would call a method to show the confirmation window with the details
# For now, let's assume the user confirms and we add them as an unactivated user
# The logic for showing the confirmation window and handling the response will be added later
add_user(first_name, last_name, user_id, email, password) # Now using the auth module
QMessageBox.information(self, 'Success', 'Registration successful!')
except sqlite3.IntegrityError as e:
QMessageBox.warning(self, 'Error', 'A user with this email or user ID already exists in the database.')

def hash_password(self, password):
# Hash a password with bcrypt
hashed = bcrypt.hashpw(password.encode('utf-8'), bcrypt.gensalt())
return hashed


class LoginRegisterWindow(CustomWindow):
def __init__(self):
super().__init__()
self.setWindowTitle('Login/Register Window')
central_widget = QWidget(self)
self.setCentralWidget(central_widget)
layout = QVBoxLayout(central_widget)
self.background_label = DraggableLabel(self)
self.background_label.resize(self.size())
layout.addWidget(self.background_label)
self.background_label.imageDropped.connect(set_global_background_image)
self.register_button = QPushButton('Register', self)
self.register_button.clicked.connect(lambda: self.create_child_window(RegisterWindow))
layout.addWidget(self.register_button)
self.login_button = QPushButton('Login', self)
self.login_button.clicked.connect(lambda: self.create_child_window(LoginWindow))
layout.addWidget(self.login_button)
self.change_color_button = QPushButton('Change Background Color', self)
self.change_color_button.clicked.connect(self.change_background_color)
layout.addWidget(self.change_color_button)
def create_child_window(self, window_class):
child_window = window_class(self)
child_window.show()
```

```python
def change_background_color(self):
color = QColorDialog.getColor()
if color.isValid():
palette = QPalette()
palette.setColor(QPalette.Window, color)
self.setPalette(palette)
QApplication.instance().setPalette(palette)
def set_background_image(self, image_path):
set_global_background_image(image_path) # This will trigger the update_background for all windows
# update 202312272338 start
#************************************************************************#
class AdminToolsWindow(QMainWindow):
def __init__(self, parent=None):
super().__init__(parent)
self.setWindowTitle('Admin Tools')
self.initUI()
def initUI(self):
# Layout and buttons go here
layout = QVBoxLayout()
self.display_users_button = QPushButton('Display Users')
self.display_users_button.clicked.connect(self.display_users)
layout.addWidget(self.display_users_button)
self.delete_user_button = QPushButton('Delete User')
self.delete_user_button.clicked.connect(self.delete_user)
layout.addWidget(self.delete_user_button)
self.update_user_button = QPushButton('Update User')
self.update_user_button.clicked.connect(self.update_user)
layout.addWidget(self.update_user_button)
self.reset_password_button = QPushButton('Reset Password')
self.reset_password_button.clicked.connect(self.reset_password)
layout.addWidget(self.reset_password_button)
# Set central widget and layout
central_widget = QWidget()
central_widget.setLayout(layout)
self.setCentralWidget(central_widget)
def display_users(self):
# Implement user display logic
pass
def delete_user(self):
# Implement user deletion logic
pass
def update_user(self):
# Implement user update logic
pass
```

```
def reset_password(self):
# Implement password reset logic
pass
#**************************************************************************#
# update 202312272338 end
>>>
config.py
Configuration parameters for the application.
<<<
# config.py
DB_PATH = 'users.db'
ADMIN_EMAIL = 'amahir@bedford.ac.uk'
ADMIN_PASSWORD = 'Bedford@2024'
>>>
utils.py
Utility functions that can be used across the application.
<<<
# utils.py
import os
def clear_terminal():
os.system('cls||clear')
>>>
```

Display the users.py
To test the results
<<<

```python
import sys
from PyQt5.QtWidgets import QApplication, QMainWindow, QTableWidget, QTableWidgetItem,
QVBoxLayout, QWidget, QScrollArea
from database import fetch_all_users # Make sure this function exists in your database module
class UserTableWindow(QMainWindow):
def __init__(self):
super().__init__()
self.setWindowTitle("User List")
self.setGeometry(100, 100, 800, 600)
self.initUI()
def initUI(self):
# Create a central widget
central_widget = QWidget(self)
self.setCentralWidget(central_widget)
# Create a vertical layout
layout = QVBoxLayout(central_widget)
# Create a table widget
self.table = QTableWidget(self)
self.table.setColumnCount(6) # Adjust the number of columns based on your user data
self.table.setHorizontalHeaderLabels(["First Name", "Last Name", "User ID", "Email", "Role","activated"]) # Set your
headers here
# Populate the table with data
self.populate_table()
# Add the table to a scroll area
scroll_area = QScrollArea(self)
scroll_area.setWidgetResizable(True)
scroll_area.setWidget(self.table)
layout.addWidget(scroll_area)
def populate_table(self):
# Fetch user data
users = fetch_all_users() # This function should now return the role_approved data as well
self.table.setRowCount(len(users))
for row_num, user in enumerate(users):
for col_num, data in enumerate(user):
# Convert boolean or integer role_approved to a readable format if needed
if col_num == 5: # Assuming role_approved is the 6th column
data = 'Yes' if data else 'No'
self.table.setItem(row_num, col_num, QTableWidgetItem(str(data)))

def main():
```

```python
app = QApplication(sys.argv)
main_window = UserTableWindow()
main_window.show()
sys.exit(app.exec_())
if __name__ == "__main__":
main()
>>>
```

Chapter 2 - A big review

213

Understanding of a general Review:

The project aims to build a research project management application tailored for the administration of student research. It requires a multi-tiered user system with distinct functionalities and privileges for Admins, Supervisors, and Students. Integration with external services like OneDrive and MS Teams is crucial for file management and communication. The application should be intuitive, performant, and secure, with a scalable and maintainable architecture.

Evaluation in Bullet Points:

- User Stories Alignment: The user stories are well-aligned with the typical workflows of a research environment, capturing essential activities across different roles.

- Use Case Comprehensiveness: The use cases cover a broad spectrum of the application's functionality, from account management to project tracking, and communications.

- Functional Requirements Suitability:

- Authentication and User Management: Robust user roles and authentication mechanisms are planned, which is fundamental for a multi-user platform.

- Project Management: The system addresses the need for creating, assigning, and tracking projects, which is central to the app's purpose.

- File Management: Integration with OneDrive for file management is a prudent choice for cloud storage and accessibility.

- Communication: Incorporating MS Teams for communication is beneficial for a seamless user experience, keeping all interactions within the platform.

- Notifications: Alerting users about deadlines and updates is a critical feature for maintaining project timelines.

- Non-Functional Requirements Analysis:

- Usability: The emphasis on an intuitive UI/UX is crucial for user adoption and satisfaction.

- Performance: The requirement for quick responses and efficient operations will ensure a smooth user experience.

- Security: A focus on data protection and secure access is essential, especially when handling sensitive research data.

- Scalability and Maintainability: Planning for future growth and ease of maintenance will safeguard the application's longevity.

- Program Architecture Reasoning:

- Front-End: Choosing PyQt suggests a preference for a native application experience, which can offer performance benefits.

- Back-End: Utilising SQLite for data storage is suitable for lightweight applications but may need reevaluation for scalability.

● External Integrations: The use of APIs for OneDrive and MS Teams integration is a sound approach to extend functionality without reinventing the wheel.

● Additional Considerations Acknowledgement:

● Testing and Validation: The plan to implement comprehensive testing will help in delivering a reliable application.

● Documentation: Providing user training and documentation is essential for end-user empowerment and system maintenance.

Complexity

The use of SQLite may need to be reconsidered if the application is expected to scale significantly. Additionally, while MS Teams integration is useful, it might increase complexity and should be designed carefully to avoid dependency issues.

Analyse and evaluate of the current code

First analysis:

main.py (Entry Point)

- The script uses PyQt5 to start a GUI application.
- A LoginRegisterWindow is created and displayed.
- The application exits cleanly upon closure.

database.py (Database Operations)

- SQLite is used for database operations, which is lightweight and appropriate for smaller-scale applications.

- There is a clear structure for managing database schemas and user data.

- The use of bcrypt for password hashing is a good practice for security.

- Functions to add users, including test users, and admin are present.

- Redundant code for adding test users; two functions with the same name (add_test_users) could lead to confusion and should be consolidated. (Fixed)

user.py (User Class)

- Represents a user and encapsulates registration and credential checking logic.

- Direct database operations are abstracted, which is good for separation of concerns.

auth.py (Authentication Logic)

- Handles password hashing and user validation.

- Provides functionality to add users and retrieve user roles and statuses.

- There's a potential issue with the add_user function being defined twice, once here and once in database.py.

ui.py (User Interface)

- Defines the GUI elements using PyQt5.

- The UI classes are well-structured with separation for login, registration, and admin tools windows.

- Image dropping and background changing functionalities are innovative.

- The CustomWindow base class helps maintain consistency across different windows.

config.py (Configuration)

- Holds the database path and admin credentials.
- Centralising configuration is a good practice.

utils.py (Utilities)

- Provides a function to clear the terminal, which is useful for cleanliness but may not be necessary for the GUI application.

Second analysis (after fixing-1):

Based on the updated code snippets provided for the ongoing Python project, here's an analysis and evaluation:

main.py

- The entry point is concise and clear, initialising the main application window.

database.py

- Implements SQLite database integration and ensures table schema upon initialization.

- Provides comprehensive functions for user management, including adding users and admins, updating user roles, and checking if a user exists.

- Utilises bcrypt for password hashing which indicates a consideration for security.

- Contains test functions to add sample users, which is useful for development and testing but should be removed or commented out for production.

user.py

- Defines a User class encapsulating user properties and methods for registration and credential checking.

- Uses methods from the auth.py module for adding users and validating credentials, which is good practice for code reusability and separation of concerns.

auth.py

- Contains functions for user authentication, including password hashing and user validation.

- There seems to be a duplicated add_user function in both auth.py and database.py, which could lead to confusion and errors; it should be consolidated into one module to avoid redundancy.

ui.py

- Constructs the user interface with PyQt5, setting up different windows for login, registration, and admin tools.

- Integrates drag-and-drop functionality for setting the background image, which enhances user experience.

- Uses signals and slots, a core feature of Qt, to handle events like background image changes, which indicates a good understanding of the framework.

config.py

- Centralises the application configuration, which simplifies the management of global settings.

utils.py

- Provides a utility function to clear the terminal, which is more relevant for CLI-based applications but still shows consideration for cleanliness in the development environment.

UserTableWindow (in Display the users.py)

- Provides a GUI to display user information in a table format, which is a practical tool for administrators to view registered users.

- The function populate_table retrieves user data and fills the table, which indicates integration between the UI and the database.

General Observations:

- Security: The application uses bcrypt for hashing passwords, which is a good practice for security.

- Code Redundancy: The project has redundant code, especially for adding users, which should be addressed to maintain code quality and avoid confusion.

- Database: SQLite is used for local storage, which is adequate for a small-scale application but may need to be scaled to a more robust database system for production.

- Error Handling: There is basic error handling in the UI components, but more comprehensive exception handling throughout the application could enhance robustness.

- Testing: There is an indication of test functions, which is good, but it would be beneficial to see a dedicated testing strategy, possibly including unit tests and integration tests.

Recommendations:

- Resolve the redundancy of add_user definitions.

- Consider implementing a robust testing strategy.

- Prepare for scalability by planning for a transition to a more scalable database if necessary.

- Ensure comprehensive error and exception handling is implemented.

- Before moving to production, remove or disable test functions and data.

This evaluation should provide a strong foundation for understanding the state of the project and planning the next steps. If there are specific areas you would like me to delve deeper into or if there are any amendments needed, please let me know.

Fixing the code:

To resolve the issue of the duplicated add_user function in both auth.py and database.py, you should decide which module is more appropriate for this functionality. Typically, database operations should be centralised in the database.py module. Here's a suggested approach:

Consolidate the add_user Function in database.py:

Since database.py is already responsible for database connections and schema, it makes sense to keep the add_user function there. It directly interacts with the database to insert new user records.

Remove the add_user Function from auth.py:

The auth.py should handle authentication-related functions, like validating credentials or hashing passwords, rather than adding new users to the database.

Refactor user.py to Use the add_user from database.py:

Update the user.py class to call the add_user function from database.py instead of auth.py.

Here is what you can do specifically in the code:

- In auth.py, remove the following block of code:

```python
# update 2023280934 start
#************************************************************************#
def add_user(first_name, last_name, user_id, email, password, role_approved):
"""Add a new user to the database with a specified approval status."""
hashed_password = bcrypt.hashpw(password.encode('utf-8'), bcrypt.gensalt())
with create_connection() as conn:
cursor = conn.cursor()
cursor.execute('''
INSERT INTO users (first_name, last_name, user_id, email, password, role_approved)
VALUES (?, ?, ?, ?, ?, ?)
''', (first_name, last_name, user_id, email, hashed_password, role_approved))
conn.commit()
#************************************************************************#
# update 2023280934 end
```

- In user.py, ensure that the import statement for add_user refers to database.py:

```python
from database import add_user
```

- In database.py, keep the add_user function as it is since this is the appropriate location for it.

By following these steps, we'll have removed the redundancy and centralised the user creation logic within database.py, which is responsible for direct database interactions. This change should be tested thoroughly to ensure that the functionality remains consistent and no new issues are introduced.

Other files:

If other files in the project also use the add_user function, you'll need to update their import statements to reference the correct location of the add_user function after the consolidation. Here's how you can manage this:

1. **Identify All References:** Look through the codebase for all files that import the add_user function. This may include the ui.py file if it's using add_user for registration purposes or any other script that might be involved in user creation.
2. **Update Import Statements:** In each file that uses the add_user function, update the import statement so that it imports from database.py instead of auth.py. For example, if ui.py currently has:

from auth import add_user

You would change it to:

from database import add_user

1. **Refactor Calls to add_user (if needed):** If the signature of the add_user function is different between auth.py and database.py, you will need to refactor the calls to add_user to match the signature used in database.py. Ensure that all parameters passed to the function are in the correct order and format as expected by the database.py version of add_user.

File	signature
| auth | ```python
def add_user(first_name, last_name, user_id, email, password, role_approved):
    """Add a new user to the database with a specified approval status."""
    hashed_password = bcrypt.hashpw(password.encode('utf-8'), bcrypt.gensalt())
    with create_connection() as conn:
        cursor = conn.cursor()
        cursor.execute('''
INSERT INTO users (first_name, last_name, user_id, email, password, role_approved)
VALUES (?, ?, ?, ?, ?, ?)
''', (first_name, last_name, user_id, email, hashed_password, role_approved))
        conn.commit()
``` |
| database | ```python
def add_user(first_name, last_name, user_id, email, password, role='Student', role_approved=0):
    """Add a new user to the database with a specified role and approval status."""
    hashed_password = bcrypt.hashpw(password.encode('utf-8'), bcrypt.gensalt())
    with create_connection() as conn:
        cursor = conn.cursor()
        cursor.execute('''
INSERT INTO users(first_name, last_name, user_id, email, password, role, role_approved)
VALUES(?, ?, ?, ?, ?, ?, ?)
''', (first_name, last_name, user_id, email, hashed_password, role, role_approved))
        conn.commit()
``` |
| Better signature | It is very clear that the add_user function in file database.py is better because it includes the role parameter with default value 0. So we will use the add_user function from database.py file. |
| add_user function from database.py | ```python
def add_user(first_name, last_name, user_id, email, password, role='Student', role_approved=0):
    """Add a new user to the database with a specified role and approval status."""
    hashed_password = bcrypt.hashpw(password.encode('utf-8'), bcrypt.gensalt())
    with create_connection() as conn:
        cursor = conn.cursor()
        cursor.execute('''
INSERT INTO users(first_name, last_name, user_id, email, password, role, role_approved)
VALUES(?, ?, ?, ?, ?, ?, ?)
''', (first_name, last_name, user_id, email, hashed_password, role, role_approved))
``` |

1. **Test Thoroughly (Unit test - Integration test - Regression test):** After making these changes, it's critical to test all functionalities that involve user creation to ensure that there are no issues due to the change in the function's location.
2. **Search for Indirect References:** Don't forget to look for indirect references where the function might be passed around as an argument to other functions or used in callbacks.
3. **Commit Changes:** Once you've made and tested the changes, commit them to your version control system with an appropriate message indicating that you've refactored the add_user function usage to a single source in database.py.
4. **Document Changes:** Update any project documentation that references the add_user function to indicate its new location.
```

Following these steps will help maintain consistency in our project and reduce confusion for anyone reading or working with the code in the future.

After fixing we got these files as in version 17:

Version 17

We fixed most of bugs and code standards according to previous analysis:

main.py
Entry point of the application, responsible for starting the application.
<<<

```
##########################################################
## Atheer Work: Research Tracker Project © 2024 A Mahir ###
##########################################################
# ******************************************************

# clear the terminal
from utils import clear_terminal
clear_terminal()
# ******************************************************
import sys
from PyQt5.QtWidgets import QApplication
from ui import LoginRegisterWindow
if __name__ == '__main__':
app = QApplication(sys.argv)
win = LoginRegisterWindow()
win.show()
sys.exit(app.exec_())
```

>>>

database.py (Database Operations)
Contains the database connection and operations.
<<<

```
##########################################################
## Atheer Work: Research Tracker Project © 2024 A Mahir ###
##########################################################
# ******************************************************

# clear the terminal
from utils import clear_terminal
clear_terminal()
# ******************************************************
import sqlite3
import bcrypt
from config import DB_PATH, ADMIN_EMAIL, ADMIN_PASSWORD
def create_connection():
"""Create a database connection to the SQLite database specified by DB_PATH."""
conn = sqlite3.connect(DB_PATH)
return conn
# update 202312272031 start
#********************************************************************#
def ensure_table_schema():
with create_connection() as conn:
cursor = conn.cursor()
```

```python
# Create table if it doesn't exist
cursor.execute('''
CREATE TABLE IF NOT EXISTS users (
id INTEGER PRIMARY KEY AUTOINCREMENT,
first_name TEXT NOT NULL,
last_name TEXT NOT NULL,
user_id TEXT NOT NULL UNIQUE,
email TEXT NOT NULL UNIQUE,
password TEXT NOT NULL
)
''')
# Check if 'role' column exists and add if not
cursor.execute("PRAGMA table_info(users)")
columns = [info[1] for info in cursor.fetchall()]
if 'role' not in columns:
cursor.execute('ALTER TABLE users ADD COLUMN role TEXT DEFAULT "Student"')
# Check if 'role_approved' column exists and add if not
if 'role_approved' not in columns:
cursor.execute('ALTER TABLE users ADD COLUMN role_approved INTEGER DEFAULT 0')
conn.commit()
#***********************************************************************#
# update 202312272031 end

# update 2023122719:29 start
#***********************************************************************#
def add_user(first_name, last_name, user_id, email, password, role='Student', role_approved=0):
    """Add a new user to the database with a specified role and approval status."""
    hashed_password = bcrypt.hashpw(password.encode('utf-8'), bcrypt.gensalt())
    with create_connection() as conn:
        cursor = conn.cursor()
        cursor.execute('''
        INSERT INTO users(first_name, last_name, user_id, email, password, role, role_approved)
        VALUES(?, ?, ?, ?, ?, ?, ?)
        ''', (first_name, last_name, user_id, email, hashed_password, role, role_approved))
        conn.commit()
def add_admin():
    """Add an admin user to the database with predefined credentials and role."""
    admin_first_name = 'Admin'
    admin_last_name = 'User'
    admin_user_id = 'admin'
    admin_email = ADMIN_EMAIL # Corrected to use the standalone variable
    admin_password = ADMIN_PASSWORD # Corrected to use the standalone variable
    # Set the role as 'Administrator' and role_approved as 1 for the admin user
    add_user(admin_first_name, admin_last_name, admin_user_id, admin_email, admin_password, 'Administrator',
```

230

```python
1)
#******************************************************************#
# update 2023122719:29 end
# update 2023122719:05 start
#******************************************************************#
# Add a function to update the user's role and approval status
def update_user_role(user_id, role, role_approved):
with create_connection() as conn:
cursor = conn.cursor()
cursor.execute('''
UPDATE users SET role = ?, role_approved = ? WHERE user_id = ?
''', (role, role_approved, user_id))
conn.commit()
#******************************************************************#
# update 2023122719:05 end
# update 2023122719:51 start
#******************************************************************#
def add_test_users():
test_users = [
# Students (role-approved)
{"first_name": "Student1", "last_name": "Approved", "user_id": "student1", "email": "student1@example.com",
"password": "password1", "role": "Student", "role_approved": 1},
{"first_name": "Student2", "last_name": "Approved", "user_id": "student2", "email": "student2@example.com",
"password": "password2", "role": "Student", "role_approved": 1},
{"first_name": "Student3", "last_name": "Approved", "user_id": "student3", "email": "student3@example.com",
"password": "password3", "role": "Student", "role_approved": 1},
# Students (role not approved yet)
{"first_name": "Student4", "last_name": "NotApproved", "user_id": "student4", "email": "student4@example.com",
"password": "password4", "role": "Student", "role_approved": 0},
{"first_name": "Student5", "last_name": "NotApproved", "user_id": "student5", "email": "student5@example.com",
"password": "password5", "role": "Student", "role_approved": 0},
{"first_name": "Student6", "last_name": "NotApproved", "user_id": "student6", "email": "student6@example.com",
"password": "password6", "role": "Student", "role_approved": 0},
# Supervisors (role-approved)
{"first_name": "Supervisor1", "last_name": "Approved", "user_id": "supervisor1", "email": "supervisor1@example.com",
"password": "password7", "role": "Supervisor", "role_approved": 1},
{"first_name": "Supervisor2", "last_name": "Approved", "user_id": "supervisor2", "email": "supervisor2@example.com",
"password": "password8", "role": "Supervisor", "role_approved": 1},
# Admins (role-approved)
{"first_name": "Admin1", "last_name": "Approved", "user_id": "admin1", "email": "admin1@example.com",
"password": "password9", "role": "Administrator", "role_approved": 1},
{"first_name": "Admin2", "last_name": "Approved", "user_id": "admin2", "email": "admin2@example.com",
"password": "password10", "role": "Administrator", "role_approved": 1}
]
```

```python
for user in test_users:
print(f"Adding user: {user['user_id']}, Role: {user['role']}, Password: {user['password']}")
# Check if the user already exists before attempting to add
if not user_exists(user["email"]):
add_user(user["first_name"], user["last_name"], user["user_id"], user["email"], user["password"], user["role"],
user["role_approved"])
else:
print(user["email"], " Test user already exists.")
def display_users():
"""Display users with their roles and hashed passwords."""
with create_connection() as conn:
cursor = conn.cursor()
cursor.execute('''
SELECT id, first_name, last_name, user_id, email, role, role_approved, password FROM users
''')
users = cursor.fetchall()
for user in users:
print(f"ID: {user[0]}, Name: {user[1]} {user[2]}, UserID: {user[3]}, Email: {user[4]}, Role: {user[5]}, Approved:
{'Yes' if user[6] == 1 else 'No'}, Hashed Password: {user[7]}")
#********************************************************************#
# update 2023122719:51 end
# update 202312272046 start
#********************************************************************#
def user_exists(email):
"""Check if a user already exists in the database based on their email."""
with create_connection() as conn:
cursor = conn.cursor()
cursor.execute('SELECT id FROM users WHERE email = ?', (email,))
return cursor.fetchone() is not None
#********************************************************************#
# update 202312272046 end

# update 20231228626 start
#********************************************************************#
def get_activated_admin_emails():
"""Retrieve email addresses of all activated admins."""
with create_connection() as conn:
cursor = conn.cursor()
cursor.execute('''
SELECT email FROM users WHERE role='Administrator' AND role_approved=1
''')
emails = cursor.fetchall()
return [email[0] for email in emails] if emails else []
#********************************************************************#
```

```python
# update 20231228626 end
# update 2023281004 start
#*********************************************************************#
def get_admin_and_supervisor_emails():
"""Retrieve email addresses of all admins and supervisors."""
emails = []
with create_connection() as conn:
cursor = conn.cursor()
# Adjust the query to match your database schema
cursor.execute("SELECT email FROM users WHERE role='Administrator' OR role='Supervisor'")
emails = [row[0] for row in cursor.fetchall()]
return emails
#*********************************************************************#
# update 2023281004 end

# update 2023281054 start
#*********************************************************************#
def fetch_all_users():
"""Fetch all user data from the database."""
users = []
with create_connection() as conn:
cursor = conn.cursor()
cursor.execute("SELECT first_name, last_name, user_id, email, role, role_approved FROM users") # Adjust the
columns based on your database schema
users = cursor.fetchall()
return users
#*********************************************************************#
# update 2023281054 end
# update 202312272046 start
#*********************************************************************#
def main():
ensure_table_schema()
# Check if the admin user already exists before attempting to add
if not user_exists(ADMIN_EMAIL):
add_admin() # Add an admin user with the Administrator role and approved status
else:
print("Admin user already exists.")
add_test_users()
display_users() # Display the list of users
if __name__ == '__main__':
main()
#*********************************************************************#
# update 202312272046 end
```

```
>>>
```

user.py (User Class)

A class that represents a user and its attributes.

```
<<<
```

```python
from auth import validate_user
from database import add_user
class User:
def __init__(self, first_name, last_name, user_id, email, password):
self.first_name = first_name
self.last_name = last_name
self.user_id = user_id
self.email = email
self.password = password
def register(self):
# Here you can include any additional validation if necessary
add_user(self.first_name, self.last_name, self.user_id, self.email, self.password)
return True
def check_credentials(self):
# This method would be used to validate the user's login credentials
return validate_user(self.email, self.password)
```

```
>>>
```

auth.py (Authentication Logic)

Contains authentication and authorization logic.

```
<<<
```

```python
import bcrypt
from database import create_connection
def hash_password(password):
"""Hash a password with bcrypt."""
return bcrypt.hashpw(password.encode('utf-8'), bcrypt.gensalt())
def validate_user(username, password):
"""Validate a user's login credentials."""
conn = create_connection()
cursor = conn.cursor()
cursor.execute('''
SELECT password FROM users WHERE user_id=? OR email=?
''', (username, username,))
user_data = cursor.fetchone()
conn.close()
if user_data:
stored_password = user_data[0]
return bcrypt.checkpw(password.encode('utf-8'), stored_password)
return False
def get_user_role_and_status(username):
```

```python
"""Retrieve the role and role approval status for a user."""
with create_connection() as conn:
cursor = conn.cursor()
cursor.execute('''
SELECT role, role_approved FROM users WHERE user_id=? OR email=?
''', (username, username,))
user_data = cursor.fetchone()
if user_data:
return user_data
else:
return None, None
>>>
```

ui.py (User Interface)

Contains all the PyQt5 UI classes.

<<<

```python
###########################################################
## Atheer Work: Research Tracker Project © 2024 A Mahir ###
###########################################################
# *****************************************************************
import os
import sys
import sqlite3
import re
import bcrypt
from PyQt5.QtWidgets import (QApplication, QMainWindow, QPushButton, QLineEdit, QMessageBox,
QColorDialog, QLabel,
QInputDialog, QVBoxLayout, QWidget, QCheckBox, QHBoxLayout)
from PyQt5.QtCore import Qt, QSize, QMimeData, QUrl, pyqtSignal, QObject
from PyQt5.QtGui import QImage, QPixmap, QDragEnterEvent, QDropEvent, QPalette, QBrush
from PyQt5.QtGui import QDesktopServices
from PyQt5.QtCore import QUrl
from PyQt5.QtWidgets import QTableWidget, QTableWidgetItem, QHeaderView # update 2023280706
# from auth import validate_user, add_user
from auth import validate_user, get_user_role_and_status # update 202312272338
from database import add_user
from database import ensure_table_schema
from database import user_exists # We need to import the user_exists function to check for existing users
from database import get_activated_admin_emails # Add this import to get the activated admin emails # update 20231228626
from database import get_admin_and_supervisor_emails # Import the function # update 2023281004

os.system('cls||clear') # clear the terminal
# Global signal class
```

```python
class GlobalSignals(QObject):
background_image_changed = pyqtSignal(str)
global_signals = GlobalSignals() # Create an instance of the global signals class
global_background_pixmap = None
def set_global_background_image(image_path):
global global_background_pixmap
global_background_pixmap = QPixmap(image_path)
global_signals.background_image_changed.emit(image_path) # Emit the signal through the instance
class CustomWindow(QMainWindow):
def __init__(self, parent=None):
super().__init__(parent)
self.setFixedSize(QSize(800, 400))
global_signals.background_image_changed.connect(self.update_background) # Connect to the global signal
def update_background(self, image_path):
if QPixmap(image_path).isNull():
QMessageBox.warning(self, 'Error', 'The image file is not valid.')
return
palette = QPalette()
brush = QBrush(QPixmap(image_path).scaled(self.size(), Qt.KeepAspectRatioByExpanding,
Qt.SmoothTransformation))
palette.setBrush(QPalette.Window, brush)
self.setPalette(palette)
def create_child_window(self, window_class):
child_window = window_class(self)
global_signals.background_image_changed.connect(child_window.update_background)
child_window.show()
class DraggableLabel(QLabel):
imageDropped = pyqtSignal(str) # Signal to emit the file path
def __init__(self, parent=None):
super().__init__(parent)
self.setAcceptDrops(True)
self.setAutoFillBackground(True)
def dragEnterEvent(self, event: QDragEnterEvent):
if event.mimeData().hasUrls():
event.acceptProposedAction()
def dropEvent(self, event: QDropEvent):
mimeData = event.mimeData()
if mimeData.hasUrls():
urls = mimeData.urls()
if len(urls) > 0:
image_path = urls[0].toLocalFile()
self.imageDropped.emit(image_path)
event.acceptProposedAction()
```

```python
class LoginWindow(CustomWindow):
def __init__(self, parent=None):
super().__init__(parent)
self.setWindowTitle('Login Window')
self.initUI()
def initUI(self):
# Add layout, labels, line edits, and buttons for login functionality
self.username = QLineEdit(self)
self.password = QLineEdit(self)
self.password.setEchoMode(QLineEdit.Password)
self.login_button = QPushButton('Login', self)
self.login_button.clicked.connect(self.login)
self.show_password_checkbox = QCheckBox('Show Password', self)
self.show_password_checkbox.stateChanged.connect(self.toggle_password_visibility)
# Set placeholder text for the password field
self.password.setPlaceholderText("Enter your password")
# Set the echo mode to hide the password initially
self.password.setEchoMode(QLineEdit.Password)
layout = QVBoxLayout()
layout.addWidget(QLabel('Enter your username:'))
layout.addWidget(self.username)
layout.addWidget(QLabel('Enter your password:'))
layout.addWidget(self.password)
layout.addWidget(self.show_password_checkbox) # Add the checkbox to the layout
layout.addWidget(self.login_button)
# "Forget Password" Button
self.forget_password_button = QPushButton('Forget Password')
self.forget_password_button.clicked.connect(self.forget_password)
layout.addWidget(self.forget_password_button)
# Set the central widget with the layout
central_widget = QWidget(self)
central_widget.setLayout(layout)
self.setCentralWidget(central_widget)
# update 202312272338 start
#***********************************************************************#
def login(self):
username = self.username.text()
password = self.password.text()
if username and password:
if validate_user(username, password):
user_role, role_approved = get_user_role_and_status(username)
if user_role == 'Administrator':
if role_approved:
self.open_admin_tools()
```

```python
            else:
                self.email_activated_admins()
        else:
            QMessageBox.information(self, 'Success', 'Login successful!')
    else:
        QMessageBox.warning(self, 'Error', 'Invalid username or password.')
    else:
        QMessageBox.warning(self, 'Error', 'Please enter both username and password.')
    def email_activated_admins(self):
        # Open default email client to email all activated admins
        # You would need to implement get_activated_admin_emails to retrieve the emails
        admin_emails = ";".join(get_activated_admin_emails())
        subject = "Activation Request"
        body = "I am an admin and require my role to be activated."
        mailto_link = f"mailto:{admin_emails}?subject={subject}&body={body}"
        QDesktopServices.openUrl(QUrl(mailto_link))
    def open_admin_tools(self):
        self.admin_tools_window = AdminToolsWindow()
        self.admin_tools_window.show()
#***********************************************************************#
# update 202312272338 end

    def toggle_password_visibility(self, state):
        if state == Qt.Checked:
            self.password.setEchoMode(QLineEdit.Normal)
        else:
            self.password.setEchoMode(QLineEdit.Password)
    def forget_password(self):
        # Open the default email client to send an email
        admin_email = "amahir@gmail.com"
        subject = "Password Reset Request"
        body = "I have forgotten my password and request assistance to reset it."
        mailto_link = f"mailto:{admin_email}?subject={subject}&body={body}"
        QDesktopServices.openUrl(QUrl(mailto_link))
# update 2023280706 start
#***********************************************************************#
class ConfirmationWindow(CustomWindow):
    def __init__(self, user_data, register_window_ref, parent=None):
        super().__init__(parent)
        self.user_data = user_data
        self.register_window_ref = register_window_ref
        self.setWindowTitle('Confirm Registration Details')
        self.initUI()
    def initUI(self):
```

```python
layout = QVBoxLayout()
# Create a read-only table to display user data for confirmation , # Setup the table without password fields
self.table = QTableWidget(4, 2, self) # Change the row count to 4 to exclude password fields
self.table.setHorizontalHeaderLabels(['Field', 'Value'])
self.table.verticalHeader().setVisible(False)
self.table.setEditTriggers(QTableWidget.NoEditTriggers)
self.table.horizontalHeader().setSectionResizeMode(QHeaderView.Stretch)
fields = ['First Name', 'Last Name', 'User ID', 'Email', 'Password', 'Confirm Password']
for i, field in enumerate(fields):
self.table.setItem(i, 0, QTableWidgetItem(field))
self.table.setItem(i, 1, QTableWidgetItem(self.user_data[field]))
layout.addWidget(self.table)
# Confirm and Edit buttons
self.confirm_button = QPushButton('Confirm')
self.confirm_button.clicked.connect(self.confirm)
layout.addWidget(self.confirm_button)
self.edit_button = QPushButton('Edit')
self.edit_button.clicked.connect(self.edit)
layout.addWidget(self.edit_button)
central_widget = QWidget(self)
central_widget.setLayout(layout)
self.setCentralWidget(central_widget)
# update 2023280911 start
#************************************************************************#
def confirm(self):
# Add the user to the database as an unactivated user here
try:
# Assuming add_user function accepts a 'role_approved' parameter indicating activation status
# Here we set 'role_approved' to 0 indicating the user is not activated
add_user(
self.user_data['First Name'],
self.user_data['Last Name'],
self.user_data['User ID'],
self.user_data['Email'],
self.user_data['Password'],
role_approved=0
)
# After confirming the user details
QMessageBox.information(self, 'Registration Confirmed', 'Your details have been confirmed. Please wait for an
admin to activate your account.')
# Prompt to send an activation request email
reply = QMessageBox.question(self, 'Activation Request', 'Do you want to send an activation request now?',
QMessageBox.Yes | QMessageBox.No, QMessageBox.No)
# update 2023281004 start
```

```python
#*******************************************************************#
if reply == QMessageBox.Yes:
# Function to retrieve admin and supervisor emails from the database
admin_and_supervisor_emails = get_admin_and_supervisor_emails()
if admin_and_supervisor_emails:
# Prepare the mailto link with all the retrieved emails
emails_string = ";".join(admin_and_supervisor_emails)
subject = "Account Activation Request"
body = f"Hello,\n\nPlease activate my account.\n\nUser ID: {self.user_data['User ID']}"
mailto_link = f"mailto:{emails_string}?subject={subject}&body={body}"
QDesktopServices.openUrl(QUrl(mailto_link))
# Close the confirmation window after user interaction
self.close()
#*******************************************************************#
# update 2023281004 end
self.register_window_ref.close()
except Exception as e:
QMessageBox.warning(self, 'Registration Failed', f'An error occurred during registration: {e}')
def edit(self):
# Close the confirmation window and bring the registration window to the front for editing
self.close()
self.register_window_ref.show()
# update 2023280911 start
#*******************************************************************#
#*******************************************************************#
# update 2023280706 end
class RegisterWindow(CustomWindow):
def __init__(self, parent=None):
super().__init__(parent)
self.setWindowTitle('Register Window')
# Initialise all QLineEdit attributes before calling initUI()
self.first_name = QLineEdit(self)
self.last_name = QLineEdit(self)
self.user_id = QLineEdit(self)
self.username = QLineEdit(self)
self.confirm_username = QLineEdit(self)
self.password = QLineEdit(self)
self.confirm_password = QLineEdit(self)
self.initUI()
def initUI(self):
layout = QVBoxLayout()
# Create horizontal layouts for each label-input pair
fields = [
('First Name:', self.first_name),
```

```python
        ('Last Name:', self.last_name),
        ('ID:', self.user_id),
        ('Enter your username (email):', self.username),
        ('Re-enter your username (email):', self.confirm_username),
        ('Password:', self.password),
        ('Rewrite Password to validate:', self.confirm_password)
    ]
    for label_text, widget in fields:
        row_layout = QHBoxLayout()
        label = QLabel(label_text)
        label.setAlignment(Qt.AlignRight | Qt.AlignVCenter)  # Align right for the label
        row_layout.addWidget(label)
        row_layout.addWidget(widget)  # Add the corresponding input field
        layout.addLayout(row_layout)  # Add the horizontal layout to the main vertical layout
    # Show Password Checkbox
    self.show_password_checkbox = QCheckBox('Show Password')
    self.show_password_checkbox.stateChanged.connect(self.toggle_password_visibility)
    layout.addWidget(self.show_password_checkbox)
    # Set placeholder text for password fields
    self.password.setPlaceholderText("Password (UpperCase, LowerCase, Special Character, Length > 8)")
    self.confirm_password.setPlaceholderText("Rewrite Password to validate")
    # Set the echo mode to hide the password initially
    self.password.setEchoMode(QLineEdit.Password)
    self.confirm_password.setEchoMode(QLineEdit.Password)
    # "Show Password" Checkbox
    self.show_password_checkbox = QCheckBox('Show Password')
    self.show_password_checkbox.stateChanged.connect(self.toggle_password_visibility)

    # Register Button
    self.register_button = QPushButton('Register')
    self.register_button.clicked.connect(self.register)
    layout.addWidget(self.register_button)
    central_widget = QWidget(self)
    central_widget.setLayout(layout)
    self.setCentralWidget(central_widget)
    def toggle_password_visibility(self, state):
        echo_mode = QLineEdit.Normal if state == Qt.Checked else QLineEdit.Password
        self.password.setEchoMode(echo_mode)
        self.confirm_password.setEchoMode(echo_mode)
    def register(self):
        # Gather all the inputs
        first_name = self.first_name.text().strip()
        last_name = self.last_name.text().strip()
        user_id = self.user_id.text().strip()
```

```python
email = self.username.text().strip()
confirm_email = self.confirm_username.text().strip()
password = self.password.text()
confirm_password = self.confirm_password.text()
# Check if the email or user ID already exists in the database
if user_exists(email) or user_exists(user_id):
QMessageBox.warning(self, 'Error', 'A user with this email or user ID already exists.')
return
# Proceed only if the password and confirmation match
if password != confirm_password or email != confirm_email:
QMessageBox.warning(self, 'Error', 'Email addresses or passwords do not match.')
return
# update 2023280706 start
#*************************************************************************#
# Gather all the inputs into a dictionary for easy passing to the confirmation window
user_data = {
'First Name': first_name,
'Last Name': last_name,
'User ID': user_id,
'Email': email,
'Password': password,
'Confirm Password': confirm_password
}
# Open the confirmation window with the user's data
# Instead of immediately closing the registration window, just hide it temporarily
self.hide()
# Pass the reference of the registration window to the confirmation window
self.confirmation_window = ConfirmationWindow(user_data, self)
self.confirmation_window.show()
#*************************************************************************#
# update 2023280706 end
def hash_password(self, password):
# Hash a password with bcrypt
hashed = bcrypt.hashpw(password.encode('utf-8'), bcrypt.gensalt())
return hashed
class LoginRegisterWindow(CustomWindow):
def __init__(self):
super().__init__()
self.setWindowTitle('Login/Register Window')
central_widget = QWidget(self)
self.setCentralWidget(central_widget)
layout = QVBoxLayout(central_widget)
self.background_label = DraggableLabel(self)
self.background_label.resize(self.size())
```

```python
layout.addWidget(self.background_label)
self.background_label.imageDropped.connect(set_global_background_image)
self.register_button = QPushButton('Register', self)
self.register_button.clicked.connect(lambda: self.create_child_window(RegisterWindow))
layout.addWidget(self.register_button)
self.login_button = QPushButton('Login', self)
self.login_button.clicked.connect(lambda: self.create_child_window(LoginWindow))
layout.addWidget(self.login_button)
self.change_color_button = QPushButton('Change Background Color', self)
self.change_color_button.clicked.connect(self.change_background_color)
layout.addWidget(self.change_color_button)
def create_child_window(self, window_class):
child_window = window_class(self)
child_window.show()
def change_background_color(self):
color = QColorDialog.getColor()
if color.isValid():
palette = QPalette()
palette.setColor(QPalette.Window, color)
self.setPalette(palette)
QApplication.instance().setPalette(palette)
def set_background_image(self, image_path):
set_global_background_image(image_path) # This will trigger the update_background for all windows
# update 202312272338 start
#*************************************************************************#
class AdminToolsWindow(QMainWindow):
def __init__(self, parent=None):
super().__init__(parent)
self.setWindowTitle('Admin Tools')
self.initUI()
def initUI(self):
# Layout and buttons go here
layout = QVBoxLayout()
self.display_users_button = QPushButton('Display Users')
self.display_users_button.clicked.connect(self.display_users)
layout.addWidget(self.display_users_button)
self.delete_user_button = QPushButton('Delete User')
self.delete_user_button.clicked.connect(self.delete_user)
layout.addWidget(self.delete_user_button)
self.update_user_button = QPushButton('Update User')
self.update_user_button.clicked.connect(self.update_user)
layout.addWidget(self.update_user_button)
self.reset_password_button = QPushButton('Reset Password')
self.reset_password_button.clicked.connect(self.reset_password)
```

```python
layout.addWidget(self.reset_password_button)
# Set central widget and layout
central_widget = QWidget()
central_widget.setLayout(layout)
self.setCentralWidget(central_widget)
def display_users(self):
# Implement user display logic
pass
def delete_user(self):
# Implement user deletion logic
pass
def update_user(self):
# Implement user update logic
pass
def reset_password(self):
# Implement password reset logic
pass
#**********************************************************************#
# update 202312272338 end
>>>
config.py
Configuration parameters for the application.
<<<
# config.py
DB_PATH = 'users.db'
ADMIN_EMAIL = 'amahir@bedford.ac.uk'
ADMIN_PASSWORD = 'Bedford@2024'
>>>
utils.py
Utility functions that can be used across the application.
<<<
# utils.py
import os
def clear_terminal():
os.system('cls||clear')
>>>
```

Testing Functions

display_the_users.py

To test the results

```python
<<<
import sys
from PyQt5.QtWidgets import QApplication, QMainWindow, QTableWidget, QTableWidgetItem,
QVBoxLayout, QWidget, QScrollArea
from database import fetch_all_users # Make sure this function exists in your database module
class UserTableWindow(QMainWindow):
def __init__(self):
super().__init__()
self.setWindowTitle("User List")
self.setGeometry(100, 100, 800, 600)
self.initUI()
def initUI(self):
# Create a central widget
central_widget = QWidget(self)
self.setCentralWidget(central_widget)
# Create a vertical layout
layout = QVBoxLayout(central_widget)
# Create a table widget
self.table = QTableWidget(self)
self.table.setColumnCount(6) # Adjust the number of columns based on your user data
self.table.setHorizontalHeaderLabels(["First Name", "Last Name", "User ID", "Email", "Role","activated"]) # Set your
headers here
# Populate the table with data
self.populate_table()
# Add the table to a scroll area
scroll_area = QScrollArea(self)
scroll_area.setWidgetResizable(True)
scroll_area.setWidget(self.table)
layout.addWidget(scroll_area)
def populate_table(self):
# Fetch user data
users = fetch_all_users() # This function should now return the role_approved data as well
self.table.setRowCount(len(users))
for row_num, user in enumerate(users):
for col_num, data in enumerate(user):
# Convert boolean or integer role_approved to a readable format if needed
if col_num == 5: # Assuming role_approved is the 6th column
data = 'Yes' if data else 'No'
self.table.setItem(row_num, col_num, QTableWidgetItem(str(data)))
```

```python
def main():
app = QApplication(sys.argv)
main_window = UserTableWindow()
main_window.show()
sys.exit(app.exec_())
if __name__ == "__main__":
main()
>>>
```

Third analysis (after fixing-2):

1. Code Structure and Organization:

- The project is modularized into distinct files, each serving a specific purpose (main.py, database.py, user.py, auth.py, ui.py, config.py, and utils.py).

- Comments and updates are used to track changes, providing a history of modifications.

- The use of separate configuration (config.py) and utility (utils.py) files indicates an attempt to adhere to the Single Responsibility Principle.

2. Database Operations (database.py):

- Utilises SQLite for data persistence, suitable for small to medium-sized applications.

- Implements bcrypt for password hashing, which is a secure choice for storing passwords.

- Contains functions for database schema initialization, user management, and retrieval of specific user data.

- Follows a pattern of opening a connection, executing a query, and committing the transaction, wrapped in context managers for better resource handling.

3. User Management (user.py):

- Defines a User class encapsulating attributes and methods related to user operations such as registration and credential checking.

- The use of classes suggests an object-oriented approach to represent entities within the system.

4. Authentication Logic (auth.py):

- Provides functions for password hashing and user validation.

- Leverages bcrypt for password comparison, which securely checks hashed passwords.

5. User Interface (ui.py):

- Implements the UI using PyQt5, a set of Python bindings for Qt libraries, allowing for a robust and cross-platform GUI.

- Defines several classes for different windows (LoginWindow, RegisterWindow, AdminToolsWindow), demonstrating an understanding of GUI components and event-driven programming.

6. Configuration and Utility Files:

- config.py centralises configuration variables, which is a good practice for maintainability.

- utils.py provides a utility function, albeit currently only for clearing the terminal, which suggests room for expansion as utilities grow.

7. Testing Utilities:

- The display_the_users.py script provides a way to visualise the user data, indicating a focus on testing and validating the application's functions.

Evaluation in Bullet Points:

- Code Quality:

- The code is well-commented, which aids maintainability.

- There is a clear attempt to separate concerns, though there are areas where UI and business logic could be more distinctly separated.

- Security:

- The use of bcrypt for hashing passwords is a secure practice.

- There is no clear indication of SQL injection protection; parameterized queries are used, which is a good sign, but further scrutiny is required.

- Performance:

- SQLite is a lightweight database, but performance under load is not addressed and may need consideration for scaling.

- There are no apparent performance inefficiencies in the code snippets provided.

- Scalability:

- The use of SQLite may limit scalability; a more robust database system may be required for a larger number of users.

- The code appears to be modular, which could ease the transition to a more scalable database if needed.

- Usability:

- The UI is being designed with user experience in mind, but actual usability would need to be tested with real users.

- The application uses native system dialogs and widgets, which typically enhance user experience.

- Maintainability:

- Code modularity and use of classes will facilitate future maintenance.

- The presence of utility functions and configuration files indicates a forward-thinking approach to code organisation.

- Testing:

- The provided display_the_users.py is a good starting point for testing, but a more comprehensive testing strategy, including unit and integration tests, would be beneficial.

Overall Evaluation:

The code demonstrates a foundational structure for a multi-user research project management application with user authentication, role-based access control, and integration with external services. Security best practices are followed for password handling, and the user interface is being built using a mature GUI framework.

However, as the project scales, the choice of SQLite and the current state of error handling may need to be revisited to ensure robustness and reliability. Furthermore, the testing suite appears to be in its infancy and will need to be expanded to ensure the application's correctness and stability.

Evaluation of the project -So far

Based on the code provided and the project requirements, let's compare how the current implementation aligns with the project's goals:

1. User Roles and Authentication:

- The code has defined user roles and an authentication system, meeting the functional requirement for different user roles and secure login.

- Admin, supervisor, and student roles are considered in the database schema updates.

- There is a function validate_user for authenticating users, aligning with the requirement for a secure login system.

2. User Management:

- The add_user and update_user_role functions in database.py align with the need for admin to manage user accounts.

- The User class provides a structured way to manage user information, although it's not fully developed for all admin functionalities like user modification or deletion.

3. Project Management:

- While the code snippets provided do not contain explicit project management functionalities, the system's structure with user roles and authentication suggests the groundwork is laid for further development.

- The requirement for supervisors to assign and track student projects is not directly addressed in the provided code.

4. File Management with OneDrive Integration:

- There is no direct evidence of OneDrive integration in the provided snippets. This feature seems to be missing and would be a significant gap in fulfilling the project's requirements.

5. Communication via MS Teams:

- Similar to OneDrive, there is no code indicating MS Teams integration, which is a necessary component of the project's communication requirements.

6. Notifications and Alerts:

- The application does not yet have the functionality for notifications and alerts, which is crucial for informing users about deadlines and updates.

7. Reporting:

- Reporting functionalities such as generating progress reports are not present in the provided code snippets.

8. Usability:

- The UI is being built with PyQt5, which is known for creating user-friendly interfaces. However, usability testing would be necessary to ensure the UI meets the intuitive and clear design specified in the non-functional requirements.

9. Performance:

- SQLite is used for the database, which may not offer the best performance for larger data volumes, a consideration for the application's scalability.

10. Security:

- Passwords are securely hashed using bcrypt, aligning with the security requirement. However, comprehensive security measures, such as protection against SQL injection and data encryption, are not verifiable from the snippets.

11. Scalability:

- The application's scalability is questionable with SQLite as the database choice, especially if the number of users and data volume increases significantly.

12. Maintainability:

- The code is well-commented and modular, which aids maintainability. However, the presence of hardcoded admin credentials in config.py could be a potential security risk and might not be best practice for maintainability.

13. Compatibility and Backup:

- There are no indications of cross-platform compatibility considerations or backup and recovery mechanisms in the provided code.

Conclusion:

The code shows a solid start towards meeting the project's primary plan and requirements, with a clear structure for user authentication and basic database operations. However, key functionalities such as project management, file and communication integrations, reporting, and advanced security measures are not yet implemented or evident in the provided snippets. Enhancements in these areas would be necessary to fully meet the project's comprehensive requirements.

This comparison should assist in identifying the next steps in development to ensure that the final product will fulfil the intended use cases and satisfy the end-users. If this evaluation aligns with your expectations, we can move to the next step; otherwise, please let me know how you would like to proceed or if there are any specific areas you would like to amend or focus on.

Next:

This comparison should assist in identifying the next steps in development to ensure that the final product will fulfil the intended use cases and satisfy the end-users.

Chapter 3 : Progressing the Research Manager: Review and Implementation

Reviewing the Project Blueprint

Analysing the Project's Primary Plan

The journey of building the Python Research Manager begins with a thorough analysis of its primary plan. The project, envisioned as a comprehensive tool for managing research activities, is anchored in a set of well-defined user stories and requirements. These narratives serve as the cornerstone, offering insights into the expectations and needs of various stakeholders - administrators, supervisors, and students. The plan, meticulously crafted, outlines the functionalities and experiences these users anticipate, forming a blueprint that guides every subsequent development decision.

Evaluating User Stories and Use Cases

User stories in the project plan are the lifeblood of user-centric design. Each story, from an admin's desire to maintain system integrity to a student's need for effective project management, encapsulates a specific functionality or experience. These stories are not just feature requests but are empathetic insights into the users' world, providing a clear path for creating features that resonate with their real-world challenges. The use cases, branching out like a tree with each limb representing a different scenario, offer a broader view of how these stories intertwine, ensuring a holistic approach to the application's functionality.

Assessing Functional and Non-Functional Requirements

The functional requirements lay out a clear roadmap for the application's capabilities. These include user authentication processes, project management tools, and integration with OneDrive for file management, among others. Each requirement is a building block, essential for creating a robust and efficient tool tailored to the needs of the research community.

In parallel, the non-functional requirements, often the unsung heroes of application development, are crucial for ensuring the application's usability, security, and scalability. These include designing an intuitive interface, ensuring data protection, and preparing the system for potential growth. Addressing these requirements is imperative for delivering a seamless user experience and safeguarding the application's reliability and sustainability.

Preparing for Development Lifecycle Management

The final step in reviewing the blueprint involves preparing for the development lifecycle. This preparation extends beyond choosing the right programming languages or frameworks. It encompasses setting up a collaborative development environment, establishing version control systems, and defining a workflow that promotes agility and adaptability. This phase is about laying the groundwork for a development process that is as dynamic and iterative as the project itself.

Deep Dive into User Expectations and Interaction Flows

Delving deeper into user stories, it becomes evident how each role within the system - Admin, Supervisor, and Student - has unique requirements and expectations. The admin users, being the system's backbone, require comprehensive control over account management and system settings to uphold data integrity and system performance. Supervisors, positioned as the bridge between administrative control and student activities, need tools for approving registrations, assigning projects, and tracking progress. These functionalities are pivotal in creating a controlled yet flexible research environment.

Students, the primary users of the system, seek an intuitive and efficient platform to register, manage, and update their research projects. Their requirements are centred around ease of use, accessibility of information, and seamless integration with external tools for file management and communication. The system must cater to these needs without compromising on the overall security and integrity of the application.

Incorporating Feedback Loops and Agile Methodology

A significant aspect of the project blueprint review involves setting up mechanisms for continuous feedback and iterative development. Adopting an agile methodology allows for rapid adaptation to changing requirements and user feedback. This approach is essential in a dynamic environment like research management, where user needs can evolve rapidly. By building in regular checkpoints for user feedback and making it a core part of the development process, the project ensures that the final product remains aligned with user expectations and industry standards.

Bridging the Gap Between Theory and Practice

The initial review process also involves bridging the gap between theoretical requirements and practical implementation. This step is crucial in identifying potential challenges in translating the project plan into a functional application. It involves scrutinising each requirement for feasibility, considering the available resources, and identifying any need for technology or skill acquisition. This proactive approach helps in anticipating and mitigating risks early in the development cycle.

Setting the Stage for Collaborative Development

Collaboration is key in a project of this magnitude. The plan review stage sets the stage for a collaborative development environment. This involves choosing the right tools for project management, issue tracking, and communication. Establishing clear guidelines for code reviews, testing, and documentation is also part of this process. The goal is to create an ecosystem where developers, designers, and stakeholders can work together seamlessly, fostering innovation and efficiency.

Enhancing Application Architecture

Refining the Technology Stack for Scalability

As we transition into the architectural phase of the Python Research Manager, a pivotal consideration is the selection and refinement of the technology stack. The choice of technologies is not just about picking the most popular or cutting-edge tools; it's about finding the right fit for the project's goals, scalability, and long-term sustainability. The stack must support the intricate functionalities required by different user roles while remaining agile enough to adapt to future enhancements and integrations.

A critical aspect of this decision-making process involves evaluating the database technology. While SQLite, used in the initial development phase, offers simplicity and ease of setup, concerns about its scalability and concurrent access capabilities in a multi-user environment necessitate exploration of more robust alternatives like PostgreSQL or MySQL. These databases offer advanced features like better concurrency control, transaction management, and scalability, which are essential for an application expected to handle significant user load and complex data relationships.

In parallel, the choice of Python as the primary programming language, complemented by PyQt for the graphical user interface, aligns well with the project's needs. Python's versatility and readability, coupled with PyQt's robustness in creating cross-platform GUI applications, form a solid foundation for building a user-friendly and efficient application. However, this choice necessitates a careful design of the application's backend architecture to ensure it can efficiently handle the processing requirements and integrate seamlessly with the frontend.

Optimising the Database Schema for Performance

The database schema design is a cornerstone in the application's architecture. It needs to be optimised for performance, data integrity, and scalability. The schema should be designed to minimise redundancy and ensure data normalisation, which reduces data anomalies and enhances data consistency.

A well-thought-out schema will have clearly defined tables for users, projects, file management, and communication logs, each with appropriate relationships and constraints. For instance, the users' table should efficiently associate with projects and roles, enabling quick queries and updates. The design should also consider future expansions, such as adding new features or adjusting existing ones without major overhauls.

Indexing is another critical aspect of the schema design. Proper indexing can significantly improve query performance, especially for common operations like looking up users, retrieving project details, or filtering data based on specific criteria. However, it's essential to strike a balance, as over-indexing can lead to unnecessary overheads and affect insert and update operations.

Designing for External Service Integrations

The project plan outlines the need for integrating external services like OneDrive for file management and Microsoft Teams for communication. These integrations are crucial for providing a seamless user experience and enhancing the application's functionality.

For OneDrive integration, the architecture needs to incorporate a reliable and secure way to connect to the OneDrive API. This involves handling authentication (possibly using OAuth), managing file uploads/downloads, and keeping track of changes in the OneDrive storage. The application architecture must include robust error handling and data synchronisation mechanisms to ensure that the file management system is reliable and user-friendly.

Similarly, integrating Microsoft Teams requires a thoughtful approach. The architecture must support real-time communication features, including messaging and meeting scheduling. This implies the need for a responsive and scalable messaging system, potentially leveraging web sockets or similar technologies for real-time data transmission.

Incorporating Security Protocols and Compliance Measures

Security in application development is not an afterthought; it's an integral part of the architecture from the ground up. For the Python Research Manager, embedding security protocols and ensuring compliance with data protection regulations are critical. This process involves several layers, from the database to user interactions.

At the database level, encryption of sensitive data, such as user passwords and personal information, is essential. Implementing techniques like salted password hashing (already in place using bcrypt) ensures that even if data breaches occur, the impact is minimised. Beyond encryption, the architecture must also include mechanisms for regular security audits, vulnerability assessments, and timely patching of any identified security gaps.

For user interactions, secure session management is crucial, especially in a multi-user environment where different roles access varied levels of data. Implementing secure authentication flows, possibly integrating two-factor authentication, adds an extra layer of security. Additionally, authorization checks must be stringent, ensuring users can only access data and functionalities pertinent to their roles.

Compliance with data protection regulations like GDPR or HIPAA (if applicable) requires careful planning. The architecture must support features like data anonymization, user consent management, and easy access to data retrieval and deletion requests. These compliance measures not only protect users' privacy but also fortify the application's credibility and trustworthiness.

Planning for User Experience and Interaction Design

The architecture of the Python Research Manager is not just about backend robustness; it's equally about frontend excellence and user experience. The application must offer an intuitive, responsive, and accessible interface. This involves a thoughtful design process where user feedback is continuously integrated.

The use of PyQt for the GUI offers flexibility in designing interfaces that are both aesthetically pleasing and functional. However, this needs to be coupled with a deep understanding of the users' workflows. For instance, the interface for the admin users should facilitate easy management of user accounts and system settings, while the interface for students should focus on ease of project management and access to resources.

Adopting a responsive design ensures that the application is accessible across various devices and screen sizes, a critical aspect considering the diverse usage scenarios in a research environment. Furthermore, accessibility features, such as keyboard navigation, screen reader support, and colour contrast considerations, ensure that the application is usable by people with different abilities.

Implementing Robust Error Handling and Logging

A resilient application architecture anticipates errors and gracefully handles them. Implementing robust error handling mechanisms prevents the application from crashing and provides users with helpful feedback in case of issues. This involves capturing exceptions at different layers of the application and responding with appropriate actions.

Logging is another vital aspect of architecture. A comprehensive logging system helps in diagnosing issues, understanding user behaviour, and improving system performance. The logs must be structured in a way that they provide actionable insights without compromising user privacy.

Embracing Microservices for Scalable Architecture

As the Python Research Manager project grows in complexity and user base, a monolithic architecture may start to show its limitations. Adopting a microservices architecture could be a strategic move to enhance scalability and maintainability. This approach involves decomposing the application into a suite of independently deployable, smaller services, each running in its own process and communicating with lightweight mechanisms, often an HTTP resource API.

Microservices offer several advantages for a project like the Python Research Manager. They allow for easy scaling of individual components of the application as needed, rather than scaling the entire application. This can be particularly useful for handling varying loads in different parts of the application, such as user authentication, project management, and file storage with OneDrive integration.

Another benefit is the ease of maintenance and faster deployment cycles. Each service can be developed, deployed, and updated independently, reducing the risk and complexity involved in deploying updates. Additionally, this architecture supports a diverse technology stack, allowing the best technology to be chosen for each service based on its specific requirements.

However, microservices also introduce challenges, particularly in terms of increased complexity in deployment and monitoring, as well as the need for careful design of the communication patterns between services. Implementing an effective strategy for service discovery, load balancing, and fault tolerance becomes crucial.

Leveraging APIs for Extensibility and Integration

One of the key requirements of the Python Research Manager is the integration with external services like OneDrive and Microsoft Teams. Leveraging Application Programming Interfaces (APIs) is the cornerstone for achieving these integrations effectively.

The architecture should include dedicated services or components that handle the communication with these external APIs. For OneDrive integration, this might involve a file management service that handles all interactions with the OneDrive API, including file uploads, downloads, and synchronisation. This service would expose its own API to the rest of the application, providing a clean and controlled interface for file operations.

Similarly, for Microsoft Teams integration, a communication service could be responsible for sending messages, managing chat rooms, and scheduling meetings. This service would handle all the complexities of interfacing with the Microsoft Teams API, presenting a simplified interface to the rest of the application.

Designing these integration components requires careful consideration of API rate limits, error handling, data caching, and synchronisation issues. The architecture should be robust enough to handle potential API changes and outages, ensuring the application remains functional and responsive.

Fostering Continuous Integration and Continuous Deployment (CI/CD)

To support a dynamic and agile development process, implementing Continuous Integration and Continuous Deployment (CI/CD) practices is vital. CI/CD automates the integration of code changes from multiple contributors, running automated tests to ensure new code does not introduce bugs or regressions.

In the context of the Python Research Manager, setting up a CI/CD pipeline would involve automating the testing of each microservice, as well as the integration testing of the entire application. This ensures that changes in one part of the application do not break other parts. Continuous Deployment can then automatically deploy the application to a staging or production environment whenever new changes are made, reducing the time and effort required for deployment and ensuring a more consistent release process.

CI/CD also aids in maintaining code quality and accelerates feedback loops. Developers receive immediate feedback on their code changes, allowing quick fixes and reducing the likelihood of bugs making it to production.

Advanced Data Management Strategies

In an application like the Python Research Manager, where data is at the core of its functionality, advanced data management strategies are crucial. This involves not just handling the storage and retrieval of data efficiently, but also ensuring data integrity, security, and compliance with privacy laws.

Data Caching and Synchronisation: Implementing a caching mechanism can significantly improve the application's performance, especially for frequently accessed data. However, this introduces the complexity of keeping the cache synchronised with the database. Strategies like cache invalidation, time-to-live (TTL) settings, and write-through or write-behind caching can be employed based on specific use cases.

Data Partitioning and Sharding: As the volume of data grows, partitioning and sharding become important to distribute the data across multiple databases or tables, helping to maintain high performance and availability. This requires a thoughtful approach to ensure that data distribution does not lead to complex queries or transaction management issues.

Data Backup and Recovery: A robust backup and recovery strategy is essential to safeguard against data loss due to system failures or security breaches. Regular backups, along with tested recovery procedures, ensure the application can quickly bounce back from unforeseen incidents.

Data Archiving: Implementing data archiving for older or infrequently accessed data can help in optimising database performance. This involves moving historical data to separate storage, keeping the operational database lean and efficient.

Preparing for Future Enhancements

Building an application like the Python Research Manager is not a one-time effort; it's an ongoing journey. The architecture must be designed with future enhancements in mind.

Modular Design: Adopting a modular design approach where different functionalities are encapsulated in separate modules or services makes it easier to update or add new features without impacting the entire application. This also simplifies testing and deployment of new functionalities.

API Versioning: As the application evolves, changes to the APIs are inevitable. Implementing API versioning allows new versions to be deployed without breaking existing integrations. This is especially important for external integrations, where changes need to be carefully managed to avoid disruptions.

Feature Flags: Implementing feature flags or toggles can be an effective way to introduce new features or changes gradually. This allows features to be tested in production with a subset of users before rolling them out to everyone, reducing the risk of deploying new functionalities.

Monitoring and Analytics: Incorporating monitoring and analytics from the beginning helps in understanding how the application is being used and where potential issues may lie. This insight is invaluable for guiding future enhancements and ensuring that the application continues to meet user needs effectively.

Emphasising Comprehensive Documentation

In the realm of software development, particularly for a complex project like the Python Research Manager, comprehensive documentation is not just helpful—it's essential. Documentation serves as a roadmap, a guide, and a reference for everyone involved in the project, from developers to end-users.

Technical Documentation: This includes detailed descriptions of the system architecture, codebase, APIs, and database schema. It should provide enough detail for new developers to understand the system's workings and contribute effectively. This documentation needs to be kept up-to-date as the system evolves, reflecting any changes in the code or architecture.

User Guides and Help Documentation: To ensure that end-users can effectively utilise the application, user guides and help documentation are necessary. These documents should be written in clear, non-technical language and provide step-by-step instructions on using the application's features. Including screenshots, videos, or interactive guides can further enhance the user experience.

API Documentation: For external integrations and for developers who will be working with the application's API, well-documented API endpoints with examples of requests and responses are crucial. Tools like Swagger or Postman can be used to create interactive API documentation that is both informative and user-friendly.

Fostering Community Involvement and Open Source Collaboration

Building a project of this scale and scope can benefit greatly from community involvement and, if applicable, open-source collaboration. Encouraging the participation of a wider community can bring in diverse perspectives, innovative ideas, and additional resources.

Open Source Contribution: If parts of the Python Research Manager are open-sourced, it is vital to create a welcoming environment for contributors. This involves setting clear guidelines for contributions, establishing a process for submitting and reviewing code, and maintaining an active and inclusive community.

Feedback Mechanisms: Implementing mechanisms for users and community members to provide feedback, report bugs, or suggest features is essential for continuous improvement. This can be facilitated through forums, issue trackers, or regular community meetings.

Regular Updates and Changelogs: Keeping the community informed about the latest developments, upcoming features, and bug fixes through regular updates and changelogs helps maintain engagement and trust.

Conclusion of Enhancing Application Architecture

In concluding this extensive examination of enhancing the application architecture for the Python Research Manager, we recognize that architecture is not just about the right technology stack or design patterns. It's about building a foundation that supports the application's current needs while being flexible and robust enough to adapt to future challenges. It encompasses a commitment to security, performance, user experience, and continuous evolution.

Through comprehensive documentation, community involvement, and a forward-thinking approach, the architecture laid out in this section sets the stage for developing an application that is not only functional and efficient but also adaptable, scalable, and sustainable in the long term.

Building the User Interface

Designing User-Friendly Interfaces with PyQt5

The user interface (UI) is the bridge between the functionality of the Python Research Manager and its users. A well-designed UI not only makes the application accessible and easy to use but also enhances user satisfaction and engagement. Utilising PyQt5 for the UI development offers a range of tools and widgets that can be used to create a professional and intuitive interface.

Layout and Design Principles: The primary step in UI development is to establish a layout that is logical, intuitive, and aligned with the users' workflow. This involves organising content and features in a way that is easy to navigate and understand. The design should follow established principles such as consistency, alignment, contrast, and hierarchy to guide the user naturally through the application.

Customization and Flexibility: PyQt5 provides the ability to customise widgets and create a unique look and feel for the application. This customization can be used to align the UI with the branding of the application or to provide different themes that users can choose from. Flexibility in the UI design also means accommodating different user preferences and accessibility needs.

Responsive Design: With users accessing the application on various devices with different screen sizes, implementing a responsive design is crucial. The UI should adapt to different screen sizes and resolutions, ensuring that the application is equally usable on desktops, laptops, and tablets.

Interactive Elements: Interactive elements such as buttons, sliders, and input fields play a crucial role in the user experience. These elements should be designed to be responsive and provide immediate feedback to the user. For example, buttons should change appearance when hovered over or clicked, and input fields should validate data in real-time and provide helpful error messages.

Implementing Navigation and Workflows

Efficient navigation is key to a positive user experience. The application should have a clear and consistent navigation structure that allows users to move between different parts of the application effortlessly.

Menu Design: A well-structured menu, whether it's a top bar, sidebar, or dropdown, should provide easy access to all major features of the application. The menu items should be logically grouped and labelled in a way that is understandable to the users.

Workflow Optimization: Understanding the users' workflow is crucial in designing the UI. The application should facilitate a smooth workflow, minimising the number of steps needed to perform common tasks. This can be achieved through the intelligent placement of features, use of shortcuts, and streamlining processes.

Breadcrumbs and Navigation Aids: For complex applications with multiple levels of navigation, providing breadcrumbs and other navigation aids helps users keep track of their location within the application. This is particularly important in the Python Research Manager, where users might navigate through various projects, documents, and settings.

Ensuring Accessibility and Usability Standards

Accessibility and usability are not just legal requirements; they are ethical obligations to ensure that the application can be used by everyone, including people with disabilities.

Accessibility Features: The UI should be designed with accessibility in mind, which includes providing keyboard navigation, screen reader support, and alternative text for images. Colours and font sizes should be chosen to ensure sufficient contrast and readability.

Usability Testing: Conducting usability tests with real users is an invaluable part of the design process. This involves observing users as they interact with the application and gathering feedback on their experience. Usability testing helps identify any issues or pain points in the UI, which can then be addressed to improve the overall user experience.

Integrating Feedback into UI/UX Improvements

Constructive feedback is a pivotal component in refining the user interface of the Python Research Manager. It provides direct insights into user preferences, difficulties they encounter, and features they desire. This feedback can be gathered through various channels such as user surveys, interviews, usability testing sessions, and analytics.

Iterative Design Process: Implementing an iterative design process is essential. This involves releasing updates, gathering feedback, making improvements, and then repeating the cycle. Such an approach ensures that the UI evolves based on actual user needs and preferences.

A/B Testing: A/B testing is an effective method to compare different versions of the UI. By presenting two or more variants to users, developers can collect data on which version performs better in terms of usability, engagement, and user satisfaction.

User Analytics: Analysing user interaction with the application can provide valuable insights. Tools like heatmaps, which show where users click most, or analytics that track user journey through the application, can highlight areas that are working well and those that need improvement.

Tools and Techniques for Creating a Dynamic User Interface

Creating a dynamic and responsive user interface requires a blend of the right tools and techniques. PyQt5 provides a robust framework, but there are additional practices and tools that can enhance the development process.

Rapid Prototyping: Tools like Balsamiq or Sketch can be used for rapid prototyping of the UI. Prototypes allow for quick visualisation of the design and can be used to gather early feedback before the actual coding begins.

Custom Widgets and Animations: PyQt5 allows for the creation of custom widgets and animations, which can be used to add interactivity and visual appeal to the UI. For instance, custom data visualisation widgets can enhance the presentation of project progress or research data.

Consistent Style and Theme: Establishing a consistent style guide and theme for the application ensures that the UI remains cohesive. This includes consistent use of colours, fonts, and widget styles. PyQt5's stylesheet and theming capabilities allow for this consistency and also provide the flexibility to change the look and feel easily.

Ensuring Responsiveness and Interaction

The responsiveness of the UI is crucial for a seamless user experience. This goes beyond just adapting to different screen sizes; it also involves ensuring that the application responds quickly to user inputs and actions.

Optimising Performance: Techniques like lazy loading, where data or components are loaded only when needed, can significantly improve performance. For complex operations, providing feedback, such as a loading indicator, keeps the user informed about the application's status.

Gesture and Touch Support: For users accessing the application on touch-enabled devices, support for gestures can enhance usability. PyQt5 offers capabilities to handle touch events, which can be utilised to make the application more intuitive for touch-based interactions.

Advanced UI/UX Considerations

Beyond the fundamental aspects of UI design, there are advanced considerations that can significantly enhance the user experience of the Python Research Manager. These elements add layers of sophistication and user-centric design to the application.

Internationalisation and Localization: Given the global reach of research and academic work, the application should be designed with internationalisation in mind. This includes the ability to support multiple languages and adapt to various cultural contexts. PyQt5 provides tools for internationalisation, allowing dynamic translation of the UI based on user preferences or location.

Error Handling in UI: Robust error handling within the UI is crucial for a professional user experience. This involves not just catching and logging errors but also presenting them to users in a non-technical, helpful manner. Providing actionable guidance or an easy way to report the error can reduce user frustration and aid in quicker resolution.

User Assistance Features: Integrating user assistance features like tooltips, help icons, or an interactive guide can improve the usability of the application, especially for new users or complex functionalities. These features should be designed to be unobtrusive yet easily accessible when needed.

Leveraging User Testing for Refined UI Design

User testing is a critical component in developing a user interface that not only meets but exceeds user expectations. It involves a series of activities designed to test the UI with real users and gather actionable insights.

Conducting Usability Testing Sessions: Organising sessions where users interact with the application in a controlled environment can provide deep insights into user behaviour, preferences, and challenges they face. These sessions should be planned to cover various user scenarios and workflows.

Feedback Loops and Iterative Improvement: Establishing feedback loops where users can easily provide their suggestions or report issues is vital. This feedback should be regularly reviewed and used as a basis for continuous improvement of the UI.

Analysing User Behavior Data: Collecting and analysing data on how users interact with the application can reveal a lot about the UI's effectiveness. Metrics like time spent on each screen, frequently used features, and common points of exit can inform decisions about UI improvements.

Ensuring Accessibility and Compliance

Accessibility is a legal and ethical requirement, ensuring that the application is usable by people with various disabilities. PyQt5 offers functionalities to make UI elements accessible, but it requires deliberate design choices.

Implementing Accessibility Standards: The UI should comply with recognized accessibility standards such as WCAG (Web Content Accessibility Guidelines). This includes providing keyboard navigation, screen reader support, and ensuring that all UI elements are accessible and labelled correctly.

Regular Accessibility Audits: Conducting regular audits of the UI to ensure accessibility compliance is important. Tools like accessibility checkers can automate some of this testing, but manual testing by users with disabilities provides invaluable insights.

Wrap-Up and Summary of UI/UX Development

The development of the user interface for the Python Research Manager is a comprehensive process that balances aesthetics, functionality, usability, and accessibility. From leveraging PyQt5's capabilities to implementing responsive designs and interactive elements, the focus has always been on creating an intuitive and engaging experience for the users. The iterative design process, enriched by user feedback and testing, ensures that the UI evolves in alignment with user needs and technological advancements.

Key takeaways from the UI/UX development process include:

- Importance of User-Centric Design: Every aspect of the UI/UX design is grounded in understanding and meeting the users' needs. This approach fosters a product that resonates with its audience and addresses their specific requirements effectively.

- Responsive and Accessible Design: Ensuring that the UI is accessible to all users, including those with disabilities, and functions seamlessly across various devices and screen sizes.

- Iterative Improvement and Testing: Continuous improvement based on user feedback and behaviour data is vital for refining the UI. Regular usability testing sessions are instrumental in achieving a polished and user-friendly interface.

Looking Ahead: Future UI Trends and Technologies

As technology evolves, so do the trends and best practices in UI/UX design. Staying abreast of these changes is crucial for keeping the application relevant and user-friendly.

- Adoption of AI and Machine Learning: Integrating AI and machine learning can enhance user experience by providing personalised experiences, predictive text input, and intelligent assistance within the application.

- Voice User Interfaces (VUIs): With the growing popularity of voice-controlled devices, considering VUIs as part of the application can offer users an alternative way to interact with the platform, enhancing accessibility and convenience.

- Virtual and Augmented Reality (VR/AR): As VR and AR technologies become more mainstream, they could offer innovative ways to visualise and interact with research data within the application.

Conclusion: A Commitment to Excellence in UI/UX

The journey of building the user interface for the Python Research Manager is marked by a commitment to excellence, innovation, and user satisfaction. The application's UI/UX is not just a static feature but an evolving entity that adapts and grows with its user base and technological advancements. The ongoing process of refining the UI will continue to play a pivotal role in the success and usability of the application.

Implementing Core Functionalities

Establishing Robust Authentication Mechanisms

In the Python Research Manager, ensuring secure access to data and features is paramount. This begins with a robust authentication system, a critical component that serves as the first line of defence against unauthorised access.

Implementing Multi-Factor Authentication (MFA): MFA adds an additional layer of security beyond just username and password. Integrating MFA, possibly using one-time passwords or authentication apps, significantly reduces the risk of unauthorised access.

Session Management: Proper management of user sessions is vital. This includes secure session creation upon login, session expiration after inactivity, and secure session termination upon logout. Techniques like token-based authentication can be employed for enhanced security and scalability.

Password Policies and Security: Enforcing strong password policies and educating users about secure password practices are essential. The system should also provide secure password reset mechanisms, ideally involving user verification steps.

Constructing Dynamic Project Management Capabilities

The core of the Python Research Manager lies in its project management capabilities, which need to be dynamic, intuitive, and comprehensive.

Project Creation and Assignment: Users should be able to easily create and define projects, setting parameters like objectives, timelines, and milestones. Supervisors should have the functionality to assign projects to students and track their progress.

Progress Tracking and Updates: Implementing a system for tracking project progress and updates is critical. This could include features like Gantt charts for timeline visualisation, task lists for tracking individual components, and progress reports.

Collaborative Tools: Facilitating collaboration among students, supervisors, and administrators is key. This might involve shared workspaces, communication tools, and real-time notifications on project updates.

Integrating OneDrive for Cloud-Based File Handling

File management is a crucial aspect of research project management. Integrating OneDrive provides a secure and efficient way to handle files.

File Upload and Download: Users should be able to seamlessly upload and download project-related files. The integration should support various file types and sizes, ensuring that users can work with a wide range of data.

Synchronisation and Version Control: Keeping files synchronised between the application and OneDrive is essential. Implementing version control can help in tracking changes and maintaining the integrity of the data.

Access Control: The system should implement fine-grained access control, ensuring that users can access only the files they are authorised to view or edit.

Embedding MS Teams for Seamless Communication

Communication is a cornerstone in managing research projects effectively. The integration of Microsoft Teams into the Python Research Manager offers a comprehensive platform for communication and collaboration.

Direct Messaging and Group Chats: Facilitate one-on-one and group conversations among students, supervisors, and administrators. This feature supports the exchange of quick messages, files, and links, enhancing collaboration and information sharing.

Meeting Scheduling and Video Conferencing: Integrate functionalities for scheduling meetings directly within the application. Leverage MS Teams' video conferencing capabilities to conduct virtual meetings, discussions, and presentations, offering a seamless experience without leaving the application.

Notifications and Alerts: Integration with MS Teams can also extend to notifications. Alerts about project updates, deadlines, or new messages can be sent directly through MS Teams, ensuring that users stay informed in real-time.

Developing a Comprehensive Notification System

A well-designed notification system is crucial in keeping users informed and engaged with their projects. This system should be intuitive, customizable, and non-intrusive.

Customizable Alerts: Users should have the ability to customise their notification settings, choosing what types of notifications they receive and how they are alerted. Options could include email, in-app notifications, or integration with external platforms like MS Teams.

Contextual and Relevant Notifications: Notifications should be relevant to the user's role and current context within the application. For example, students might receive notifications about upcoming deadlines, while supervisors might be alerted to new project submissions or updates from their students.

Unobtrusive Design: While keeping users informed is important, notifications should not become a source of distraction. Designing them to be subtle yet noticeable ensures that they serve their purpose without disrupting the user's workflow.

Incorporating Advanced Reporting Tools

The ability to generate and view detailed reports is crucial in a research project management application. These reports provide valuable insights into project progress, resource allocation, and overall performance.

Project Progress Reports: Develop functionalities for generating reports that track the progress of individual projects. These should include metrics like milestones achieved, pending tasks, and overall timeline adherence.

Activity and Resource Utilisation Reports: Implement reporting tools that provide insights into how resources are being utilised. This could include data on user activity, resource allocation efficiency, and time spent on various tasks.

Customizable Report Generation: Allow users to generate customised reports based on specific parameters they choose. This flexibility ensures that users can extract the exact information they need, tailored to their particular requirements.

Enhancing User Management and Administration

With multiple user roles in the Python Research Manager, robust user management and administrative functionalities are key to maintaining system integrity and efficiency.

Admin Dashboard: Create a comprehensive admin dashboard that provides a quick overview of the system's status, user activities, and project progress. The dashboard should offer easy access to administrative functions like user account management, system settings, and data backups.

Role-Based Access Control (RBAC): Implement RBAC to ensure that users have access only to the features and data relevant to their roles. This not only enhances security but also streamlines the user experience by presenting a customised interface based on the user's role.

User Onboarding and Training: Develop features that facilitate easy onboarding of new users. This could include interactive tutorials, help sections, and user guides that assist users in navigating and utilising the application effectively.

Preparing for Future Feature Expansions

As the needs of the research community evolve, so should the Python Research Manager. Preparing the application for future expansions is critical for its long-term success.

Scalable Architecture: Ensure that the application's architecture is scalable, allowing for the easy addition of new features and modules. This involves adopting coding practices that are modular and maintainable.

Feedback Mechanisms for Feature Requests: Establish channels through which users can submit feature requests or suggestions. Regularly reviewing this feedback can provide valuable insights into how the application can be further developed to meet emerging needs.

Staying Ahead of Technological Advances: Continuously monitor technological trends and advancements. This proactive approach ensures that the application can leverage new technologies to enhance its capabilities and offer cutting-edge features to its users.

Testing, Deployment, and Maintenance

Developing a Comprehensive Testing Strategy

Testing is an integral part of the software development lifecycle, particularly for an application as complex as the Python Research Manager. A comprehensive testing strategy ensures the application is reliable, secure, and performs as expected.

Unit Testing: Begin with unit testing, which involves testing individual components or functions of the application. This is crucial for ensuring that each part of the codebase works correctly in isolation.

Integration Testing: Once unit testing is complete, integration testing checks how different parts of the application work together. This step is vital for identifying issues in the interactions between various components, such as database, backend logic, and the user interface.

Functional and User Acceptance Testing: Functional testing involves testing the application against the functional requirements to ensure all features are working as expected. User acceptance testing, ideally conducted with actual users, ensures the application meets user needs and is ready for deployment.

Automated Testing: Implementing automated testing tools can significantly streamline the testing process. Automation helps in regularly executing a suite of tests, ensuring ongoing code changes do not introduce new bugs.

Automating Deployment Processes

Deployment automation is key to ensuring smooth and efficient delivery of the application to production. Automating the deployment process minimises human error, saves time, and ensures a consistent deployment environment.

Continuous Integration/Continuous Deployment (CI/CD): Set up a CI/CD pipeline to automatically build, test, and deploy the application. This process allows for rapid, reliable, and repeatable deployment of application updates.

Configuration Management Tools: Utilise configuration management tools to automate the setup and maintenance of servers and environments. Tools like Ansible, Chef, or Puppet can manage server configurations, ensuring all environments are consistent and up to date.

Containerization and Orchestration: Consider using containerization technologies like Docker for deploying the application. Containers package the application and its dependencies together, simplifying deployments across different environments. Orchestration tools like Kubernetes can manage these containers at scale.

Planning for Scalability and Performance

Scalability is a critical factor in the success of any application, especially one expected to handle a growing number of users and data.

Load Testing: Regularly perform load testing to understand how the application behaves under different levels of user load. This testing helps identify performance bottlenecks and areas that need optimization.

Scalable Architecture: Design the application architecture to be scalable from the start. This might involve using microservices architecture, as discussed earlier, which allows individual components of the application to be scaled as needed.

Database Performance Optimization: Continuously monitor and optimise database performance. This can involve query optimization, indexing, and using database caching to improve response times.

Establishing a Sustainable Maintenance and Update Cycle

The lifecycle of the Python Research Manager extends beyond deployment. Regular maintenance and updates are essential to keep the application running smoothly, secure, and aligned with user needs.

Scheduled Maintenance: Implement a regular maintenance schedule to update the application, fix bugs, and apply security patches. This process should be communicated transparently to users to minimise inconvenience.

Monitoring for Bugs and Performance Issues: Use monitoring tools to continuously track the application's performance and identify any issues. Tools like log analyzers and performance monitoring solutions can provide real-time insights into the health of the application.

Gathering User Feedback: Continuously engage with users to gather feedback on the application's performance and any issues they encounter. This feedback is crucial for identifying areas for improvement in future updates.

Security Updates and Compliance Checks

In an environment where security threats are constantly evolving, keeping the application secure is an ongoing challenge.

Regular Security Audits: Conduct regular security audits to identify vulnerabilities and address them before they can be exploited. This includes reviewing code for security best practices, checking for vulnerabilities in dependencies, and penetration testing.

Compliance with Data Protection Regulations: Regularly review and update the application to ensure compliance with data protection laws and regulations. This is particularly important given the sensitivity of research data.

Updating Encryption and Data Protection Methods: Stay updated with the latest encryption techniques and data protection methods. Regularly update these measures in the application to safeguard user data against emerging threats.

Leveraging Analytics for Continuous Improvement

Data analytics can provide valuable insights into how the application is being used, which features are most popular, and where users encounter difficulties.

User Behavior Analytics: Implement analytics to track how users interact with the application. This information can guide future updates and feature development, ensuring that the application evolves in line with user needs.

Performance Analytics: Use performance analytics to monitor the application's responsiveness and efficiency. This data can help identify performance bottlenecks and areas where optimization is needed.

Predictive Analytics: As the application matures, consider using predictive analytics to anticipate user needs and potential system issues. This proactive approach can enhance user satisfaction and reduce downtime.

References List:

Bennett, T. (2023). *Applying AI in Software Development: Best Practices and Examples - DreamFactory Software- Blog.* [online] blog.dreamfactory.com. Available at: https://blog.dreamfactory.com/applying-ai-in-software-development-best-practices-and-examples / [Accessed 30 Dec. 2023].

Beres, J. (2023). *A Software Developer's Guide to Generative AI | Built In.* [online] builtin.com. Available at: https://builtin.com/software-engineering-perspectives/generative-ai-tips-for-software-development [Accessed 30 Dec. 2023].

Dryka, M. and Pluszczewska, B. (2023). *Is There a Future for Software Engineers? The Impact of AI [2023].* [online] brainhub.eu. Available at: https://brainhub.eu/library/software-developer-age-of-ai#:~:text=AI%20can%20assist%20in%20automating[1] [Accessed 30 Dec. 2023].

Wang, L. (2017). *AI in Software Engineering: Case Studies and Prospects.* [online] ar5iv. Available at: https://ar5iv.labs.arxiv.org/html/2309.15768 [Accessed 30 Dec. 2023].

---

1.   https://brainhub.eu/library/software-developer-age-of-ai#_853ae90f0351324bd73ea615e6487517__4c761f170e016836ff84498202b99827__853ae90f0351324bd73ea615e6487517_text_43ec3e5dee6e706af7766ff fea512721_AI_0bcef9c45bd8a48eda1b26eb0c61c869_20can_0bcef9c45bd8a48eda1b26eb0c61c869_20assist_0bcef9c45bd8a48eda1b26eb0c61c869_20in_0b cef9c45bd8a48eda1b26eb0c61c869_20automating

Appendices

272

Appendix A: Python Project Blueprint - A Practical Guide for Beginners

1. Introduction to the Project Blueprint

- 1.1 Overview of the Research Project Management Application
- 1.2 Objectives and Learning Outcomes for Beginners

2. Setting Up Your Development Environment

- 2.1 Installing Python and Necessary Libraries
- 2.2 Introduction to Visual Studio Code on Apple Machines
- 2.3 Configuring the Development Environment

3. Understanding the Code Structure

- 3.1 Overview of the Project's Directory and File Structure
- 3.2 Explanation of Key Files and Their Roles
- 3.3 Navigating the Code in Visual Studio Code

4. Deep Dive into Main Components

- 4.1 Understanding main.py: The Entry Point
- 4.2 Breakdown of database.py: Managing Data Operations
- 4.3 Insights into user.py and auth.py: User and Authentication Logic
- 4.4 Exploring ui.py: Building the User Interface

5. Working with the Database

- 5.1 Introduction to SQLite and Database Concepts
- 5.2 Step-by-Step Guide to Database Operations in the Code
- 5.3 Best Practices for Database Management in Python

6. Front-End Development with PyQt5

- 6.1 Basics of PyQt5 for GUI Development
- 6.2 Analysing UI Code Components
- 6.3 Customising and Experimenting with the UI

7. Understanding and Implementing Authentication

- 7.1 Concept of User Authentication and Security

1. Introduction to the Project Blueprint

1.1 Overview of the Research Project Management Application

Welcome to a journey through the intricate world of building a Python-based application. In this appendix, we will delve into the Research Project Management Application, a comprehensive software designed to facilitate the management and tracking of academic and research projects. This application stands as a testament to the power and versatility of Python, offering a blend of user-friendly interface and robust backend functionalities.

The Research Project Management Application is more than just a tool; it's a practical implementation of numerous Python concepts. It encompasses database management, user authentication, graphical user interfaces (GUIs), and more. Designed with real-world utility in mind, this application provides an ideal platform for learners to see how different pieces of a software project come together to form a cohesive and functional whole.

1.2 Objectives and Learning Outcomes for Beginners

The primary objective of this appendix is to guide beginner programmers through understanding and working with a real Python project. By the end of this journey, you will have gained:

- Comprehensive Understanding: You'll gain a deep understanding of how a Python application is structured, from its foundational code to the more complex functionalities that make it work.

- Practical Skills: You'll learn how to set up a Python development environment, navigate through the code, understand the purpose of different files and components, and how they interact within the application.

- Hands-On Experience: Through guided walkthroughs, you'll get hands-on experience in modifying and adding functionalities to the application. This experience is invaluable in transitioning from a beginner to an intermediate-level Python programmer.

- Problem-Solving Abilities: By troubleshooting and debugging as you work through the code, you will enhance your problem-solving skills, an essential asset in any programmer's toolkit.

- Confidence in Application Development: The knowledge and experience gained will boost your confidence in developing and managing your Python projects.

This appendix is designed to be both informative and interactive. You are encouraged to experiment with the code, explore its functionalities, and even try your hand at customising the application. Each section is structured to build upon the last, gradually enhancing your understanding and skills.

As you progress through this guide, remember that the journey of learning to code is as important as the destination. Each challenge you encounter and overcome is a step forward in your journey as a Python developer.

Let's embark on this exciting journey of discovery and learning in the world of Python programming!

2. Setting Up Your Development Environment

2.1 Installing Python and Necessary Libraries

To begin working with the Research Project Management Application, the first step is to set up Python on your machine. Python is a versatile programming language, and it's essential to have the right version and libraries installed to ensure compatibility with the project.

Step-by-Step Installation:

Download Python:

- Visit the official Python website (python.org[1]).

- Navigate to the Downloads section and choose the version recommended for your Apple machine (typically, Python 3.x).

- Download the installer and run it. Ensure you select the option to 'Add Python to PATH' during installation.

Verify Installation:

- Open the Terminal on your Apple machine.

- Type python—version (or python3—version) and press Enter. You should see the installed Python version displayed.

Install Necessary Libraries:

- The application might require specific Python libraries. You can install these using pip, Python's package manager.

- In the Terminal, install each required library using the command: pip install library-name.

- Common libraries used in Python projects include PyQt5 (for GUI development), SQLite3 (for database operations), and bcrypt (for hashing and security).

2.2 Introduction to Visual Studio Code on Apple Machines

Visual Studio Code (VSC) is a powerful, free code editor from Microsoft. It's widely used in the programming community for its versatility and extensive feature set.

Setting Up VSC:

Download and Install:

- Download Visual Studio Code from code.visualstudio.com.

---

1. https://www.python.org/

- Open the downloaded file and drag VSC to the Applications folder.

Familiarising Yourself with VSC:

- Launch VSC from the Applications folder.

- Explore the interface, which includes the editor window, file explorer, and integrated terminal.

- Familiarise yourself with the command palette (Cmd + Shift + P), which allows you to access various commands and features.

Customising VSC:

- Customise the look and feel by changing the theme (under Code > Preferences > Colour Theme).

- Install extensions for Python development by searching in the Extensions view (Cmd + Shift + X).

2.3 Configuring the Development Environment

Configuring your development environment is crucial for a seamless coding experience. This involves setting up your project workspace and ensuring all tools are properly integrated.

Configuring for Python Development:

Open the Project in VSC:

- Clone or download the project repository to your machine.

- Open the folder in VSC (File > Open Folder).

Setting Up a Python Interpreter:

- Open any Python file in the project.

- Click on the Python interpreter version displayed in the status bar at the bottom.

- Select the appropriate Python interpreter for the project (usually the one you installed earlier).

Installing Project Dependencies:

- Check if the project has a requirements.txt file. This file lists all the Python libraries needed for the project.

- Open the integrated terminal in VSC (Terminal > New Terminal).

- Run pip install -r requirements.txt to install all dependencies.

By following these steps, your development environment will be ready, and you can begin exploring and working on the Python Research Project Management Application.

Advanced Configuration and Usage of VSC for Python Development

Once you have Visual Studio Code installed and configured with the necessary Python interpreter and libraries, you can enhance your development experience with advanced features and best practices.

Advanced Features of VSC for Python Development:

Debugging in VSC:

- VSC provides an integrated debugging tool, essential for any development process.

- To start debugging, open a Python file and click on the 'Run and Debug' icon in the sidebar or press F5.

- Set breakpoints by clicking to the left of the line number where you want the execution to pause.

- Utilise the debugging panel to watch variables, inspect call stacks, and navigate through your code during runtime.

Using Git for Version Control:

- VSC integrates seamlessly with Git, a version control system, allowing you to track changes and collaborate effectively.

- Initialise a Git repository in your project folder if it's not already version-controlled (Git: Initialize Repository in the command palette).

- Commit changes, create branches, and push to remote repositories directly from VSC.

Efficient Code Navigation and Refactoring:

- Use features like 'Go to Definition' and 'Find All References' to navigate large codebases quickly.

- Refactor code with ease using VSC's built-in refactoring tools, such as 'Rename Symbol,' which updates all instances of a variable or function name.

Utilising Code Linters and Formatters:

- Linters like Pylint or Flake8 can be integrated into VSC to identify potential errors and enforce a coding standard.

- Use auto-formatters like Black or autopep8 to ensure your code adheres to Python's PEP 8 style guide.

Customising User Workspace:

- Tailor your workspace by modifying settings in settings.json (accessible through Preferences: Open Settings (JSON) in the command palette).

- Customise settings like font size, tab size, and enable autosave for a personalised coding experience.

Exploring Extensions and Shortcuts:

- Enhance your VSC experience with extensions specific to your development needs. Extensions like Python, GitLens, and Coderunner add useful functionalities.

- Familiarise yourself with VSC shortcuts for increased efficiency. For example, Cmd + / for commenting code, Cmd + B to toggle the sidebar.

Best Practices:

- Consistent Coding Practice: Follow consistent coding standards for readability and maintainability. VSC's linters and formatters can help enforce these standards.

- Regular Commits: Make regular commits to your Git repository with descriptive commit messages. This practice is crucial for tracking changes and collaborating with others.

- Stay Updated: Keep VSC, Python, and all extensions updated to the latest versions to benefit from security updates, bug fixes, and new features.

3. Understanding the Code Structure

After setting up your development environment, the next step is to understand the structure and organisation of the Python Research Project Management Application. A well-organised codebase is essential for efficient development and maintenance.

3.1 Overview of the Project's Directory and File Structure

When you first open the project in Visual Studio Code, you'll notice a structured layout of directories and files. Here's a brief overview:

- main.py: This is the entry point of the application. It initialises and launches the main window of the GUI.

- database.py: Contains all the database-related operations, such as connecting to the database, creating tables, and handling data queries.

- user.py and auth.py: These files manage user-related functionalities, including user registration, authentication, and role management.

- ui.py: Holds the code for the graphical user interface (GUI), defining how different elements of the application look and behave.

- config.py: Contains configuration settings, like database path and admin credentials.

- utils.py: Includes utility functions that can be used across different parts of the application, like clearing the terminal screen.

- Sub-directories: Depending on the project's complexity, there might be sub-directories for organising different modules or functionalities.

Understanding this structure helps in navigating through the code and knowing where to look when making changes or debugging.

3.2 Explanation of Key Files and Their Roles

Each file in the project serves a specific purpose:

- main.py: The starting point of the application. It sets up the PyQt application instance and loads the main window.

- database.py: A crucial file for data persistence. It handles all interactions with the SQLite database, from creating tables to inserting and fetching data.

- user.py and auth.py: These work together to handle user data and authentication. user.py defines the User class and methods for user actions, while auth.py deals with password hashing and verification.

● ui.py: This is where the application's user interface is designed. It uses PyQt5 to create windows, buttons, text fields, and other GUI components.

● config.py: Centralizes configuration settings, making it easier to manage and modify them without searching through the entire codebase.

● utils.py: Provides utility functions, enhancing code reusability and reducing redundancy.

3.3 Navigating the Code in Visual Studio Code

Visual Studio Code offers several features to help you navigate the codebase efficiently:

● File Explorer: Use the sidebar file explorer to browse through the project's files and folders.

● Search Functionality: Quickly find files, symbols, or even specific lines of code using the search feature (Cmd + Shift + F).

● Go to Definition: Right-click on a function or variable and select 'Go to Definition' to jump to its declaration.

● Code Outline: The outline view provides a hierarchical structure of the file currently open, allowing you to quickly navigate through different classes and methods.

By familiarising yourself with the project structure and utilising VSC's navigation tools, you'll be well-equipped to understand and work with the code effectively.

4. Deep Dive into Main Components

Now that you have a general understanding of the project structure and navigation, let's dive deeper into the main components of the Research Project Management Application. This detailed exploration will help you understand the functionality and interconnectivity of different parts of the application.

4.1 Understanding main.py: The Entry Point

Part 1: Introduction to import and from ... import ...

Understanding import:

1. What is import?

● The import statement in Python is used to bring in other Python modules (collections of functions, classes, and variables) into your script. It's akin to having access to tools from various toolboxes without needing to create them from scratch.

2. Why Use import?

● It promotes code reusability.

● It keeps your code organised by segmenting functionalities into different files or modules.

● It helps in managing namespace by preventing naming conflicts.

3. Examples:

```
# Example 1: Importing a complete module
import math
print(math.sqrt(16)) # Outputs: 4.0
# Example 2: Importing a module with alias
import datetime as dt
current_date = dt.date.today()
print(current_date) # Outputs: Current date
# Example 3: Importing a specific function
from math import factorial
print(factorial(5)) # Outputs: 120
# Example 4: Importing multiple classes/functions from a module
from os.path import join, exists
file_path = join('folder', 'file.txt')
print(exists(file_path)) # Check if the file exists
# Example 5: Conditional Import
try:
import numpy
except ImportError:
print("Numpy is not installed")
```

Understanding from ... import ...:

1. What Does from ... import ... Mean?

- This syntax is used to import specific elements (functions, classes, variables) from a module. This is useful when you only need certain parts of a module, not the entire module.

2. Benefits of Using from ... import ...:

- Reduces memory consumption by importing only required components.

- Enhances readability by explicitly stating which elements are being used.

- Allows directly using the imported element without the module prefix.

3. Examples:

```python
# Example 1: Importing a single class from a module
from threading import Thread
t = Thread(target=lambda: print("New thread"))
t.start() # Outputs: New thread
# Example 2: Importing multiple elements from a module
from sys import argv, exit
print(argv) # Prints command-line arguments
exit() # Exits the program
# Example 3: Importing with alias
from datetime import datetime as dt
print(dt.now()) # Outputs: Current date and time
# Example 4: Importing all elements from a module (not recommended)
from math import *
print(sqrt(9)) # Outputs: 3.0
# Example 5: Using imported functions in a list comprehension
from math import factorial
factorials = [factorial(x) for x in range(5)]
print(factorials) # Outputs: [1, 1, 2, 6, 24]
```

In the context of main.py, import sys brings in the system-specific parameters and functions provided by the Python Standard Library, while from PyQt5.QtWidgets import QApplication specifically imports the QApplication class from the PyQt5.QtWidgets module, a necessary component for creating any PyQt5 application.

Understanding these import statements is crucial as they lay the foundation for utilising Python's extensive libraries and modules, which greatly expand the functionality available in any Python script.

Next, we will delve deeper into understanding variables, assignment, and the instantiation of classes and objects in Python, as seen in the app = QApplication(sys.argv) line of main.py. Let me know if you're ready to proceed or if there's anything specific you'd like to focus on!

Part 2: Variables, Assignment, Classes, and Indentation in Python

Variables and Assignment:

1. What is a Variable?

- In programming, a variable is a storage location identified by a name (an identifier) that holds data or information.

2. Assignment in Python (=):

- The assignment operator = is used to assign values to variables. The variable is on the left of =, and the assigned value is on the right.

3. Examples:

```python
# Example 1: Simple Assignment
age = 30
# Example 2: Assigning String Value
name = "Alice"
# Example 3: Reassignment
age = 31 # Age is now updated to 31
#Boolean Assignment
is_student = True
# Example 4: Assigning Computed Value
total = age + 10 # total is 41
# Example 5: Multiple Assignments
x, y, z = 5, 10, 15
# Example 6: Swapping Values
x, y = y, x # x becomes 10, y becomes 5
# Example 7: Unpacking from a Collection
data = [1, 2, 3]
a, b, c = data # a=1, b=2, c=3
# Example 8: List Assignment
fruits = ["apple", "banana", "cherry"]
# Example 9: Dictionary Assignment
person = {"name": "Alice", "age": 30}
# Example 10: Compound Assignment
x += 5 # Same as x = x + 5
```

Classes and Instantiation:

1. What is a Class?

● A class in Python is a blueprint for creating objects. It defines a set of attributes (variables) and methods (functions) that characterise any object of the class.

2. Instantiating Classes:

● Instantiation is the process of creating an instance (an object) of a class. In Python, this is done by calling the class as if it were a function.

3. Examples:

```python
# Example 1: Class Definition and Object Creation
class Person:
def __init__(self, name):
self.name = name
person1 = Person("John")
# Example 2: Method in a Class
class Person:
def greet(self):
print("Hello!")
person1 = Person()
person1.greet() # Outputs: Hello!
# Example 3: Returning Values from Methods
class Calculator:
def add(self, a, b):
return a + b
calc = Calculator()
result = calc.add(5, 3) # result is 8
# Example 4: Class with Multiple Methods
class Dog:
def __init__(self, name):
self.name = name
def bark(self):
print("Woof!")
def greet(self):
print(f"My name is {self.name}")
dog = Dog("Rex")
dog.bark() # Outputs: Woof!
dog.greet() # Outputs: My name is Rex
# Example 5: Inheritance
class Animal:
def speak(self):
pass
class Cat(Animal):
def speak(self):
print("Meow")
cat = Cat()
cat.speak() # Outputs: Meow
# Example 6: Static Methods
class Math:
@staticmethod
def add(a, b):
return a + b
result = Math.add(2, 3) # result is 5
# Example 7: Class Attributes
```

```python
class Circle:
pi = 3.14 # Class attribute
def __init__(self, radius):
self.radius = radius
def area(self):
return Circle.pi * self.radius ** 2
circle = Circle(5)
print(circle.area()) # Outputs: Area of the circle
```

Indentation in Python:

1. Role of Indentation:

- Indentation is crucial in Python. It defines the scope of loops, functions, classes, and other structures. Unlike many other languages that use braces {}, Python uses indentation to define blocks of code.

2. Examples:

```python
# Example 1: Correct Indentation in a Function
def hello():
print("Hello, World!")
hello()
# Example 2: Indentation in a Loop
for i in range(3):
print(i) # Outputs: 0, 1, 2
# Example 3: Indentation in Conditional Statements
age = 20
if age >= 18:
print("Adult")
else:
print("Not Adult")
# Example 4: Indentation in Class Definition
class MyClass:
def my_method(self):
print("Method of MyClass")
obj = MyClass()
obj.my_method() # Outputs: Method of MyClass
# Example 5: Indentation in Multiline Statements
total = (1 + 2 + 3 +
4 + 5)
print(total) # Outputs: 15
# Example 6: Using Indentation to Define Scope
def calculate_sum(a, b):
sum = a + b
return sum
print(calculate_sum(5, 10)) # Outputs: 15
# Example 7: Indentation Error
def greeting():
print("Hello!") # This will cause an IndentationError
```

Class attributes and static methods in Python

We will cover various scenarios and use cases, helping to clarify when and why each concept is used. We'll start with class attributes.

Class Attributes in Python

What are Class Attributes?

- Class attributes are variables declared within a class but outside any methods. They are shared across all instances of the class.

Why Use Class Attributes?

- To define properties that should be the same for every instance of the class.

- Useful for constants or default values.

Examples and Explanations:

Example 1: Basic Class Attribute
class Vehicle:
wheels = 4 # Class attribute shared by all instances
car = Vehicle()
truck = Vehicle()
print(car.wheels) # Outputs: 4
print(truck.wheels) # Outputs: 4

Here, wheels is a class attribute of Vehicle, representing a common property shared by all vehicles.
Example 2: Modifying Class Attribute
class Vehicle:
wheels = 4
Vehicle.wheels = 6
bus = Vehicle()
print(bus.wheels) # Outputs: 6

Modifying wheels at the class level changes this attribute for all instances of the class.
Example 3: Class Attribute Used in a Method
class Circle:
pi = 3.14
def __init__(self, radius):
self.radius = radius
def area(self):
return Circle.pi * self.radius ** 2
circle = Circle(5)
print(circle.area()) # Outputs: 78.5

pi is a class attribute used within the area method to calculate the area of a circle.
Example 4: Shared Data Among Instances

```python
class Database:
connected = False # Class attribute
@classmethod
def connect(cls):
cls.connected = True
@classmethod
def disconnect(cls):
cls.connected = False
Database.connect()
print(Database.connected) # Outputs: True
Database.disconnect()
print(Database.connected) # Outputs: False
```

connected is a class attribute representing the database connection status shared among all instances.

Example 5: Counting Instances

```python
class Product:
count = 0 # Class attribute
def __init__(self):
Product.count += 1
p1 = Product()
p2 = Product()
print(Product.count) # Outputs: 2
```

count is used to keep track of the number of Product instances created.

Example 6: Class Attribute as Default Value

```python
class Employee:
company_name = "XYZ Corp" # Default value
def __init__(self, name):
self.name = name
emp = Employee("Alice")
print(emp.company_name) # Outputs: XYZ Corp
```

company_name serves as a default value for the company name of all employees.

Example 7: Class Constants

```python
class MathConstants:
PI = 3.14159
E = 2.71828
print(MathConstants.PI) # Outputs: 3.14159
```

Constants like PI and E are defined as class attributes.

Example 8: Class Attributes in Inheritance

```python
class Animal:
kingdom = "Animalia"
class Dog(Animal):
pass
dog = Dog()
print(dog.kingdom) # Outputs: Animalia
```

kingdom is inherited from the Animal class.

Example 9: Class Attribute for Configuration

class Config:

DEBUG = True

if Config.DEBUG:

print("Debugging mode is on.")

DEBUG is used as a configuration setting for the application.

Example 10: Class Attributes as Enums

class Colors:

RED = 1

GREEN = 2

BLUE = 3

print(Colors.RED) # Outputs: 1

Colors class uses class attributes to represent enum-like values.

In each example, the class attribute serves a specific purpose, from representing shared data to providing default values and configuration settings.

Next, we will explore static methods in a similar detailed manner.

Static Methods in Python

What are Static Methods?

- Static methods are functions defined inside a class but not associated with any instance of that class. They don't require access to self (the instance) or cls (the class).

Why Use Static Methods?

- To group utility functions related to a class but that don't need access to class or instance-specific data.

- For organisational purposes, keeping all functions relevant to a class within its scope.

Examples and Explanations:

Example 1: Basic Static Method

class Math:

@staticmethod

def add(a, b):

return a + b

print(Math.add(5, 3)) # Outputs: 8

add is a static method that performs addition without needing any data from a Math instance.

Example 2: Static Method for Validation

```python
class User:
@staticmethod
def is_valid_email(email):
return "@" in email
print(User.is_valid_email("test@example.com")) # Outputs: True
```

is_valid_email checks if an email address is valid, which is a common utility for User objects.

Example 3: Static Method without Decorator

```python
class Calculator:
def multiply(a, b):
return a * b
multiply = staticmethod(multiply)
print(Calculator.multiply(4, 5)) # Outputs: 20
```

Defining multiply as a static method without using the @staticmethod decorator.

Example 4: Static Method for Data Conversion

```python
class Temperature:
@staticmethod
def celsius_to_fahrenheit(celsius):
return (celsius * 9/5) + 32
print(Temperature.celsius_to_fahrenheit(30)) # Outputs: 86
```

Converting temperatures from Celsius to Fahrenheit.

Example 5: Static Method Used in Class Method

```python
class Circle:
@staticmethod
def validate_radius(radius):
return radius > 0
@classmethod
def create(cls, radius):
if cls.validate_radius(radius):
return cls(radius)
else:
raise ValueError("Invalid radius")
# Usage
circle = Circle.create(5)
```

validate_radius is a static method used by the class method create.

Example 6: Multiple Static Methods

```python
class StringUtils:
@staticmethod
def is_palindrome(string):
return string == string[::-1]
@staticmethod
def first_char(string):
return string[0]
print(StringUtils.is_palindrome("radar")) # Outputs: True
print(StringUtils.first_char("hello")) # Outputs: h
```

Grouping related utility functions in a class.

Example 7: Static Method as an Alternative Constructor

```python
class Date:
def __init__(self, day, month, year):
self.day = day
self.month = month
self.year = year
@staticmethod
def from_string(date_string):
day, month, year = map(int, date_string.split('-'))
return Date(day, month, year)
date = Date.from_string("25-12-2020")
```

from_string is used to create a Date object from a string.

Example 8: Static Methods for Mathematical Operations

```python
class SimpleMath:
@staticmethod
def square(x):
return x * x
@staticmethod
def cube(x):
return x * x * x
print(SimpleMath.square(4)) # Outputs: 16
print(SimpleMath.cube(3)) # Outputs: 27
```

Performing basic mathematical operations.

Example 9: Static Method in Inheritance

```python
class Base:
@staticmethod
def greet():
return "Hello from Base"
class Derived(Base):
pass
print(Derived.greet()) # Outputs: Hello from Base
```

Inheriting a static method.

Example 10: Using Static Methods in External Functions

```
class Validator:
@staticmethod
def is_number(string):
return string.isdigit()
def process_data(data):
if Validator.is_number(data):
print("Processing number")
else:
print("Invalid data")
process_data("123") # Outputs: Processing number
```

Using a static method in an external function to validate data.

Each example demonstrates a practical scenario where static methods are useful, highlighting their role in organising utility functions within classes. They contribute to the overall design by providing encapsulated functionalities related to but not dependent on class instances.

In this part, we've covered the basics of variables, class creation, and the importance of indentation in Python, all of which are foundational concepts for understanding the main.py script in your PyQt5 application.

Next, we will look into other key aspects of main.py, such as understanding the special operators __name__ and __main__, and more about PyQt5's QApplication. Let me know if you're ready to move on to these topics or if there's anything else you'd like to focus on!

Part 3: Special Operators, __name__, and __main__ in Python

Understanding Special Operators (__name__ and __main__):

What are __name__ and __main__?

- __name__ is a special built-in variable in Python that represents the name of the current module.

- __main__ is the string assigned to __name__ when the script is run as the main program.

Purpose of __name__ == '__main__':

- This statement is used to check whether the script is being run directly or being imported into another script. It helps in controlling the execution of code segments.

Examples:

```python
# Example 1: Basic Usage in a Script
if __name__ == '__main__':
print("Script is running directly.")
# Explanation:
# This is the most basic form of using __name__. When this script is run directly,
# it prints the message. This example is chosen to illustrate the fundamental use case of __name__.
# Example 2: Skipping Code on Import
def function():
print("Function is called.")
if __name__ == '__main__':
function() # This will only execute if the script is not imported.
# Explanation:
# Here, the function call is wrapped inside the __name__ check. The function is
# only called when the script is run directly. This example demonstrates how to
# prevent certain code from executing when the script is imported as a module.
# Example 3: Protecting Code from Being Run on Import
def main():
print("Main function")
if __name__ == '__main__':
main() # Ensures 'main' is called only when script is the main program.
# Explanation:
# The use of a main() function is a common pattern. This structure is used to
# organise the main executable code. This example is chosen to show a clean and organised way
# to structure a Python script.
# Example 4: Using in Modules
# In a file named 'module.py'
print(f"Module name: {__name__}") # Will display '__main__' or 'module' based on how it's run.
# Explanation:
# This showcases how __name__ behaves differently when a script is run directly
# versus being imported. It helps in understanding the dynamic nature of __name__.
# Example 5: Differentiating Module Functionality
def run_only_when_main():
print("This runs only as a main program.")
def run_always():
print("This runs always.")
if __name__ == '__main__':
run_only_when_main()
run_always()
# Explanation:
# This example demonstrates the flexibility of __name__. It allows certain
# parts of the script to run only when it's the main program, while others run
# regardless. It illustrates how to control script behaviour in different contexts.
# Example 6: Testing Purposes
# 'main.py' can include tests that are only executed when it's not imported.
```

```python
def add(a, b):
return a + b
def test_add():
assert add(2, 3) == 5
assert add(-1, 1) == 0
if __name__ == '__main__':
test_add()
# Explanation:
# This example demonstrates how to include test functions within the script.
# The tests are run only when the script is executed directly, not when imported as a module.
# This is beneficial for developers to test their code without affecting the module's functionality when used
elsewhere.
# Example 7: Running Main Functions from Different Scripts
# This pattern allows the script to act as both a reusable module and a standalone script.
def main_function():
print("This is the main function.")
if __name__ == '__main__':
main_function()
# Explanation:
# This example illustrates how a script can have dual functionality: it can be run as a standalone program or be
imported as a module in other scripts.
# The main_function() is executed only when the script is the main program, demonstrating the flexibility in script
usage.
# Example 8: Organizing Code
# Ensuring the main execution logic of the script is clearly separated and identifiable.
def initialize():
print("Initialization code")
def main_logic():
print("Main logic of the script")
if __name__ == '__main__':
initialize()
main_logic()
# Explanation:
# This example is chosen to show how code can be organised within a script. The initialization and main logic are
kept separate and are only executed when the script runs directly.
# This approach promotes code readability and maintainability, especially in larger projects.
# Example 9: Conditional Initialization
# Initialise certain variables or settings only when the script is the main program.
configuration = {}
def setup_config():
global configuration
configuration = {"mode": "debug", "version": "1.0"}
if __name__ == '__main__':
setup_config()
```

# Explanation:
# This example demonstrates conditional setup or initialization that should only occur when the script is not imported.
# For instance, setting up configuration or debugging options. It helps in creating scripts that are flexible to be used in different environments or modes.
# Example 10: Debugging
# Useful for adding debugging code that only runs when the script is executed directly, not when imported.
def complex_function():
# Some complex logic
return True
if __name__ == '__main__':
result = complex_function()
print(f"Debug: The result of complex_function is {result}")
# Explanation:
# This example is about adding debug statements that help in the development and testing phase.
# The debug print statement is executed only when running the script directly, ensuring that these messages do not appear during normal usage when the script is imported as a module.

In each of these examples, the choice is driven by a specific aspect of using __name__ and __main__ in Python scripts. They demonstrate various scenarios ranging from basic usage, code organisation, conditional execution, to debugging and testing. These examples aim to provide a comprehensive understanding of these special operators in different practical situations, particularly relevant for scripts that can act both as modules and standalone programs.

Understanding __name__ and __main__ is crucial in Python programming, especially in scripts forming part of larger applications, where the distinction between running as a main script or being imported as a module matters significantly.

Next, we will explore PyQt5's QApplication, focusing on its role and functionalities within the context of GUI applications. Let me know if you're ready to proceed with this or if you have any other specific areas to explore!

Part 4: Understanding PyQt5's QApplication

Introduction to PyQt5 and QApplication

What is PyQt5?

- PyQt5 is a set of Python bindings for The Qt Company's Qt application framework. It is used for developing graphical user interfaces (GUIs) and also for developing non-GUI tools.

Role of QApplication in PyQt5:

- QApplication is a core class in PyQt5. It manages application-wide resources and settings. It must be created before any other GUI components, and it encapsulates the main event loop where all events from the window system and other sources are processed and dispatched.

Detailed Explanation of QApplication with Examples

1. Creating an Instance of QApplication:

```
app = QApplication(sys.argv)
# Explanation:
# sys.argv contains a list of command-line arguments. QApplication uses it to handle command-line arguments that are GUI-related.
# This instance is essential for any PyQt5 application. It initialises the application's resources and settings.
```

1. Basic PyQt5 Application Structure:

```
if __name__ == '__main__':
app = QApplication(sys.argv)
window = QWidget()
window.show()
sys.exit(app.exec_())
# Explanation:
# This code snippet demonstrates the minimal setup required to create a PyQt5 application.
# A QWidget object is created as the main window, shown, and the application's event loop is started with app.exec_().
```

1. Handling Application-wide Settings:

```
app.setStyle('Fusion')
# Explanation:
# QApplication provides the setStyle() method to change the global style of the application. 'Fusion' is a built-in style provided by Qt.
```

1. Event Loop in PyQt5:

```
sys.exit(app.exec_())
# Explanation:
# The exec_() method of QApplication starts the application's main event loop. This loop waits for events like mouse clicks or keypresses and dispatches them to the appropriate widgets.
# sys.exit ensures a clean exit, allowing the application to close down resources neatly.
```

1. Global Accessibility of QApplication:

```
print(QApplication.instance())
# Explanation:
# QApplication.instance() returns the current instance of the application, making it globally accessible. This is useful for accessing application-wide settings and features from anywhere within the application.
```

1. Integration with System Events:

app.aboutToQuit.connect(on_app_exit)
# Explanation:
# The aboutToQuit signal is emitted before the application quits. Here, it is connected to a function on_app_exit, which can be used to perform cleanup tasks or save settings before the application closes.

1. Customising Application Appearance:

app.setStyleSheet("QPushButton { margin: 10ex; }")
# Explanation:
# QApplication allows setting a style sheet for the entire application, which changes the visual appearance of widgets. This example sets a custom margin for all QPushButton widgets in the application.

1. Multilingual and Localization Support:

translator = QTranslator()
translator.load("de_DE", "/path/to/translations")
app.installTranslator(translator)
# Explanation:
# PyQt5 supports internationalisation. Here, a QTranslator object is used to load a German translation file, enabling the application to display text in German.

1. Handling Command-Line Arguments:

if "—debug" in sys.argv:
enable_debug_mode()
# Explanation:
# This shows how to use command-line arguments (sys.argv) in a PyQt5 application. If '—debug' is passed as an argument, the application can enable a debug mode or perform other actions based on the argument.

1. Customizing Widget Behaviour:

window = QMainWindow()
window.statusBar().showMessage("Ready")
# Explanation:
# QMainWindow provides a statusBar method. Here, a message is displayed in the status bar of the main window, demonstrating how to customise widget behaviour in the application.

Why These Examples?

These examples are chosen to illustrate various aspects of QApplication in PyQt5, from the basics of setting up and running an application, handling global settings and styles, to more advanced features like event handling, localization, and customising behaviour. They provide a comprehensive understanding of QApplication, which is essential for developing PyQt5 applications.

With this understanding of QApplication, we can further explore other components and functionalities of PyQt5, or delve into another aspect of your PyQt5 application. Let me know your preference for the next step!

In summary:

Purpose and Functionality:

- main.py is the starting point of your Python application. When you run the program, the code in this file executes first.

- It initialises the core part of the application, which in this case, is a graphical user interface (GUI) built using PyQt5.

Code Breakdown and Explanation:

```python
import sys
from PyQt5.QtWidgets import QApplication
from ui import LoginRegisterWindow
if __name__ == '__main__':
app = QApplication(sys.argv)
win = LoginRegisterWindow()
win.show()
sys.exit(app.exec_())
```

- Import Statements: import sys brings in necessary system-specific parameters and functions used by Python. PyQt5 modules are imported to use GUI components.

- Creating QApplication Instance: app = QApplication(sys.argv) creates an application object. It's a requirement for any PyQt5 application to handle widget management, event handling, etc.

- Initialising the Main Window: win = LoginRegisterWindow() creates an instance of the LoginRegisterWindow class (defined in ui.py), which sets up the main window of your application.

- Displaying the Window: win.show() makes the window visible.

- Starting the Event Loop: sys.exit(app.exec_()) starts the event loop for the application, allowing it to wait for events such as user input.

Alternative Methods:

- Instead of using PyQt5, other GUI frameworks like Tkinter or Kivy could also be used to create the main window and run the application. Each has its syntax and features.

4.2 Breakdown of database.py: Managing Data Operations

Purpose of the File:

- database.py manages all interactions with the database. It contains functions to connect to the database, create tables, and handle data.

Sample Code Explanation:

```python
def create_connection():
    """Create a database connection to the SQLite database specified by DB_PATH."""
    conn = sqlite3.connect(DB_PATH)
    return conn
```

- Database Connection: The function create_connection() establishes a connection to an SQLite database. SQLite is chosen for its simplicity and ease of integration into applications.

- Return Connection Object: The function returns a connection object, which is used in other functions to execute SQL queries.

Alternatives and Options:

- Other databases like MySQL or PostgreSQL can also be used. However, they require additional setup and might not be as straightforward as SQLite for beginners.

4.3 Insights into user.py and auth.py: User and Authentication Logic

Understanding User Management:

- These files are crucial for handling user data and ensuring secure access to the application.

- user.py defines how user data is managed, while auth.py deals with authentication and password security.

Code Example from auth.py:

```python
def hash_password(password):
    """Hash a password with bcrypt."""
    return bcrypt.hashpw(password.encode('utf-8'), bcrypt.gensalt())
```

- Password Hashing: This function demonstrates how to securely hash a password using bcrypt, a popular hashing algorithm. This is crucial for security.

Why This Matters:

- Understanding user authentication and secure password handling is essential for protecting user data and privacy in any application.

4.4 Exploring ui.py: Building the User Interface

Building the GUI:

- ui.py contains the code for the application's user interface. It's where the visual components like buttons, text fields, and layouts are defined.

Code Snippet and Explanation:

```python
class LoginWindow(QMainWindow):
# ... other code ...
def initUI(self):
self.username = QLineEdit(self)
self.password = QLineEdit(self)
self.login_button = QPushButton('Login', self)
# ... additional setup code ...
```

- Defining Widgets: This snippet shows how to create input fields and a button in the login window.

- Layout and Design: The position, size, and behaviour of these widgets are also defined in this class.

Importance for Beginners:

- Understanding how to create and manipulate GUI components is essential for building interactive applications.

5. Working with the Database

The database.py file is a central component of the Research Project Management Application. It handles all interactions with the SQLite database, a lightweight, disk-based database that doesn't require a separate server process. Understanding how to work with the database is crucial for managing and persisting data within your application.

5.1 Introduction to SQLite and Database Concepts

SQLite is an excellent choice for applications that require a simple yet powerful database solution. It stores the entire database (definitions, tables, indices, and the data itself) in a single cross-platform file.

Key Concepts:

- Database File: SQLite databases are stored in a single file, making them easy to manage and deploy.

- SQL (Structured Query Language): SQLite uses SQL to interact with the database, allowing you to execute queries to create, read, update, and delete data.

- Tables and Schemas: A database schema defines the structure of your database, including the tables and the type of data each can hold.

5.2 Step-by-Step Guide to Database Operations in the Code

The database.py file contains several functions that interact with the SQLite database. Here's a guide to understanding these operations:

- create_connection: Establishes a connection to the SQLite database. The connection object is used to interact with the database.

- ensure_table_schema: Checks if the necessary tables exist and creates them if they don't. This function is essential for initialising the database schema.

- CRUD Operations: The file includes functions for CRUD operations:

- Create: add_user inserts a new user into the database.

- Read: fetch_all_users retrieves data from the database.

- Update: update_user_role changes data in the database.

- Delete: While not explicitly defined in the provided code, a delete operation would remove data from the database.

5.3 Best Practices for Database Management in Python

When working with databases in Python, there are several best practices to follow:

- Use Parameterized Queries: To prevent SQL injection attacks, use parameterized queries instead of string concatenation.

- Handle Database Connections Carefully: Always close database connections when they're no longer needed to avoid database locks and resource leaks.

- Error Handling: Implement robust error handling around your database operations to catch and respond to any issues that may arise.

- Database Transactions: Use transactions (committing or rolling back) to ensure data integrity, especially when performing multiple related operations.

Working with the database is a critical aspect of backend development in Python applications. Understanding how to perform and manage database operations is key to building robust and reliable software.

6. Front-End Development with PyQt5

Developing the front-end, or the graphical user interface (GUI), of your Python application is a crucial aspect that directly impacts user experience. PyQt5, a set of Python bindings for the Qt application framework, is used in the Research Project Management Application for this purpose. It offers a wide range of tools and widgets to create professional-looking and functional GUIs.

6.1 Basics of PyQt5 for GUI Development

PyQt5 simplifies the process of GUI creation in Python. It allows developers to design visually appealing and user-friendly interfaces with less manual coding.

Key Concepts:

- Widgets: In PyQt5, widgets are the basic building blocks of a GUI application. They can be windows, buttons, text fields, labels, etc.

- Layouts: Layouts determine how widgets are arranged in the window. PyQt5 offers various layout managers to organise widgets, such as QVBoxLayout, QHBoxLayout, and QGridLayout.

- Signals and Slots: A key feature in PyQt5, signals and slots are used for communication between objects. When a user interacts with a widget (like clicking a button), a signal is emitted. Slots are functions that get called in response to a signal.

6.2 Analysing UI Code Components

In the ui.py file, you'll find the definition of the application's UI. Here's an overview of its components:

- Window Classes: Each window in the application (like the login window, registration window, etc.) is defined as a class that extends QMainWindow or another appropriate base class.

- Setting Up Widgets: Within these classes, widgets are instantiated (like QLineEdit for text input, QPushButton for buttons).

- Configuring Layouts: The arrangement of widgets is handled using layout managers, which are applied to containers or entire windows.

- Event Handling: Functions are defined to handle events, such as clicking a button or submitting a form.

6.3 Customising and Experimenting with the UI

Customising the UI to fit the needs of your application is a critical part of development. PyQt5 provides extensive options for customization:

- Styling Widgets: You can modify the appearance of widgets using stylesheets, similar to CSS in web development.

● Adding Functionality: Extend the functionality of widgets by writing new slots (functions) that respond to signals emitted by the widgets.

● Experimentation: Don't hesitate to experiment with different widgets, layouts, and styles to achieve the desired look and functionality. The PyQt5 documentation is a valuable resource for learning about available options.

7. Understanding and Implementing Authentication

In any application handling user data, ensuring secure access is paramount. In the Research Project Management Application, this security is managed through effective user authentication mechanisms. The user.py and auth.py files play a central role in this process.

7.1 Concept of User Authentication and Security

User authentication is the process of verifying a user's identity. It's a critical security measure to prevent unauthorised access to the application.

Key Elements:

- Username and Password: The most common form of authentication. The application verifies if the entered username and password match the stored credentials.

- Hashing Passwords: Storing passwords in plain text is a security risk. Instead, passwords are hashed using algorithms like bcrypt. This means even if the data is compromised, the actual passwords are not easily decipherable.

7.2 Walkthrough of the Authentication Process in the Code

The authentication process involves several steps, each managed by functions within user.py and auth.py.

- user.py: User Class

- Represents users of the application.

- The register method adds a new user, calling add_user from database.py.

- The check_credentials method verifies login details.

- auth.py: Authentication Functions

- hash_password: Converts a plain text password into a hashed version for secure storage.

- validate_user: Checks if the entered username and password are correct. It compares the entered password (after hashing) with the stored hashed password.

7.3 Enhancing Security Features

While the basic authentication is a good start, consider the following enhancements for added security:

- Implementing Multi-Factor Authentication (MFA): Adds an extra layer of security by requiring users to provide two or more verification factors to gain access.

- Account Lockout Mechanisms: Temporarily lock out accounts after several unsuccessful login attempts to prevent brute force attacks.

- Security Questions or Email Verification: For password recovery, use security questions or email verification instead of displaying or sending the password directly.

Understanding and implementing robust authentication mechanisms is crucial for the security and integrity of your application. It's not only about protecting data but also about building trust with your users.

8. Adding New Features: A Hands-On Approach

One of the most exciting aspects of software development is the ability to continually evolve and improve an application by adding new features. For beginners, this practice not only enhances the functionality of the project but also significantly contributes to skill development and understanding of Python programming.

8.1 Guidelines for Extending the Application

When planning to add new features to the Python Research Project Management Application, consider the following guidelines:

- Identify the Need: Start by identifying what new feature or improvement is needed. It could be something that enhances user experience, increases efficiency, or adds a new functionality.

- Plan Your Approach: Before diving into coding, plan your approach. Sketch out how the new feature will fit into the existing architecture, the changes needed, and any new components you will have to create.

- Understand Dependencies: Understand the dependencies and interactions between various parts of the application. Ensure that your new feature integrates smoothly without disrupting existing functionalities.

8.2 Suggested Beginner-friendly Features to Implement

For beginners looking to expand the application, here are some manageable yet impactful features you can start with:

- User Profile Management: Allow users to view and edit their profiles, including changing passwords, updating email addresses, or adding profile pictures.

- Enhanced Search Functionality: Implement a more advanced search for projects or users, with filters and sorting options.

- Notification System: Develop a system to notify users about important events like project deadlines, new messages, or system updates.

8.3 Tips for Debugging and Testing New Code

As you add new features, debugging and testing become crucial to ensure that your additions work as intended and don't introduce bugs into the system.

- Test Incrementally: Test your code frequently as you write it. This approach helps in identifying and fixing issues early in the development process.

- Use Debugging Tools: Leverage the debugging tools available in Visual Studio Code. Set breakpoints, step through your code, and inspect variables to understand the flow and state of your application.

- Write Unit Tests: If possible, write unit tests for your new features. Unit testing helps in validating that your code performs as expected in isolated conditions.

9. Version Control and Best Practices

In software development, especially when working on complex projects like the Python Research Project Management Application, employing version control and adhering to best practices is vital. Version control systems, such as Git, provide a way to track changes, collaborate with others, and manage different versions of your code efficiently.

9.1 Introduction to Using Git in VSC

Git is a distributed version control system that helps you keep track of changes made to your code over time. Using Git with Visual Studio Code (VSC) enhances your development workflow.

Getting Started with Git in VSC:

- Initialise a Git Repository: If your project isn't already a Git repository, you can initialise one directly in VSC by opening the Command Palette (Cmd + Shift + P) and running the Git: Initialize Repository command.

- Commit Changes: As you make changes to your code, regularly commit these changes. This process involves 'staging' your changes and then committing them with a descriptive message.

- Branching: Use branches in Git to work on new features or fixes without affecting the main codebase. This practice is especially useful for testing new functionalities or making significant changes.

9.2 Managing Code Versions and Collaborating

Using Git, you can manage different versions of your code and collaborate with others more effectively.

- Push and Pull: Sync your local repository with a remote repository (like GitHub) using push (to send your commits) and pull (to fetch the latest updates).

- Merge and Resolve Conflicts: When multiple people work on the same project, merge conflicts can occur. VSC provides tools to help you resolve these conflicts and merge changes seamlessly.

- Code Reviews: If working in a team, use pull requests for code reviews. This process allows team members to discuss, review, and suggest changes to the code before it's merged.

9.3 Adopting Coding Best Practices

Maintaining high-quality code is essential for the health and longevity of your project. Here are some best practices:

- Readable and Maintainable Code: Write code that is easy to read and understand. Use meaningful variable names, consistent indentation, and include comments where necessary.

- Regular Refactoring: Periodically review and refactor your code. This means restructuring existing code without changing its external behaviour to improve its internal structure.

- Staying Informed and Updated: Keep up with the latest Python features and best practices. Regularly update your libraries and tools to incorporate new improvements and security fixes.

Incorporating version control and following best practices in software development not only helps in managing your code more effectively but also ensures that the development process is smooth and efficient. These practices are crucial, especially as you start adding more features or collaborating with others.

10. From Code to Execution: Running the Application

After setting up your development environment, understanding the code structure, and possibly making modifications or adding new features, the next step is to run the application. This process involves executing the code and interacting with the application's interface, which is a critical phase to ensure that everything functions as expected.

10.1 Steps to Run the Project on Your Machine

To run the Python Research Project Management Application on your Apple machine using Visual Studio Code, follow these steps:

Open the Project in VSC:

- Launch Visual Studio Code and open the project folder containing the application code.

Run the Main Script:

- Locate the main.py file in the file explorer. This file is the entry point of your application.

- Right-click on the file and select 'Run Python File in Terminal' or use the play button in the upper right corner of the editor. This will start the application.

Interact with the Application:

- Once the application starts, you should see the main window, typically the login or registration screen, depending on how the application is structured.

- Test the functionalities you have worked on or modified to ensure they are working correctly.

10.2 Troubleshooting Common Issues

When running the application, you might encounter various issues or errors. Here are some common troubleshooting steps:

- Check for Syntax Errors: Python will output any syntax errors in the terminal. Review the error messages for clues on where and what the issue might be.

- Debugging: Utilise VSC's debugging tools to step through the code and inspect variables at runtime. This can help identify logical errors or unexpected behaviours.

- Dependency Issues: Ensure all required libraries (as listed in requirements.txt, if available) are installed. Use the command pip install -r requirements.txt in the terminal.

10.3 Interpreting and Utilising Application Logs

If your application is configured to generate logs (which is a good practice for complex applications), use them to understand the application's behaviour and troubleshoot issues.

- Locate Log Files: Find out where the application stores its log files. This could be in a dedicated directory or file within the project.

- Read Log Messages: Review the log messages for any warnings, errors, or other informative messages that could help you understand what the application is doing or where it might be encountering problems.

- Using Logs for Debugging: Use the information in the logs to trace back issues. Logs can provide insights into the sequence of actions leading up to an error or unexpected behaviour.

Running and interacting with the application is a crucial part of the development cycle. It's where you get to see the fruits of your labour in action and make sure that everything works as intended. This phase also provides valuable learning experiences in debugging and problem-solving.

11. Concluding Thoughts and Further Learning Paths

As we reach the conclusion of "Appendix A: Python Project Blueprint - A Practical Guide for Beginners," it's important to reflect on the journey you've embarked upon and to look ahead to the paths that lie open for further exploration in the world of Python programming and software development.

11.1 Recap and Reflection on the Learning Journey

Throughout this guide, you have navigated the intricacies of setting up a Python development environment, delved deep into the structure and functionality of a real-world Python project, and gained hands-on experience in running and modifying an application. These skills form the bedrock of your journey as a Python developer and provide a solid foundation for building more complex and sophisticated applications.

- From Theory to Practice: You've translated theoretical knowledge into practical skills, moving beyond basic Python syntax to understanding how a complete application is structured and functions.

- Problem-Solving and Debugging: The hands-on experience in debugging and problem-solving has prepared you to tackle challenges and errors with confidence and a systematic approach.

- Understanding the Big Picture: You've learned not just about writing code, but also about project organisation, version control, and best practices in software development.

11.2 Additional Resources for Continued Learning

To further enhance your skills and knowledge, consider exploring the following resources and avenues:

- Advanced Python Courses: Online platforms like Coursera, Udemy, and edX offer advanced courses in Python that cover specialised topics like data science, machine learning, and web development.

- Open Source Contribution: Contributing to open source projects on platforms like GitHub can provide real-world coding experience and an opportunity to collaborate with other developers.

- Building Personal Projects: Start your own Python projects based on your interests. This could be anything from a simple automation script to a full-fledged web application.

11.3 Encouragement for Future Project Development

The journey of learning and development in programming is ongoing. Each project you work on enhances your skills and broadens your understanding. Remember:

- Stay Curious and Keep Exploring: The field of technology is ever-evolving. Stay curious and open to learning new languages, frameworks, and tools.

- Embrace Challenges: Each challenge you encounter is an opportunity to learn and grow. Don't be afraid to tackle complex problems or to step out of your comfort zone.

● Join the Community: Engage with the Python community through forums, social media, and local meetups. Networking with fellow developers can provide support, inspiration, and opportunities for collaboration.

Appendix B: Understanding Layered Architecture in Software Development

Introduction to Layered Architecture

Layered architecture is a cornerstone design pattern in software engineering, especially relevant in complex applications. By dividing an application into distinct, hierarchical layers, each with a designated responsibility, this architecture promotes organisation and clarity.

Defining Layered Architecture:

- Concept: It's about structurally organising an application into separate layers, each handling specific aspects of the application. This separation ensures that each layer is independent but cooperates closely with the others.

- Purpose: The primary goal is to separate the concerns, making the application more manageable, scalable, and maintainable.

- Advantages: This approach brings several benefits, including enhanced modularity, easier maintenance, and the ability to upgrade or modify individual layers without impacting others significantly.

Layered architecture is particularly beneficial in projects where different skill sets are required for different aspects of the application, such as in the Research Project Management Application, where different technologies and expertise come into play in various layers.

Core Layers in a Layered Architecture

In a typical layered architecture, an application is divided into several layers, each focusing on a specific aspect of the application. Here's a breakdown of these layers and their roles:

1. Presentation Layer (Front-End):

● Functionality: This layer is where the user interacts with the application. It's responsible for displaying information to the user and handling user inputs.

● Components: In a desktop application like the Research Project Management Application, this includes the graphical user interface elements such as windows, buttons, text fields, etc., often created with tools like PyQt for Python applications.

● Role: It decouples the user interface from the business logic, ensuring that changes in the UI design do not affect the core application logic.

2. Business Logic Layer (Application Layer):

● Functionality: This layer is the brain of the application. It processes data from the presentation layer, applies business rules and logic, and prepares information to be stored or retrieved from the data layer.

● Components: It contains the code that executes specific business rules and algorithms, crucial for the functioning of the application.

● Role: It acts as a mediator between the presentation layer and the data access layer, ensuring a separation of concerns between user interface and data storage.

3. Data Access Layer (Persistence Layer):

● Functionality: This layer manages data storage and retrieval. It interacts with databases or other forms of data storage and provides data to the business logic layer.

● Components: This typically includes database access code, ORM (Object-Relational Mapping) frameworks, and other mechanisms for interacting with data storage systems.

● Role: It centralises the data access within the application, making it easier to manage data sources and maintain data integrity.

Application of Layered Architecture in the Research Project Management Application

In the context of the Research Project Management Application, implementing a layered architecture involves a clear and strategic alignment of each layer with the application's specific needs.

1. Implementing the Presentation Layer:

● In the Research Project Management Application, the Presentation Layer is developed using PyQt. This layer comprises all the graphical elements like login forms, project management interfaces, and communication panels.

● The focus here is on user experience — ensuring the interface is intuitive, responsive, and aesthetically pleasing.

2. Building the Business Logic Layer:

● This layer is where the application's rules and logic are executed. For example, it handles the logic for user registration, project assignment, and progress tracking.

● In Python, this would involve writing classes and functions that encapsulate the business processes. These components work independently of the user interface but use data supplied by the Presentation Layer.

3. Configuring the Data Access Layer:

● The Data Access Layer in this application interacts with an SQLite database, managing all data storage, retrieval, and updates.

● It includes Python scripts for database connection, query execution, and handling CRUD (Create, Read, Update, Delete) operations. This layer ensures that the business logic layer can access and manipulate the necessary data without direct interaction with the database.

4. Integrating External Services:

● The application also incorporates external integrations, like APIs for OneDrive and MS Teams. This layer manages these external communications and integrates them seamlessly into the application.

● Such integrations enhance the application's functionality, offering additional services like cloud storage and in-app communication.

Advantages in the Context of the Application

● Modularity: Each layer can be developed, tested, and debugged independently. For instance, the UI can be redesigned without altering the business logic.

● Scalability: As the application grows, each layer can be scaled or modified as needed. For example, the database can be migrated to a more robust system with minimal impact on other layers.

● Maintainability: Changes and updates can be made in one layer without affecting the entire application. This separation simplifies maintenance and updates.

Conclusion

Layered architecture provides a structured and efficient way to build and manage complex applications like the Research Project Management Application. By understanding and applying this architecture, developers can ensure their applications are robust, scalable, and easy to maintain. This approach not only facilitates current development needs but also paves the way for future enhancements and growth.

Appendix C: registered your application in the Azure portal

To ensure that you have correctly registered your application in the Azure portal and obtained the necessary client ID, client secret, and tenant ID, follow these steps:

Step 1: Register Your Application

Go to the Azure Portal: Open your web browser and navigate to theAzure Portal[1]. https://portal.azure.com/

Sign In: Log in with your Microsoft credentials.

Navigate to Azure Active Directory:

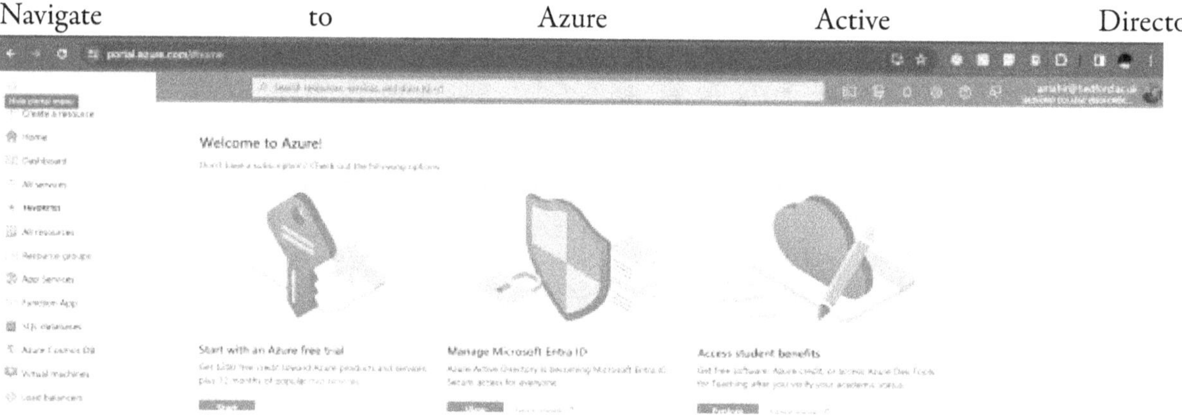

- In the left-hand navigation pane, click on "Azure Active Directory".

App Registrations:

- Within Azure Active Directory, find and select "App registrations".

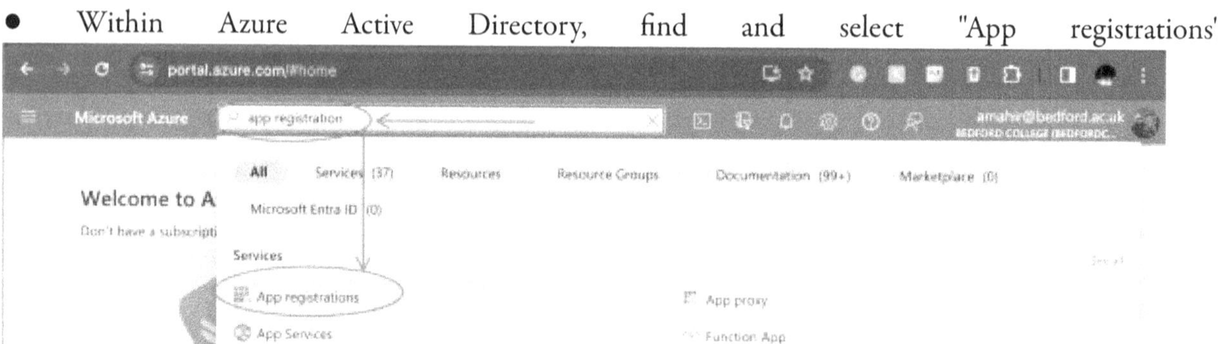

New Registration:

- Click on "New registration" at the top of the page.

- Enter a name for your application.

- Specify who can use the application (usually select "Accounts in this organisational directory only").

---

1. https://portal.azure.com/

- You may leave the "Redirect URI" field blank for now, or fill it in if you already know the URI.

- Click "Register".

Step 2: Obtain Client ID and Tenant ID

After registering your app, you'll be taken to the app's overview page where you can find the Application (client) ID and the Directory (tenant) ID.

Application (client) ID: This is your client ID. Note it down.
Directory (tenant) ID: This is your tenant ID. Note it down as well.

Step 3: Create a Client Secret

Certificates & Secrets:

- From the app's page, find and click on "Certificates & secrets" in the left-hand navigation menu.

New Client Secret:

- Click on "New client secret".

- Add a description and choose an expiry period for the secret.

- Click "Add".

Note Down the Client Secret:

- Once the client secret is created, it will be displayed. Make sure to copy and save it immediately, as you won't be able to retrieve it again after leaving this page.

Step 4: Set Permissions (if necessary)

If your application needs specific permissions to access certain resources (like Microsoft Graph API):

API Permissions:

- Click on "API permissions" in the left-hand navigation menu.

Add a Permission:

- Click on "Add a permission".

- Choose the API you want to access (e.g., Microsoft Graph).

- Select the type of permissions (Delegated or Application permissions) and the specific permissions needed.

- Click "Add permissions".

Step 5: Grant Admin Consent (if required)

For certain permissions, you might need to grant admin consent:

Grant Consent:

- Still under "API permissions", click on "Grant admin consent for [Your Organization]".

- Confirm the action.

Important Security Note

- Keep your client secret secure. Do not expose it in your source code or any public areas.

- Use environment variables or secure vaults to store and access these credentials in your application.

After completing these steps, your application will be registered with Azure, and you'll have the necessary credentials (client ID, client secret, and tenant ID) to authenticate and access Microsoft's services, such as the Microsoft Graph API.

Implementing:

Implementing:

1. Install the Correct Packages:
- You might need requests for making HTTP requests.
- For authentication with Microsoft Graph API, use msal.
- Install them using pip:

```
pip install requests msal
```

2. Update Your Code:

- Replace the microsoftgraph import with the correct way to interact with Microsoft Graph API.

- For example, use msal for authentication and requests to make API calls.

Sample Updated Code:

Here's an example of how you might authenticate and make a request to Microsoft Graph API using msal and requests:

```python
import msal
import requests
# Your Microsoft Azure configuration
client_id = 'YOUR_CLIENT_ID'
client_secret = 'YOUR_CLIENT_SECRET'
authority = 'https://login.microsoftonline.com/YOUR_TENANT_ID'
scope = ['https://graph.microsoft.com/.default']
# Create a confidential client instance
app = msal.ConfidentialClientApplication(client_id, client_secret, authority)
# Acquire a token
result = app.acquire_token_for_client(scopes=scope)
if 'access_token' in result:
# Use this token to call Microsoft Graph API
graph_api_endpoint = 'https://graph.microsoft.com/v1.0/...'
token = result['access_token']
headers = {'Authorization': 'Bearer ' + token}
response = requests.get(graph_api_endpoint, headers=headers)
# Process the response from Microsoft Graph API
else:
print("Could not acquire token: ", result.get("error"), result.get("error_description"))
```

Important Notes:

- Ensure that you have registered your application in the Azure portal and have the correct client ID, client secret, and tenant ID.

- The scope and endpoints in the requests will depend on the specific operations you're performing with the Microsoft Graph API.

- Always handle sensitive data like client secrets securely and do not expose them in your code. Use environment variables or other secure methods to store such information.

Appendix D: Glossary

API (Application Programming Interface): *Set of protocols for building software applications.* **More:** An Application Programming Interface (API) is a collection of protocols and definitions that allows different software applications to communicate and interact. It enables the integration of separate software components, allowing them to exchange data and functions seamlessly. APIs are essential in modern computing, making it possible for various applications and services to work together, enriching user experiences and expanding software capabilities.

Agile Methodology: *An iterative approach to project management and software development.* **More:** Agile methodology is an iterative approach to project management and software development focused on collaboration, flexibility, and continuously incorporating user feedback throughout the development life cycle.

Authentication: *Process of verifying identity in a computer system.* **More:** Authentication is the process of verifying the identity of a user or process, often as a prerequisite to allowing access to resources in a system. It typically involves the presentation of an identifier and credentials.

Automated Testing: *Using software to execute tests on an application automatically.* **More:** Automated testing is the use of software tools to control the execution of tests, the comparison of actual outcomes to predicted outcomes, the setting up of test preconditions, and other test control and reporting functions.

Back-End: *Server-side of an application.* **More:** The back-end of a software application contains behind-the-scenes systems handling data access logic, security, storage, servers and databases rather than front-facing client-side interfaces and display rendering.

Bandwidth: *Range of frequencies within a given band.* **More:** Bandwidth measures data transmission capacity. In computing it quantifies the amount of data that can be sent over a network connection within a measure of capacity and routers manage allocations for traffic volumes.

Bcrypt: *A password hashing function.* **More:** Bcrypt is an algorithm used to securely hash and store passwords. It incorporates salting and multiple rounds of encryption to protect against rainbow table and brute force attacks.

Cache: *Hardware or software component that stores data.* **More:** A cache is a high-speed data storage layer used to temporarily retain frequently accessed data to speed up future requests by avoiding slower storage access. Caching accelerates compute tasks and improves performance.

CI/CD (Continuous Integration/Continuous Deployment): *Automated software integration and deployment.* **More:** CI/CD is a set of software engineering practices that speed up development cycles by automatically building, testing and deploying code changes. CI/CD bridges the gap between developers and operations teams to ensure quality releases.

Class: *Blueprint for creating objects in OOP.* **More:** A class defines properties and behaviours shared among object instances in object-oriented programming. Classes act as templates or blueprints encapsulating data structures and functions to construct distinct objects and model domain concepts.

Compiler: *Program that converts code into executable instructions.* **More:** A compiler is a computer program that transforms source code written in high-level languages into executable machine code to create an executable application. Compiled languages provide optimization capabilities compared to interpreted ones.

Concurrency: *Ability of a database to allow multiple transactions.* **More:** Concurrency in databases enables handling multiple transactions simultaneously while preserving consistency, isolation and integrity constraints through locking mechanisms and multi-versioning. It improves throughput via parallelism.

Containerization: *Encapsulation of an application and its environment.* **More:** Containerization encapsulates applications in containers with their own operating environments, libraries, configurations and dependencies, ensuring consistent deployments across environments.

Data Encryption: *Encrypting data for security.* **More:** Data encryption translates information into cipher code to prevent unauthorised access during storage or transmission. It scrambles sensitive data like credentials or financial details into unreadable formats decipherable only to holders of cryptographic keys.

Database: *Organised collection of structured information or data.* **More:** A database is an organised collection of data stored in tables and managed by software called a database management system. Databases enable storage, rapid search and retrieval by users or applications.

Debugging: *Identifying and removing errors from software.* **More:** Debugging is the process of detecting, diagnosing and removing bugs, errors or defects in computer programs during software development. Debugging provides insight into runtime states, facilitates program logic correctness and improves reliability.

Dependency: *A software component that another component relies on.* **More:** A dependency in software development refers to an external package or library that another piece of code requires in order to function properly. Identifying dependencies avoids conflicts and manages software versions systematically.

Deployment: *Process of making software active.* **More:** Software deployment instals and activates applications on user devices or servers enabling execution after development stages. Automated deployments allow reliable, frequent, rapid releases of business applications to scale with agile workflows.

Docker: *A platform for developing and running applications in containers.* **More:** Docker provides containerization functionality, allowing developers to package applications with dependencies into standardised units for software development. It includes container runtime, management tools and services.

Encryption: *Process of encoding information.* **More:** Encryption converts data or messages into coded formats protecting confidentiality against unauthorised access. Secure encryption protocols encode financial, identity or transmission data providing privacy and information security.

Firewall: *Network security system.* **More:** Firewalls control access permissions for network traffic entering or leaving private networks and computers. They establish barriers blocking unauthorised connections while permitting approved communications based on predefined security rules.

Framework: *A platform for developing software applications.* **More:** A software framework is a universal reusable structure facilitating development of concrete applications, products and solutions. Frameworks expedite construction of new software systems by providing generic capabilities via abstract interfaces.

Front-End: *Part of the application that interacts with the user.* **More:** The front-end is the part of a software system or application interacting directly with users. It focuses on client-side display rendering and interface actions, accessibly presenting data for user input and interpretation.

Functionality: *The range of operations that can be run in a system.* **More:** Functionality refers to the range of operations, tasks and activities that can be run on a system or application. It relates to the capabilities of the software.

Gantt Chart: *A visual project schedule representation.* **More:** A Gantt chart is a type of bar chart that illustrates project schedules. Gantt charts show activities, tasks or events displayed against time, making it easy to determine project duration and track dependencies.

Git: *Version control system.* **More:** Git is an open source distributed version control system developed to coordinate work among multiple developers on software change tracking. Git manages source code history and collaboration across teams through branches, commits, pushes and merges.

Graphical User Interface (GUI): *Interface featuring graphical elements.* **More:** A graphical user interface (GUI) allows users to interact with electronic devices through visual indicators and graphics, like icons and menus, instead of text-based interfaces. It provides an intuitive way to interact with a system.

Hashing: *Generating value from a string of text.* **More:** Hashing generates a numeric value or fingerprint from input data used in cryptography or data storage/retrieval applications. Sensitive data like passwords are hashed using algorithms providing one-way encryption preventing reverse engineering.

HTTP (Hypertext Transfer Protocol): *Protocol used for transmitting web pages.* **More:** The Hypertext Transfer Protocol is an application protocol that defines communication rules for transferring web page data between browsers and servers on the World Wide Web. It forms the foundation of web data communication.

IDE (Integrated Development Environment): *Software suite for coding.* **More:** An integrated development environment (IDE) is a software suite that consolidates tools required for application development like code editors, compilers, debuggers and builders into a common graphical user interface. IDEs maximise programmer productivity.

IDE (Integrated Development Environment): *Application providing comprehensive facilities to programmers.* **More:** Integrated Development Environments (IDEs) integrate code editing, debugging, project management, builds, testing and other development tools into a single application suite tailored for efficiently writing, running and debugging software.

Integration Testing: *Testing combined parts of an application.* **More:** Integration testing is a software testing approach in which individual software modules are combined and tested to evaluate interactions between integrated components and detect interface defects or integration errors.

Iteration: *Repetition of a process.* **More:** Iteration means repeatedly applying a process to refine an output or result. Iterative software development cycles prototypes and user feedback to converge on requirements through successive iterations focusing on continuous improvement.

JSON (JavaScript Object Notation): *Data interchange format.* **More:** JSON (JavaScript Object Notation) is an open standard data format that encodes JavaScript objects as human-readable text for representing and transmitting structured data over networks. It facilitates data interchange due to compatibility across programming languages.

Kubernetes: *An open-source platform for managing containerized applications.* **More:** Kubernetes is an open-source system for automating containerized application deployment, scaling and management. It groups containers with similar requirements together for efficiency and provides mechanisms for container scaling and failover.

Library: *Collection of non-volatile resources.* **More:** A software library or code library is a collection of precompiled routines that programs can share. Library code abstracts complexity so developers avoid rewriting standard algorithms integrated through libraries speeding development. Libraries manage version changes systematically.

Load Testing: *Assessing application performance under expected load.* **More:** Load testing subjects an application to simulated workloads to evaluate its performance, stability, reliability and resource usage under expected load conditions. It helps determine maximum operating capacity and identify bottlenecks.

Microservices: *Architecture of loosely coupled services.* **More:** Microservices architecture structures applications as independently deployable modular services that communicate through APIs. It enables continuous delivery and scaling while allowing teams to use different tech stacks for different components.

Module: *A file containing Python statements and definitions.* **More:** A module in Python is a file containing related code components like functions, classes, or attribute definitions grouped for organisation and reuse. Modules compartmentalise namespaces clarifying relationships and scoping dependencies between components.

MVC (Model-View-Controller): *Software design pattern for developing interfaces.* **More:** The Model-View-Controller (MVC) pattern separates data (Model), presentation (View) and business logic (Controller) into three interconnected components. This promotes modular app development enabling efficiency through division of related tasks.

MS Teams: *Microsoft's communication platform.* **More:** Microsoft Teams is a unified communication and collaboration platform that combines workplace chat, video meetings, file storage and application integration. It allows teams to share conversations, files and resources in a common space.

Network: *A group of interconnected computers.* **More:** A computer network refers to multiple devices like PCs, servers, printers etc interconnected for communications and resource sharing via cables, protocols, software, signals or wireless links enabling data transfer and access to distributed services.

Object: *Instance of a class in OOP.* **More:** An object in object-oriented programming (OOP) is a bundle of code and data represented by an instance of some class which defines methods and attributes the object can contain and expose based on its type. Objects model real-world entities.

Object-Oriented Programming (OOP): *Programming model organised around objects.* **More:** Object-Oriented Programming represents concepts as objects defined by attributes and behaviours. OOP models real-world interactions, accelerates development through modularity and reusability with concepts like inheritance, encapsulation and polymorphism.

OneDrive: *Microsoftâ€™s file hosting and synchronisation service.* **More:** OneDrive is a file hosting and synchronisation service operated by Microsoft as part of its web version of Office. It allows users to store files and personal data like Windows settings or BitLocker recovery keys in the cloud.

Parameter: *Variable used in a function.* **More:** Parameters are variables in a method or function definition used to pass arguments into the function call controlling execution. Parameters enable passing inputs to customise function behaviour without modifying source code.

Patch: *A set of changes to a computer program.* **More:** A patch modifies or updates existing application code after release to fix bugs or security flaws in software systems. Vendors provide patch updates improving application performance, stability or safeguarding programs against threats or defects.

Platform: *Underlying computer system.* **More:** A computing platform includes system architecture, software frameworks and hardware infrastructure enabling software development and execution through abstracted resources consistent across devices and applications via common interfaces.

Prototype: *Early sample or model of a product.* **More:** A prototype is a rudimentary working model used to demonstrate functionality, design and implementation progress. Software prototypes provide simulations of final products for feasibility testing before full development.

PyQt5: *Python bindings for the Qt application framework.* **More:** PyQt5 provides Python bindings for the Qt cross-platform application framework. It enables building desktop GUIs, 2D graphics painting systems and 3D scenes visualisation for Python applications.

Python: *High-level programming language.* **More:** Python is a widely used general-purpose, high-level programming language emphasising code readability with clear syntax rules. Python supports multiple coding paradigms: object-oriented, structured and functional programming styles within minimalist yet powerful standard libraries.

Query: *Request for data or information from a database.* **More:** A query is a request made to a database to retrieve specific data or information based on defined constraints or filters. SQL and other querying languages structure requests to selectively extract records matching criteria.

Query Language: *Language for making queries in databases.* **More:** Query languages like SQL provide syntaxes for requesting data from databases to access, manipulate, insert, update or remove records in tables. Queries filter retrieved data sets reducing complexity in application development.

RBAC (Role-Based Access Control): *Access control based on user roles.* **More:** Role-based access control (RBAC) restricts system access based on the roles of individual users within an organisation. RBAC permissions and access are assigned to specific roles rather than to individuals.

Refactoring: *Process of restructuring code.* **More:** Code refactoring improves internal structure without altering external behaviours to enhance readability, reduce complexity, eliminate repetitions, and facilitate maintenance. Refactoring makes code more concise and modular for easier testing and extensions.

Repository: *Storage location for software packages.* **More:** A repository in software development stores and manages collections of code, documentation and other metadata resources. Repositories facilitate version control, component sharing and distribution for software projects collaborating on developing, testing or deploying applications.

Responsive Design: *Design that adapts to user environments.* **More:** Responsive web design adapts page layout and elements to optimise viewing and interaction experience across a wide range of devices from desktop computers to mobile phones. It uses flexible layouts, CSS media queries and fluid images.

Scalability: *Ability of a system to handle growth.* **More:** Scalability is the property of a system to handle increased workload by adapting its architecture. A scalable system can expand to accommodate heavier demand and improve performance by increasing processing power, memory, bandwidth etc.

Script: *Simple program.* **More:** A script is a list of commands or instructions written to automate processes or tasks. Scripts execute sequenced commands saving effort compared to manually entering commands one by one repeatedly. They run without compilation.

SDK (Software Development Kit): *Collection of software tools.* **More:** A software development kit (SDK) bundles tools like APIs, debug testing, code samples and documentation to help developers use technologies, programming interfaces or services to build applications based on frameworks and platforms like hardware, OS, storage systems etc.

Server: *A computer or system providing resources.* **More:** Servers are computers or systems delivering resources, data, services, or programs to other computers over a local network or the Internet. Servers host networks with specialised hardware and software maximising performance and availability.

Session Management: *Handling user sessions in web applications.* **More:** Session management controls user sessions in web applications by generating session IDs to represent each session. It tracks logged in users over multiple pages and requests to keep them authenticated and maintain application state.

SQLite: *A relational database management system.* **More:** SQLite is a lightweight, zero-configuration, open source relational database management system included in many operating systems and embedded in mobile apps and other software. It uses SQL syntax and manages databases as single files.

SSL/TLS (Secure Sockets Layer/Transport Layer Security): *Protocols for secure communications.* **More:** SSL/TLS protocols establish encrypted links between web servers and browsers for secure transmission of data and user credentials. They enable data encryption, source authentication and data integrity checks to secure connections over computer networks.

Syntax: *Set of rules defining how to write configurations.* **More:** Syntax refers to the grammatical rules governing structure of expressions and statements in a language. Programming languages have precise syntaxes specifying valid configurations of instructions computers can parse to execute operations.

Thread: *Smallest sequence of programmed instructions.* **More:** A thread represents the smallest sequence of instructions that can be processed independently by a CPU scheduler. Multi-threaded environments execute threads in parallel overlapping processing of shared resources improving overall application performance.

UI (User Interface): *Space where interactions between humans and machines occur.* **More:** The user interface (UI) facilitates interactions between humans and machines through controls, displays and feedback mechanisms embedded in software. Well-designed UIs optimise user experience and simplify human-computer interactions.

UI Kit: *Library for building user interfaces.* **More:** A user interface kit (UI Kit) provides standardised components like buttons, menus, inputs etc facilitating graphical user interface (GUI) development by abstracting front-end design building blocks into reusable libraries speeding construction.

Unit Testing: *Testing individual software components.* **More:** Unit testing is a software testing approach that focuses on testing individual units or components of an application in isolation from each other to verify proper functioning before integration.

Usability Testing: *Testing a product with its actual users.* **More:** Usability testing has actual users test a product or prototype to directly observe how users interact with it and identify strengths, weaknesses and areas for improvement in user interfaces and workflows. It provides insights into ease-of-use issues.

User Acceptance Testing (UAT): *Final phase of software testing.* **More:** User acceptance testing (UAT) is the final phase of software testing in which intended users test newly developed systems to validate compliance with business requirements and certify system readiness for operational use.

UX (User Experience): *Overall experience of a person using a product.* **More:** User experience (UX) describes the overall experience, perceptions and responses people have as they use a product or system. It encompasses accessibility, usability and pleasure provided during interaction with interfaces.

Variable: *Storage location paired with an identifier.* **More:** A variable associates a symbolic name with a stored value allowing efficient references in programs without using literal constants each time. Variables label memory addresses where values are allocated so the data can be used in computations.

Version Control: *System for tracking changes in files over time.* **More:** Version control systems track changes made over time to code, documents or other information stored in a file system or repository enabling reversion back to previous versions. Version control improves collaboration among teams.

Virtual Machine: *Emulation of a computer system.* **More:** A virtual machine emulates physical computer hardware, creating a virtual operating system allowing applications to function identically to running natively on dedicated hardware while abstracting underlying resources.

Web Application: *Software application that runs on a web server.* **More:** Web applications are application programs accessible with a web browser over the Internet or private network. Popular web apps provide services like social networking, online retail sales, web-based email etc serving dynamic content to users.

Widget: *An element of the user interface.* **More:** User interface widgets are modular interface components enabling interactive features like buttons, menus, date pickers, sliders within graphical user interfaces providing reusable building blocks that can be composed in application front ends.

Workflow: *Sequence of processes.* **More:** A workflow comprises automated logical processes and tasks coordinating sequenced operations streamlining work for users, applications or services. Workflows aim to complete tasks consistently and efficiently through standardisation.

XML (eXtensible Markup Language): *Markup language for encoding documents.* **More:** XML (eXtensible Markup Language) provides a standardised system to tag elements in a document to encode metadata along with content making it machine-readable. This facilitates data interchange as XML data exports to multiple platforms.

YAML (YAML Ain't Markup Language): *Human-readable data serialisation standard.* **More:** YAML is a human-friendly data serialisation standard for encoding configuration files and structured data exchange between systems or processes with support for common data types like strings, integers, floats, lists, dictionaries.

Zero-Day: *Unknown exploit in the software.* **More:** Zero-day refers to an exploit targeting undisclosed software vulnerabilities providing pathways for attackers before developers implement fixes or mitigations. Zero-day exploits can allow threat actors to infiltrate networks to avoid antivirus or defensive countermeasures.

Don't miss out!

Visit the website below and you can sign up to receive emails whenever ATHEER Mahir publishes a new book. There's no charge and no obligation.

https://books2read.com/r/B-A-LCXX-UTPAD

BOOKS 2 READ

Connecting independent readers to independent writers.

Did you love *Python Project Foundations- Building and Evolving Research Management Applications - A Series Opener*? Then you should read *Chat GPT Prompt Engineering With Tech Trends*[1] by ATHEER Mahir!

Welcome to "ChatGPT Prompt Engineering With Tech Trends, A Comprehensive Guide to Emerging Technologies" your ultimate guide to the cutting-edge world of emerging technologies. Written by an experienced academic professional with over 25 years in the field, this book offers a comprehensive exploration of the latest advancements in AI, programming, web3, security, and more.

Inside, you'll uncover the intricacies of AI-assisted programming, the power of GPT-4, and the art of prompt engineering, a skill that can elevate your ChatGPT interactions to new heights. We'll also delve into Ethereum merge, decentralized internet, cross-platform app compatibility, and the ever-evolving digital marketplaces.

Designed with both beginners and seasoned tech enthusiasts in mind, this book takes a step-by-step approach, explaining complex concepts in an easy-to-understand manner. Our hands-on examples and practical insights will empower you to stay ahead in this rapidly changing industry.

Dive into the exciting realm of emerging technologies and embrace the future with confidence. Join us on this journey and unlock the full potential of the tech world today!

Read more at https://www.linkedin.com/in/atheermahir/.

---

1. https://books2read.com/u/4j59W5

2. https://books2read.com/u/4j59W5

Also by ATHEER Mahir

Python Project Foundations
Python Project Foundations- Building and Evolving Research Management Applications - A Series Opener

Tech trends
Chat GPT Prompt Engineering With Tech Trends

Watch for more at https://www.linkedin.com/in/atheermahir/.

About the Author

Atheer Mahir, a leading AI engineer and researcher with over three decades of experience across varied sectors, is also an accomplished author with several published books. Holding advanced degrees in Science, Computer Science, Mathematics, and Physics, he exhibits a profound command of diverse programming languages. His expertise in AI is further distinguished by a creative approach, particularly visible in his specialization in photography. Committed to lifelong learning, Mahir enhances his knowledge through many platforms like LinkedIn Learning and Coursera. As a recognized authority on AI detection tools, he counsels against their use in academic settings due to their potential inaccuracies. Mahir's innovative work, coupled with his advisory insights, plays a crucial role in the advancement of AI applications in education and research.

Read more at https://www.linkedin.com/in/atheermahir/.

www.ingramcontent.com/pod-product-compliance
Lightning Source LLC
Chambersburg PA
CBHW081910120726
47996CB00010B/3273